English Learners Left Behind

BILINGUAL EDUCATION AND BILINGUALISM
Series Editors: Professor Nancy H. Hornberger, *University of Pennsylvania, Philadelphia USA* and Professor Colin Baker, *University of Wales, Bangor, Wales, Great Britain*

Recent Books in the Series
Negotiation of Identities in Multilingual Contexts
Aneta Pavlenko and Adrian Blackledge (eds)
Beyond the Beginnings: Literacy Interventions for Upper Elementary English Language Learners
Angela Carrasquillo, Stephen B. Kucer and Ruth Abrams
Bilingualism and Language Pedagogy
Janina Brutt-Griffler and Manka Varghese (eds)
Language Learning and Teacher Education: A Sociocultural Approach
Margaret R. Hawkins (ed.)
The English Vernacular Divide: Postcolonial Language Politics and Practice
Vaidehi Ramanathan
Bilingual Education in South America
Anne-Marie de Mejía (ed.)
Teacher Collaboration and Talk in Multilingual Classrooms
Angela Creese
Words and Worlds: World Languages Review
F. Martí, P. Ortega, I. Idiazabal, A. Barreña, P. Juaristi, C. Junyent, B. Uranga and E. Amorrortu
Language and Aging in Multilingual Contexts
Kees de Bot and Sinfree Makoni
Foundations of Bilingual Education and Bilingualism (4th edn)
Colin Baker
Bilingual Minds: Emotional Experience, Expression and Representation
Aneta Pavlenko (ed.)
Raising Bilingual-Biliterate Children in Monolingual Cultures
Stephen J. Caldas
Language, Space and Power: A Critical Look at Bilingual Education
Samina Hadi-Tabassum
Developing Minority Language Resources
Guadalupe Valdés, Joshua A. Fishman, Rebecca Chávez and William Pérez
Language Loyalty, Language Planning and Language Revitalization: Recent Writings and Reflections from Joshua A. Fishman
Nancy H. Hornberger and Martin Pütz (eds)
Language Loyalty, Continuity and Change: Joshua A. Fishman's Contributions to International Sociolinguistics
Ofelia Garcia, Rakhmiel Peltz and Harold Schiffman
Bilingual Education: An Introductory Reader
Ofelia García and Colin Baker (eds)
Disinventing and Reconstituting Languages
Sinfree Makoni and Alastair Pennycook (eds)
Language and Identity in a Dual Immersion School
Kim Potowski
Bilingual Education in China: Practices, Policies and Concepts
Anwei Feng (ed.)

For more details of these or any other of our publications, please contact:
Multilingual Matters, Frankfurt Lodge, Clevedon Hall,
Victoria Road, Clevedon, BS21 7HH, England
http://www.multilingual-matters.com

BILINGUAL EDUCATION AND BILINGUALISM 65
Series Editors: Nancy H. Hornberger and Colin Baker

English Learners Left Behind
Standardized Testing as Language Policy

Kate Menken

MULTILINGUAL MATTERS LTD
Clevedon • Buffalo • Toronto

Library of Congress Cataloging in Publication Data
Menken, Kate
English Learners Left Behind: Standardized Testing as Language Policy/Kate Menken
Bilingual Education and Bilingualism: 65
Includes bibliographical references and index.
1. Achievement tests–United States. 2. English language–Study and teaching–Foreign speakers. 3. Language policy–United States. I. Title.
LB3060.3.M46 2008
306.44'973–dc22   2007040068

British Library Cataloguing in Publication Data
A catalogue entry for this book is available from the British Library.

ISBN-13: 978-1-85359-998-9 (hbk)
ISBN-13: 978-1-85359-997-2 (pbk)

Multilingual Matters Ltd
UK: Frankfurt Lodge, Clevedon Hall, Victoria Road, Clevedon BS21 7HH.
USA: UTP, 2250 Military Road, Tonawanda, NY 14150, USA.
Canada: UTP, 5201 Dufferin Street, North York, Ontario M3H 5T8, Canada.

The policy of Multilingual Matters/Channel View Publications is to use papers that are natural, renewable and recyclable products, made from wood grown in sustainable forests. In the manufacturing process of our books, and to further support our policy, preference is given to printers that have FSC and PEFC Chain of Custody certification. The FSC and/or PEFC logos will appear on those books where full certification has been granted to the printer concerned.

Typeset by Techset Composition Ltd.
Printed and bound in the United States of America.

Contents

Acknowledgements

I would like to thank the many educators and students in New York City who have taken time out of extremely busy lives to share their stories with me in recent years, and who welcomed me into their schools. Standardized testing is a topic about which people in schools tend to have extremely strong opinions and, in spite of rigid scheduling, I found that interviews often went beyond the confines of a single class period. I also found that people would bend the rules and seek me out in school cafeterias and hallways for a chance to talk about their experiences. I am grateful for their generosity in doing so, and for their passion and dedication which made them want everyone to know about what really happens inside schools, so that policies can be adopted that are best for students. This book is dedicated to you.

I am grateful to Craig Shapiro, the principal of Grace Dodge High School in the Bronx (not one of the schools in this study, for inquiring minds), who has informed me about the inner workings of New York City public high schools and who, just when I'd finish an idea and feel confident I'd gotten it right, would say, 'What, you need a doctorate to know that? Come on. But did you also think about . . . .' Thank you Craig for expanding my ideas.

I have had wonderful editors. Thank you to Colin Baker and Nancy Hornberger, who carefully read each chapter and gave such knowledgeable and thoughtful feedback. It was a special treat to work with Nancy Hornberger, who was my professor at the University of Pennsylvania when I got my Master's Degree and the first person to ever introduce me to language policy (which, if you are interested in this area, is addictive). I am also so thankful to Tommi Grover, Ken Hall, Sarah Williams and others on the team at Multilingual Matters for your immediate interest in this topic, for your constant communication and support, and for tolerating long waits when I managed to break both wrists mid-way through the writing process. Oops. Thank you all!

There are others whose imprints can be seen throughout the pages of this book. Ofelia García has been a mentor to me in the truest sense, always available, and constant in her feedback, guidance, and ongoing support.

Many thanks to Tatyana Kleyn and Tori Hunt, as well as Laura Valdiviezo and Monisha Bajaj, for reading and talking about this book in its different stages. I would also like to thank wonderful faculty at Teachers College – Jo Anne Kleifgen, Jay Heubert and Thomas Sobol – for your contributions to my thinking about this work. I am grateful to my colleagues at Queens College and the Graduate Center of the City University of New York, and particularly Bob Vago and Ricardo Otheguy, for their support of my research.

To my wonderful friends and family, for teaching me so much, and for your support and encouragement – thank you. Special thanks to my mother for continuous interest and for all of your advice.

And most of all, thank you Stephen for spending countless hours and far too much time on weekends by my side while I worked, for your genuine enthusiasm about the content of this book, and for your own interests and work towards social justice. I admire and love you.

Part 1
Language Policy Context

Chapter 1
Introduction

In a movement that has rapidly accelerated in recent years, testing has become a central part of education for all students in the United States – including English Language Learners (ELLs).[1] At the same time, more immigrants arrived in the United States in the past decade than ever before, such that there are now more than five million ELLs from all over the world attending public schools in the United States and speaking at least 460 different languages (Kindler, 2002), reflecting an increase of 84.4% in this student population over the past decade (National Clearinghouse for English Language Acquisition, 2004). When an immigrant who speaks a language other than English at home enters a school in the United States today, she or he not only enters a new country, language and culture, but also a testing culture in which an assortment of different tests are administered regularly to determine everything from that student's placement into a program to help her or him learn English, to whether the student can advance to the next grade, and even to assess the performance of his or her school and state education system. It is therefore a pressing concern that language proficiency mediates performance on the standardized tests being used, which makes language a liability for ELLs when test results are the primary criteria for high-stakes decisions. Furthermore, testing has come to determine language policies in education in an implicit way, removed from explicit public debate.

In the United States, federal education policy (called the Elementary and Secondary Education Act) was amended in 1994, mandating the creation and adoption of academic standards and corresponding assessment systems inclusive of ELL students. The recently reauthorized federal education policy, entitled *No Child Left Behind*, was passed into law by Congress in 2001 and places even greater emphasis on assessment for all students, requiring that ELLs make 'adequate yearly progress' towards meeting state standards and 'demonstrated improvements in English proficiency' (US Department of Education, 1994, 2001). According to the law, each state must show the federal government that students in their schools are achieving

3

or progressing towards scores of 'proficient' on assessments; the law's rationale is that such assessments will ensure there is accountability for the educational progress of all students. While each state is allowed to design their own assessment system, most states are relying on standardized tests to meet these federal mandates. Tests now carry higher stakes than ever before for individual students, as they are used in most states as the primary criteria for high school graduation, grade promotion, and placement into tracked programs (Blank *et al.*, 1999; Heubert & Hauser, 1999).

Yet the standardized tests that most states currently employ were developed for the assessment of native English speakers – not for ELLs. In this way, these tests are first and foremost language proficiency exams, not necessarily measures of content knowledge (García & Menken, 2006; Menken, 2000). As a result, English language learners across the United States are performing poorly on the standardized tests being used in compliance with *No Child Left Behind*, and their scores are being used to make high-stakes decisions. According to national data, ELLs typically perform 20–40 percentage points below other students on statewide assessments (Abedi & Dietal, 2004; Center on Education Policy, 2005).

Research for this book was conducted in New York City, where students must pass a set of Regents exams in order to graduate from high school and to comply with state and federal regulations. In this multinational and multiethnic city, where approximately 40% of all school students come from homes where a language other than English is spoken and 14% are currently categorized English language learners (New York City Department of Education, 2006a, 2006b), ELLs in the past four years have performed an average of 47 percentage points below native English speakers on these high school exit exams. Like in other states requiring exams to attain a high school diploma, ELLs graduate from high school at rates far lower than other students. The unfortunate irony of current education reforms is that English language learners are disproportionately being 'left behind'.

This book shares the human stories of how recent testing policy is affecting schools and the daily lives of teachers and students. I spent a year in ten high schools in New York City studying how the national emphasis on testing is lived in schools, offering one local example of this critical national and international issue. Because of the high-stakes consequences attached to standardized tests in combination with consistently lower test scores among ELLs, the tests greatly impact the instruction and educational experiences of ELLs. Specifically, tests shape what content is taught in school, how it is taught, by whom it is taught, and in what language(s) it is taught. In this way, tests have become *de facto* language policy in schools.

No Child Left Behind is in actuality a language policy, even though this is rarely discussed and nor is the law presented to the public as such. This book shows how language education policy in the United States is currently being negotiated, as the law is interpreted by people at every level of the educational system, from the federal government to classrooms, with teachers acting as the final arbiters of language policy implementation. Although research has until recently often overlooked local or bottom-up language policy implementation (Canagarajah, 2005), language policy is examined in this book from the top-down to the bottom-up, in both a practical and theoretical way. Tests are a defining force for ELLs and the educators who serve them, and analyzing this movement through the lens of language policy allows us to document the practical realities and yet also explore the wider sociopolitical implications.

Defining Language Policy

Before moving into this discussion, it is first necessary to establish a definition of language policy, and particularly language education policy, which will be used in this book. Language policy is concerned with such topics as which language(s) will be taught in school, how language education is implemented, as well as orientations towards language and language ideology (Cooper, 1989; Corson, 1999; Crawford, 2000; Fettes, 1997; Fishman, 1979, 1991; Hornberger, 1996, 2006b; Kaplan & Baldauf, 1997; Ricento & Hornberger, 1996; Ruiz, 1984). While there are many definitions within this emerging field and remaining ambiguities (Hornberger, 2006b), in this book I favor the broad definition offered by Spolsky (2004). For Spolsky (2004:9), language policy encompasses all of the 'language practices, beliefs and management of a community or polity'. Language policies can be overt or covert, and include all of the decisions people make about language in society (Shohamy, 2006; Spolsky, 2004). While language policy research focuses primarily on the policies of official bodies, such as governments, this book will show how there can be policymakers at all different positions in society. The term language policy is therefore used on its own in this book, apart from language planning, because the language policies currently being created in US schools as a byproduct of testing policy occur in an *ad hoc* way, without careful language planning as traditionally depicted in the literature (Fettes, 1997; Kaplan & Baldauf, 1997). As such, it would be misleading to refer to language planning when discussing how standardized tests create current language policies in education.

Schools serve as a primary vehicle for language policy implementation. Acknowledging the importance of schooling in language policy, Cooper

(1989) introduced the term 'language acquisition planning' into the literature. This is similar to what Kaplan and Baldauf (1997) term 'language in education policy' and Shohamy (2003, 2006) calls 'language education policy', and these terms are used interchangeably in this book. While some schools have contributed to language loss, others have contributed to language maintenance, revitalization and reversing language shift.[2] Examples of language loss include the imposition of English-only policies in Ireland (Wright, 1996), and English and Afrikaans in apartheid South Africa which led to the loss of minority languages (Alexander, 1999; Heugh, 1999). By contrast, examples of minority language maintenance and reversing language shift in schooling include recent efforts to revitalize Navajo in the United States (Cummins, 2000; McCarty, 2003), Quechua bilingual education in Peru (Hornberger, 1996), as well as Basque in Spain (Gardner, 2000).

Recent research has focused on ways that language policies create and/or perpetuate social inequities (Corson, 1999; Phillipson, 1992; Phillipson & Skutnabb-Kangas, 1996; Skutnabb-Kangas, 2000; Tollefson, 1991). A great deal of scholarly attention is now being paid to ensuring that school language policies do not contribute to language loss or disparities because of language (Corson, 1999; Cummins, 2000; Skutnabb-Kangas, 2000; Tollefson, 1991). Corson (1999) explains this movement in the following passage:

> When school language policies are put into action, they are linked with power and with social justice in a range of ways. Whenever schools set out to plan their response to the language problems they face, matters of language variety, race, culture, and class always affect the planning process, and an effective language policy process will always look critically at the impact of these and other aspects of human diversity. (Corson, 1999: 6)

This book is located within recent language policy research that is concerned by issues of power, particularly within educational contexts, and seeks to ensure that language policies in education promote equity rather than inequity.

The body of research in language policy offers a helpful lens for analyzing the inclusion of ELLs in testing, because the preparation of students who are non-native speakers of English to take high-stakes standardized tests necessitates decisionmaking at the school and classroom levels with regard to language. Yet research in this area has far-reaching implications, in that language education policies paint in full relief the power dynamics within schools and the wider society which schools reflect, and help us to understand real national priorities. While debates over bilingual education wage on in the United States and elsewhere, decisions are being made in educational systems around the world about which languages will hold an official place in schools. However, these debates are not simply about language. Decisions about which languages to teach in school and how to teach them are deeply intertwined with the status of each language and its speakers within international and local sociolinguistic hierarchies. In actuality, these are conversations about how society chooses to treat diversity, culture, immigration and, mainly, the people who are the speakers of different languages.

Why is Testing a Language Policy Issue?

At present, there is no official language or language policy in the US, as clarified in the following:

> Strictly speaking, the United States has never had a language policy, consciously planned and national in scope. It has had language **policies**– ad hoc responses to immediate needs or political pressures – often contradictory and inadequate to cope with changing times. Government cannot avoid language policymaking. Yet no federal agency is charged with coordinating decisions, resources, or research in this area. (Crawford, 2000)

The *ad hoc* creation of a wide array of language policies that Crawford describes has serious implications for language in education; standards and corresponding assessments for ELLs offer one example. In the absence of official language policy in the United States, unofficial or *de facto* policies carry great significance.

Recent education reforms in the United States have dramatically affected language education, and assessments are currently assuming the place of a language plan and policy. The following citation refers to the efforts of various professional associations to create standards that plan language acquisition, in the absence of national language policy in the United States:

> As the development of language-in-education policy may seem very complex, it may be instructive to look at the recent development of 'standards statements' by professional associations in the United States. There, in the absence of a national policy on languages (or even clear guidelines), these elements of the education sector have taken policy development into their own hands ... (Kaplan & Baldauf, 1997: 140–141)

Standards were the precursor to the current focus on standardized tests, and this quotation accurately portrays this movement as language policy development. In fact, standards are now primarily symbolic in many places in the United States, hanging on classroom walls and occasionally referenced in lesson plans, when in actuality tests carry far greater weight in influencing curriculum and teaching because of the consequences attached to them.

The reality is that tests offer a highly potent and expedient method for changing school curricula and classroom practices, particularly when the stakes attached to them are high. The effects of tests on teaching and learning are called testing 'washback' in language education research (Cheng *et al.*, 2004), and policymakers in countries such as the United Kingdom, New Zealand, China and Israel turn to assessment as a vehicle for driving curricula and promoting their agendas (Baker, 1995; Hayes & Read, 2004; Qi, 2005; Shohamy, 2006). Yet when used as an instrument for change, tests are found making teaching and testing essentially synonymous (Menken, in press; Qi, 2005; Shohamy, 2001).

Testing has therefore emerged as a new development in language policy. Shohamy (2001) describes why testing is a language policy issue in the introduction to her book, *The Power of Tests*. As she writes:

> In recent years I have been conducting research in the area of language policy. Professor Bernard Spolsky and I were asked to propose a new language policy for Israel. Given my background and interest in language testing, I again learned about the power of tests as it became clear to me that the 'language testing policy' was the *de facto* 'language policy'. Further, no policy change can take place without a change in testing policy as the testing policy becomes the *de facto* language policy. It was clear that documents and statements about language policy were marginal in comparison to the power of the testing policy. I thus concluded that through the study of testing practices it is possible to learn about the existing educational policies. It was then that I realized what an excellent mirror tests could be for studying the real priorities of those in power and authority, as these are embedded in political, social, educational, and economic contexts. (Shohamy, 2001: xiii)

Shohamy's perspective is aligned to recent language policy research that is attentive to the political nature of language teaching and concerned by issues of social equity. By turning our attention to the intersection between testing and language policy, Shohamy lays the groundwork for the research presented in this book. It is exactly within this perspective towards language that my research is set, based on the assumption that high-stakes testing in the United States (and specifically New York City) is *de facto* language policy.

In recent years, several authors have argued that *No Child Left Behind* is likely to promote English-only language education policy due to its assessment mandates (Crawford, 2004; Evans & Hornberger, 2005; Wiley & Wright, 2004). The law has entirely removed the term 'bilingual' from federal education legislation, and repeals the *Bilingual Education Act* that preceded it. Because the law requires assessments of English proficiency and content knowledge, in tests that are usually in English only, these authors draw a clear connection between current testing policy and language policy. This book furthers these findings, bringing to life how *No Child Left Behind* exemplifies implicit language policy. Testing is therefore an extremely significant language policy issue, because high-stakes tests become *de facto* language policy in education when schools respond to the pressures they create.

My focus in this book is less on the technical, psychometric challenges of high-stakes testing. Shohamy (1998, 2001) notes how language testers have typically overlooked the social and political dimensions of testing. Though the technical complications of including ELLs into standardized tests are very important and are described in this book, my primary interest is in the even less explored area of how testing impacts the instructional practices and the learning experiences of ELLs, and analyzing the implications of this through the lens of language policy. In a country characterized by the absence of an official, explicit national language policy, implicit language policies become central.

Background and Organization of the Book

Before I entered the secondary classrooms of New York City for the purposes of this research, I imagined that testing was somehow affecting what educators and students do in their everyday lives at school. At the time when I began teaching English as a Second Language in the mid-1990s, there were statewide standardized tests that my students would take at the end of the year, and yet I fully assumed that the skills I was teaching in class were close enough to what would be on the tests that I need not directly align my instruction to them. Significantly, the exams that my students took were not attached to any high-stakes decisions then.

Times have changed. Even in New Jersey, where I held my first public school teaching position, it is now required that students pass an exit exam in order to graduate from high school. When I returned to classrooms in 2003 as a researcher in New York City, I was surprised by the extent to which New York's Regents exams define curriculum, teaching, and learning for English language learners. Since the passage of *No Child Left Behind* in 2001, testing has been increasingly emphasized at the federal level. At the local level, I met educator after educator, and student after student who could identify by name and describe for me in detail each part of the Regents exams. I observed hours of test preparation in classrooms where this occurs every day, and listened to many educators and ELL students describing their experiences and how testing has personally affected them.

Figure 1.1 is a sign collected from the focal school involved in this study, which captures the way that testing permeates so many aspects of schooling for English language learners who attend high school in the United States. This sign uses the image of 'Uncle Sam', the national personification of the United States, to encourage students to enroll in tutoring to help them pass the Math A Regents examination, one of the exams required for graduation in New York. This sign is an alteration of a famous

Figure 1.1 Sign collected from the hallway near the English as a Second Language and Foreign Language Office, Focal School #1

poster of Uncle Sam that was used in 1917 to recruit citizens to join the Army during World War I. The symbolism of this militaristic and national-istic image, when used to greet the arrival of new immigrants in US schools, cannot be overstated.

The first part of this book describes past and present testing and language policies in the United States. Chapter 2 documents the linguistic diversity of the United States and overviews key language policy decisions in the history of this country, with particular attention to language educa-tion policy and the treatment of English language learners in federal edu-cation legislation, and detailing current *No Child Left Behind* regulations within this historical perspective. Chapter 3 explores legislation and poli-cies for ELLs in New York City and describes the study of high school exit exams I conducted, as an example of how these complicated national issues play out in one local context.

This discussion of testing and ELLs is brought into the real life world of schools in Part 2 of this book, by considering the content of the tests and the impact they have on students and educators. Chapter 4 provides a detailed linguistic analysis of different exams being used to determine high school graduation in New York, California and Texas – the states with the largest ELL populations – showing how all of the exams are linguistically complex, regardless of the subject area and the accommodations provided. This chap-ter thereby highlights the unequal 'playing field' of testing and accounts for the lower tests scores of ELLs. Chapter 5 shows that testing culture is now a defining force in how immigrant students experience schooling in the United States, reflecting new language education policy which attempts to speed up the process of English language learning and a focus on ELLs' deficits. Many ELLs experience a test-focused curriculum, and must habitually retake the exams in order to pass. In addition, it was found in this study that the difficulty of high-stakes exams creates a pressure for ELLs to leave school and attend alternative diploma programs, drop out or return to their country of origin.

Educators are now very focused on ensuring that their ELL students can pass the tests, causing radical changes to curriculum, teaching, and classroom language policies that are described in Chapter 6. The tests them-selves leave the task of interpretation to teachers and schools, who decipher their demands and use them to create a complex and wide array of school-level language policies. While it is tempting to assume that top-down pol-icy will simply be unidirectional in implementation, and that if *No Child Left Behind* implicitly promotes English then English will always be favored in instruction. In actuality, however, this assumption is overly simplistic; while most schools in this sample indeed increased the amount of English instruction students receive to improve their test performance, one school and certain teachers were found doing exactly the opposite, and instead increased native language instruction as a test preparation strategy.

Part 3 of this book moves outward to examine the broader implications of recent testing policy for ELLs. Chapter 7 weighs the benefits and drawbacks of test-based accountability for this student population, and concludes that while the testing movement has brought ELLs into the national spotlight and in many ways raised educational standards for them, the drawbacks currently outweigh the benefits as language has become a liability within this context. The testing policies of *No Child Left Behind* are ultimately discriminatory against ELLs, by penalizing schools with large ELL populations and creating a disincentive for schools to serve these students. Chapter 8 is theoretical, analyzing the findings of this study from a language policy perspective, and describing the complex ways that testing contributes to language standardization, negotiations of language status and the creation of language hierarchies in schools. The chapter concludes by arguing that the term language 'planning' is a misnomer in the US context, where language policies are created at every level of the educational system in uncoordinated and often competing ways, and offers a new view of language education policy. Feeling that a purely theoretical conclusion simply would not be sufficient for a book like this one, Chapter 9 offers a practical set of recommendations and considerations for policymakers and practitioners.

Chapter 2

Language Policy, Federal Education Legislation and English Language Learners in the United States

In the absence of an official national language in the United States, language policies have primarily been created through our legal and educational systems, resulting in a complex mixture of legal mandates, ballot initiatives and educational policies. In the United States, implicit language policies often take on the role of the more explicit official ones in the absence of a national language. Research in language policy within this context therefore involves a good deal of detective work on the part of the researcher, to understand the language policies embedded within mandates or educational policies. Specifically, I argue in this book that *No Child Left Behind* is actually a language policy, even though this is not stated in the law and nor is the law presented to the general public as such. Yet the results are the same as official language policy would be, in that this federal legislation is changing language use and language learning in schools, which will have a lasting impact on minority languages and their speakers in this country. In specific, NCLB pushes English at the expense of minority language education, as English is the language that 'counts' on the high-stakes tests associated with current federal education legislation. It is critical that implicit languages policies are exposed to ensure that language minorities are receiving a high-quality education.

This chapter offers an overview of key language policy decisions in the history of the United States, with particular attention to language education policy. The chapter is divided into the following sections: (1) Past US Language Policies in Education, (2) History of the Testing Movement in the United States, (3) The Multilingual Landscape of Today's United States, (4) Program Models for English Language Learners in the United States, (5) Return to Anti-Immigrant Backlash and English-Only Policy, (6) Paving the Pathway towards *No Child Left Behind*: The 1994 Reauthorization of the

Elementary and Secondary Education Act, (7) *No Child Left Behind*: The Era of Assessment and Accountability for ELLs and (8) Growing National Debate over *No Child Left Behind* and the Assessment of ELLs. In order to appreciate the tremendous impact of current educational policy, it is necessary to first understand where it fits into past policies. The first section sets recent federal legislation within a broader historical context, describing the treatment of cultural and linguistic diversity in federal education policy over time. The second section examines how testing – the focus of current federal education legislation – in the past has typically evaluated immigrants and minorities, and served as a gatekeeper. The third section describes the diverse linguistic landscape in the United States today, with attention to demographics and the dramatic growth in immigration over the past decade. The fourth section addresses the treatment of English language learners in public schools, and describes current services and educational programs provided to them. The fifth section details recent anti-bilingual education legislation and efforts to promote English only. The sixth and seventh sections offer a detailed portrait of the two most recent federal education laws passed by Congress, the *Improving America's Schools Act* and *No Child Left Behind*, highlighting their significance for students who are ELLs. The eighth section describes debates increasing nationally over how best to assess English language learners within the context of NCLB assessment and accountability.

Past US Language Policies in Education

Like a pendulum swinging between opposing ends, US schooling has historically approached linguistic diversity with alternating restriction and tolerance. When the US Constitution was written, linguistic diversity was the norm in the United States. Though English was the dominant language of the 13 colonies by the end of the 17th century, many other languages were spoken. These included German, Dutch, French, Spanish, Swedish, Irish, Welsh, along with hundreds of Native American languages and African-based creoles (Ricento, 1995). Yet, like England, the United States never mandated an official language, nor did it instate a government-sanctioned body to regulate language use (such as the Academie Française in France or the Hebrew Academy in Israel), and the Constitution makes no mention of language. The 'founding fathers' in the United States did not seem to think that cultural and linguistic diversity was an issue; as Crawford (1992b: 33–34) states, 'in 1787 cultural pluralism was a concept yet to be invented'.

As a result, instruction was multilingual in US schools during colonial times and several states passed legislation protecting and promoting education in languages other than English. For example, bilingual German-English schooling was authorized by law in several states during the 19th century and took place elsewhere without the benefit of official recognition. In addition, pressure from immigrant groups resulted in European languages other than German being taught as well (Crawford, 1992a; Kloss, 1977).

With a wave of Jewish, Italian, Greek and Slavic immigrants in the early 20th century, however, the pendulum swung in the direction of anti-immigrant sentiment during what is known as the 'Americanization' campaign. In this period, languages other than English were restricted and the dominance of English grew. Several states passed legislation and mandates banning the use of German in classrooms, churches, meeting halls, or other public arenas after the United States entered World War I in 1917 (Crawford, 1999). For example, in 1919 the state of Nebraska adopted a statute which stated that 'no person, individually or as a teacher, shall, in any private denominational, parochial, or public school teach any subject to any person in any language than that English language' (National Clearinghouse for English Language Acquisition [NCELA], 2006b). This language restrictionism also affected Japanese, Chinese, Korean and Spanish, as efforts were made to prohibit these languages from being taught in the states of California, Hawaii and New Mexico respectively. However, in 1923 the US Supreme Court ruled in the case of *Meyer v. Nebraska* that the 1919 anti-bilingual education statute was a violation of the Fourteenth Amendment of the US Constitution. The Ninth Circuit Court of Appeals overturned laws prohibiting instruction in languages other than English in 1926 in at least 22 other states (Ricento, 1995).

The US Congress considered a bill to make English the official 'American language' in 1923 and, though this did not pass, together with other laws prohibiting languages other than English, it greatly impacted public sentiment. From the period of the Industrial Revolution, when immigration rates soared in the United States, and into the 1960s, English was the sole medium of instruction and few or no special services were provided to English language learners in schools. During that time period, the education of ELLs was characterized by a 'sink or swim' approach.

The *Civil Rights Act* was passed in 1964, marking the first time that federal legislation acknowledged that language can be a source of educational inequity and demanding that language support services be provided for students learning English. The *Civil Rights Act*, or Title VI of the Elementary and

Secondary Education Act (ESEA), prohibited discrimination on the basis of race, color or national origin. This was followed by Title VII of the ESEA, entitled the *Bilingual Education Act*, which was passed by Congress in 1968. The *Bilingual Education Act* sought to address the challenges faced by students arriving to the US speaking languages other than English, and funded programs to meet the needs of these students such as bilingual education and English as a second language (ESL) programs (these programs are described in the fourth section of this chapter). Although the law did not offer a definition of bilingual education, and nor did it specify which program model schools should adopt for ELLs, it did acknowledge bilingual education as a viable approach for meeting the needs of poor, language minority students (NCELA, 2006b). This remained true through various reauthorizations and amendments until 2001, as 'Title VII consistently made space for bilingual education in one form or another' (Evans & Hornberger, 2005: 88).

The passage of Title VII in 1968 was followed by an extremely significant Supreme Court case in 1974, entitled *Lau v. Nichols*, which was a lawsuit on behalf of Chinese students in the San Francisco public schools who did not speak English. Such students were placed in mainstream English-medium classrooms and, the lawsuit argued, were unable to learn and perform well in school due to their limited English. This case set a legal precedent by ruling that '*identical* education does not constitute *equal* education under the Civil Rights Act ... by merely providing students with the same facilities, textbooks, teachers and curriculum; for students who do not understand English are effectively foreclosed from any meaningful education' (as cited in NCELA, 2002). According to this ruling, school districts must take 'affirmative steps' to address the challenges that language poses for ELLs, by offering programs such as bilingual education or ESL. This was followed in 1975 by the *Lau Remedies*, created by the Office of Civil Rights of the US Department of Education, which applied the *Lau* ruling to all schools – beyond just those receiving Title VII funding. This offered the federal government a means of enforcement to ensure that school districts were providing services for ELLs (Wright, 2005). As a result, many in the field of bilingual education and ESL maintain that the *Bilingual Education Act* was not enough on its own, and that programs to meet the needs of ELLs were only truly implemented after the *Lau* ruling. This case continues to be referenced in schools with regard to the creation and implementation of programming to meet the linguistic needs of ELLs.

Though minor amendments were made to Title VII throughout the 1980s, ELLs were not systematically included in comprehensive school reform efforts. In part this was because Title VII provisions remained separate from other federal policy under the ESEA. As discussed later in this chapter, this

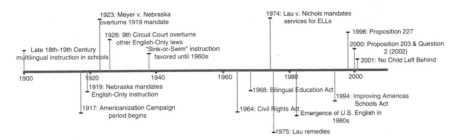

Figure 2.1 Brief historical overview of US language education policy

changed with the reauthorization of the ESEA in 1994, which brought sweeping reforms based on standards that, for the first time, also mandated the inclusion of ELLs, and ultimately culminated in the termination of the *Bilingual Education Act* in 2001 with the passage of *No Child Left Behind*.

As described in this chapter, language education policy is constantly shifting, and has undergone many changes with the sociopolitical climate surrounding schools. The timeline in Figure 2.1 offers an overview of some of the key language policies in education in the history of the United States. The events from 1980-present are detailed later in this chapter.

History of the Testing Movement in the United States

Testing English language learners is a central component of recent federal education policy, but is by no means new. In fact, testing in the United States has historically been tied to the status of immigrants and minorities, serving a gatekeeping function that perpetuates the power of the dominant groups. Alfred Binet created the first intelligence quotient (IQ) test in 1904 for the French government to identify students in need of special education services and distinguish these students from those with behavior problems. This test was translated into English and implemented in the United States in 1917, galvanizing a testing movement within the United States which later flourished globally (Spolsky, 1995). Coinciding with the Americanization period of the early 20th century, these tests were used by H.H. Goddard to evaluate immigrants to the United States who passed through Ellis Island and, failing to recognize the critical role of English proficiency on such tests, Goddard concluded that 25 of the 30 Jews tested were unintelligent (Hakuta, 1986). IQ tests were also taken by two million World War I draftees so that Carl Brigham, one of the founders of the 'objective testing movement' (Spolsky, 1995), could compare the performance of recent immigrants to those in the United States for 20 years or more. He found that test takers identified as members of the 'Nordic' race outperformed members of the 'Alpine' and 'Mediterranean' races (Hakuta, 1986; Wiley & Wright, 2004; Wright, 2004). IQ test scores also determined the placement of students into tracked educational programs, and were used to uphold racial segregation in the 20th century (Mensh & Mensh, 1991 as cited in Menken, in press). Significantly, Brigham went on to develop the Scholastic Achievement Test (SAT) which is still used to determine university admissions in the United States (Wright, 2004).

IQ testing and SATs in the United States have remained extremely powerful tools for high-stakes decisionmaking, in spite of ongoing criticism of cultural bias favoring the white middle class. For instance, research by Heath (1983) has exposed how ethnic groups differ in their notions of intelligence, exposing the cultural problems inherent in intelligence testing. Even though work by Heath and others has been extremely influential, in that IQ tests are now largely seen as passé within education circles, they continue to be used today in certain school districts, for example to determine placement of children into selective 'gifted' programs. Not surprisingly, the overrepresentation of white students in gifted programs has been widely documented, while the inverse is true of special education programs in which African-American, Hispanic and ELLs are overrepresented instead (see e.g. Artiles & Trent, 1994; Harris & Ford, 1991; Orfield, 2001).

Similarly, English literacy testing has historically provided a legal means for discrimination in civic participation and citizenship. Although the Fifteenth Amendment to the US Constitution in 1870 made it illegal to prohibit any male citizen over the age of 21 from voting, southern states adopted literacy tests as a way to bar blacks from participation. This practice was ongoing until the passage of the *Voting Rights Act of 1965*, which sought to address this problem by banning literacy tests and other educational pre-requisites to voting (Liebowitz, 1969). While this ban changed voting rights, since 1917 literacy testing has remained a requirement for naturalization as a US citizen. Although literacy in any language had been acceptable previously, in 1950 the Federal Code established literacy in English as a condition of naturalization. The role of English literacy as a gatekeeper in immigration and naturalization has expanded over time, and English literacy is now valued over first language literacy when compared to earlier periods of US history (McKay & Weinstein-Shr, 1993).

Specifically, the law requires that applicants for naturalization demonstrate an ability to read, write, speak, and understand English and display knowledge of US history and government, by passing tests of English and Civics (US Citizenship and Immigration Services, 2004). In his historical overview of laws mandating English literacy in the United States, a forward thinking Liebowitz (1969) wrote:

> The thesis of this article is that, in general, English literacy tests and other statutory sanctions in favor of English were originally formulated as an indirect but effective means of achieving discrimination on the basis of race, creed or color. (Leibowitz, 1969: 7)

English literacy testing has provided a means to bar unwanted immigrants from naturalization and to prevent blacks from voting.

It is important to clarify that testing policy has not been solely directed towards immigrants in the United States, but rather affects all students and serves dominant educational ideology as a whole, which is characterized by a belief in the need for standards and accountability. Yet the testing movement has historically been tied to racism and linguicism, rising in response to record rates of immigration to this country (Wiley & Wright, 2004). Tests are presented to the public as objective and their power is largely unquestioned (Shohamy, 2001), yet historically they have served to legitimize the marginalization of racial and ethnic minorities.

The Multilingual Landscape of Today's United States

Before moving onto a discussion of recent federal education policy, it is necessary to first contextualize these new policies within an increasingly diverse US population, as they reflect societal attitudes and an unwelcoming political climate which is responding to these new Americans by restricting the languages that they speak. More immigrants arrived in the United States during the 1990s than any other single decade. The population of non-English speakers has expanded by 42% in the last decade, while the population of native English speakers has remained relatively static (US Census Bureau, 2000). Table 2.1 below shows the demographics on linguistic diversity in the United States today. The 2000 US Census reports that 17.9% of all Americans, or nearly one in five, speaks a language other than English at home, with Spanish being the predominant minority language. The linguistic and cultural diversity of the United States derives from both internal and external populations, through immigration to the United States and also from Native American and other indigenous communities. As shown in the table, which is organized according to language group, Spanish and Chinese are the most widely spoken languages after English in the United States today.

Though popular opinion holds otherwise, recent census data indicate that immigrants to the United States are quickly learning English. Even

Table 2.1 Language spoken at home: US Census 2000, by population five years and over, by language

Language	Number	%
Population 5 years and over	262,375,152	100.0
Speak only English	215,423,557	82.1
Speak a language other than English	46,951,595	17.9
Indo-European languages		
Spanish or Spanish Creole	28,101,052	10.7
French (incl. Patois, Cajun)	1,643,838	0.6
French Creole	453,368	0.2
Italian	1,008,370	0.4
Portuguese or Portuguese Creole	564,630	0.2
German	1,383,442	0.5
Yiddish	178,945	0.1
Other West Germanic languages	251,135	0.1
Scandinavian languages	162,252	0.1
Greek	365,436	0.1
Russian	706,242	0.3
Polish	667,414	0.3
Serbo-Croatian	233,865	0.1
Other Slavic languages	301,079	0.1
Armenian	202,708	0.1
Persian	312,085	0.1
Gujarathi	235,988	0.1
Hindi	317,057	0.1
Urdu	262,900	0.1
Other Indic languages	439,289	0.2
Other Indo-European languages	327,946	0.1
Asian and Pacific Island languages		
Chinese	2,022,143	0.8
Japanese	477,997	0.2
Korean	894,063	0.3
Mon-Khmer, Cambodian	181,889	0.1
Miao, Hmong	168,063	0.1
Thai	120,464	0.0

(Continued)

Table 2.1 (Continued)

Language	Number	%
Laotian	149,303	0.1
Vietnamese	1,009,627	0.4
Other Asian languages	398,434	0.2
Tagalog	1,224,241	0.5
Other Pacific Island languages	313,841	0.1
Other languages		
Navajo	178,014	0.1
Other Native North American languages	203,466	0.1
Hungarian	117,973	0.0
Arabic	614,582	0.2
Hebrew	195,374	0.1
African languages	418,505	0.2
Other and unspecified languages	144,575	0.1

Source: US Census Bureau, Census 2000, Summary File 3

though 42% of language minorities are foreign-born, data from the 2000 US Census indicate that more than half of all language minorities speak English 'very well', as shown in Table 2.2.

The data in this table show that 9.8% of the 17.9% of people who speak a language other than English at home (more than half) report speaking English 'very well', exceeding the number who report speaking English 'less than very well'. This is very significant because, as Crawford (2002a: 1) notes, 'the pace of Anglicization in this country has never been faster'. This is consistent with research which indicates not only that immigrants to the United States learn English, but in fact that their native language is typically lost to English by the third generation (Fishman, 1991, 2001; Rumbaut *et al.*, 2006).

It is estimated that approximately 5,119,561 ELLs were enrolled in United States public schools during the 2004–2005 school year; this represents approximately 10.5% of total public school student enrollment and reflects a 60.8% increase over the reported 1994–1995 enrollment (National Clearinghouse for English Language Acquisition, 2006a). During this same period, the growth in enrollment of all students in public schools increased by only 2.6%. It is predicted that ELLs will comprise 25% of all school students by the year 2025 (US Department of Education, 2006). Figure 2.2 shows the dramatic growth in the ELL student population over the previous decade, as compared with the relatively static pattern of total school enrollment.

Table 2.2 Language spoken at home and English-speaking ability, 1980–2000

	1980	%	1990	%	2000	%	Change (%)
All speakers, age 5+	210,247,455	100.0	230,445,777	100.0	262,375,152	100.0	+24.8
English only	187,187,415	89.0	198,600,798	86.2	215,423,557	82.1	+15.1
Other language	23,060,040	11.0	31,844,979	13.8	46,951,595	17.9	+103.6
Speaks English 'very well'	12,879,004	6.1	17,862,477	7.8	25,631,188	9.8	+99.0
Speaks English 'less than very well'	10,181,036	4.8	13,982,502	6.1	21,320,407	8.1	+109.4

Source: 1980 Census of population, vol. 1, chap. D, pt. 1; US Census Bureau, Language spoken at home and ability to speak English for United States, regions, and states: 1990; Census 2000, Summary File 3, Table DP-2 as cited in Crawford, 2002a: 1

According to a survey from the US Department of Education to state education associations, as reported by Kindler (2002), ELLs in the United States speak 460 languages. Spanish is the predominant native language, spoken by 84% of ELLs attending school in the United States. Vietnamese (3.1%), Chinese (3.0%), French (2.4%) and Korean (1.7%) ranked next highest overall. The top ten languages spoken by ELLs can be seen in Figure 2.3.

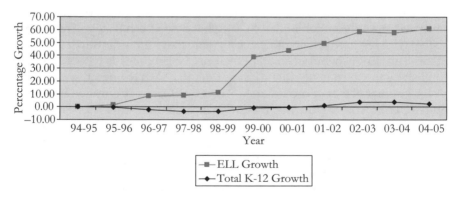

Figure 2.2 Growth of ELL population in US public schools as compared to total enrollment, 1994–1995 to 2004–2005
Source: National Clearinghouse for English Language Acquisition, 2006a

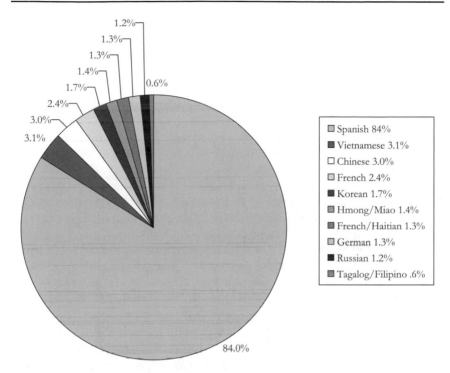

Figure 2.3 Top ten languages spoken by ELLs, pre-K to 12th grade, 2000
Source: US Census of Population and Housing, 1% PUMS, 2000 Census as cited in Capps *et al.* (2005)

Other languages with over 10,000 speakers include (in alphabetical order): Arabic, Armenian, French, Haitian Creole, Hindi, Hmong, Japanese, Khmer, Lao, Mandarin, Navajo, Polish, Portuguese, Punjabi, Russian, Serbo-Croatian, Tagalog and Urdu. There are significant regional variations in language diversity as well. For instance, Hmong is the most common language of ELLs in Minnesota, Ilocano in Hawaii, French in Maine, Serbo-Croatian in Vermont, Lakota in South Dakota and Yup'ik in Alaska (Kindler, 2002).

Program Models for English Language Learners in the United States

Since the passage of the *Bilingual Education Act* and the *Lau v. Nichols* ruling, a wide array of language programming models have been implemented in US schools to address the needs of English language learners.

These programs are divided between those where students' native languages are used in instruction, and those where instruction is solely in English. In order to define the different types of educational programs that are available for ELLs in United States public schools, the characteristics of these program models can be seen in Table 2.3 below. It is important to note from the outset that program models are rarely implemented in their 'pure' form, but rather are adapted at the school level; in this way, the descriptions below identify general characteristics with the recognition that a good deal of school-level variation occurs. As indicated in the table below, some models have the same components, but are known by different names in differing locations. For example, what are called 'dual language' programs in New York City are referred to as 'two-way' programs in Washington, DC. Models that have shared instructional goals and elements but different names are placed together in a box in Table 2.3.

As indicated in Table 2.3, programs are distinguished between those which promote bilingualism and those which promote English acquisition. Although some students receive bilingual education in their native language and English, ELLs most often find themselves in classrooms where English is the only language of instruction, as in the prevalent English as a second language (ESL) programs. Of programs in US schools that do permit native language use in instruction, 'weak' forms of bilingual education such as transitional bilingual education programs which focus on English acquisition are pervasive (Baker, 2001; García, 1997). Programs in which the linguistic goal is English acquisition, rather than bilingualism, are typically 'subtractive', in that adding a new language results in a student's first language and culture being lost or lessened (Baker, 2001). Such programs cultivate language shift over time, whereby entire communities move from speaking one language to another (Fishman, 1991, 2001). By contrast, 'additive' bilingual programs that emphasize native language maintenance as well as English acquisition, such as dual-language bilingual education programs, are far less common. Choice of program model is extremely important, because programs can either promote language shift or language maintenance over time.

Return to Anti-Immigrant Backlash and English-Only Policy

With the rise in immigration rates, bilingual education has become a primary target of English-only efforts in recent years, causing this diversity in program models to dwindle. While English assumes the role of official language in most contexts in the United States, this issue has been hotly debated in recent years, particularly in the controversies surrounding

Table 2.3 Characteristics of the major program models for English language learners in the United States

Language(s) of Instruction	Typical program names	Native language of ELL students	Language of content instruction	Language arts instruction	Linguistic goal of program
English and the native language	• Two-way bilingual education or • Dual language immersion	50% English-speaking and 50% ELLs who share the same native language	Both English and the native language	English and the native language	Bilingualism
	• Late-exit bilingual education or • Developmental bilingual education	All students speak the same native language	Both; at first, mostly the native language is used. Instruction in English increases as students gain proficiency	English and the native language	Bilingualism
	• Early-exit bilingual education or • Transitional bilingual education	All students speak the same native language	Both at the beginning, with quick progression to all or most instruction in English	English; Native language skills are developed only to assist transition to English	English acquisition rapid transfer into English-only Classroom
English only	• Sheltered content, Structured immersion or Content-based ESL	Students share the same native language or speak different languages	English adapted to the students' proficiency level, and supplemented by gestures and visual aids	English	English acquisition
	• Pull-out ESL	Students share the same native language or speak different languages; students may be grouped with a mix of ages and grade levels	English adapted to the students' proficiency level, and supplemented by gestures and visual aids	English; students leave their English-only classroom to spend part of their day receiving ESL instruction	English acquisition

Source: Adapted from Zelasko and Antunez (2000)

bilingual education. There was a resurgence of language debates in the 1980s that, like the debates in the early 20th century, linked proficiency in the English language to patriotism and national unity. Unlike earlier language battles, however, when efforts were sporadic and kept at the state and local levels, a very well-funded lobby called 'US English' emerged in the 1980s that began an orchestrated nationwide campaign to make English the sole official language of the United States (Crawford, 1992a, 1992b). Like earlier debates during the period of Americanization, current debates seem to be about more than language; rather, they are defining what it means to be American at a time when immigration rates soar and minority communities are more visible.

At the federal level, English Only legislation first appeared in 1981 as a constitutional English Language Amendment. However, this measure has never come to a Congressional vote. The English Only movement has had greater success at the state level where 28 states have adopted various forms of Official English legislation. By March of the 2007 session, official English legislation had been introduced in 15 more states.

Even now, federal legislation is again being considered to make English the sole official language of the United States. Under President George W. Bush, immigration reform has been placed high on this administration's agenda. Specifically, a wide range of bills have been drafted addressing different aspects of immigration, such as the status of illegal immigrants, the citizenship process, border control and regulation, immigration law enforcement and immigrant rights. Tagged onto this agenda of immigration reform, the topic of Official English has yet again resurfaced and on 27 July 2006, the second in a series of meetings by the House of Representatives' Education Committee was held. This meeting not only focused on aspects of the proposed changes to US border security and enforcement, but also addressed the language issue (Lakshmi, 2006). A federal bill to make English the official language of the United States, called H.R. 997, is currently pending in the US House of Representatives. Last session, an official English measure passed the US Senate with 160 votes in support (Marketwire, 2007).

Galvanized by the movement to make English the official language of the United States, a millionaire software entrepreneur named Ron Unz founded an organization called 'English for the Children' which has supported several anti-bilingual education ballot measures at the state level. In the states targeted by Unz, citizens have voted directly on whether or not bilingual education should be permitted. Voters in California, the state with the largest population of ELLs in the United States, overwhelmingly approved Proposition 227 in 1998, a ballot initiative aimed at eliminating bilingual education. As a result, most English language learners in California are now placed in educational programs where English is the sole language of instruction, and where the time period of enrollment in language support programs has been greatly diminished.

Arizona voters followed suit by passing a similar Unz measure called Proposition 203 in 2000. While the California initiative has reduced the percentage of ELLs in bilingual education programs from 29% to 12%, Arizona's Proposition 203 may end bilingual education entirely in that state; this legislation makes it even more difficult than in California for parents to seek waivers that would permit some bilingual education to continue (Crawford, 2001). In 2002, voters in Massachusetts approved Question 2, another state ballot initiative, doing away with the oldest bilingual education law in the nation. At the same time, however, Colorado voters rejected the initiative in their state and preserved bilingual education there.

The federal government still has not established an official language, and continues to allow states to decide language policy in governance and education. As a result, there is no protection for mother-tongue education in current US laws. However, in international policy, the 1996 United Nations *Universal Declaration of Linguistic Human Rights* upholds the right to maintain one's language and culture and use it in public and private. In 1999, it was ruled at a hearing in The Hague that California's Proposition 227 is a violation of human rights (Skutnabb-Kangas, 2000). However, there is no real accountability to the 1996 United Nations Declaration by the United States, so there is little chance that such a ruling would be upheld.

In marked contrast to the states that have adopted English Only legislation, it is worth noting that the following states have adopted what they term 'English Plus' mandates: New Mexico, Oregon, Rhode Island and Washington. This is best described in New Mexico's legislation, in the following excerpt from their 1989 legislation:

NOW THEREFORE BE IT RESOLVED ... that the First Session of the Thirty-Ninth Legislature of the State of New Mexico hereby reaffirms its advocacy of the teaching of other languages in the United States and its belief that the position of English is not threatened. Proficiency on the part of our citizens in more than one language is to the economic and cultural benefit of our state and the nation, whether that proficiency derives from second language study by English speakers or from home language maintenance plus English acquisition by speakers of other languages. Proficiency in English plus other languages should be encouraged throughout the State. (House Joint Memorial 16, New Mexico legislature, 1989 as cited in Menken, 2006a: 5)

'English Plus' orientations can also be found in language policies in education. For instance, the states of Alaska, Connecticut, Indiana, New York, New Jersey, Illinois, Texas, Washington and Wisconsin currently mandate bilingual education, while New Mexico and Michigan effectively require bilingual education by only funding this type of program (Menken, 2006a).

Paving the Pathway Towards *No Child Left Behind:* The 1994 Reauthorization of the Elementary and Secondary Education Act

This chapter began by describing the history of language policy in the United States as a pendulum, swinging back and forth between language restriction and language tolerance over time. Now the pendulum has swung again into a period of language restriction, and a dramatic shift in orientations towards minority languages can be observed in the changes made to federal education legislation for ELLs from the 1994 reauthorization of the Elementary and Secondary Education Act (ESEA) to the 2001 reauthorization. In many ways, the 1994 amendments to the law were favorable towards bilingual education. At the same time, however, they equally reflected a movement away from the focus on educational access and equality found in legislation such as the *Civil Rights Act* (1964), and towards a new emphasis on educational standards, outcomes and excellence instead (Fowler, 2000; Kaestle, 2001). The testing movement has thus reemerged in the United States in a new form.

For more than a decade, standards and assessment have remained central themes in federal education legislation passed by Congress. The standards identify 'what students should know and be able to do as they progress through school ... [and] are meant to be anchors, aligning curriculum, instruction and assessment' (Menken, 2001: 4). In 1994, Congress passed six education reform goals for all students in *Goals 2000: Educate America Act*, and the law specifically mentioned the inclusion of 'students or children with limited English proficiency' (US Department of Education, 1994). Building on *Goals 2000*, the ESEA was reauthorized and amended in 1994, and entitled the *Improving America's Schools Act*. This law mandated that states develop academic content and performance standards, and corresponding assessments (Riddle, 1999).

In an attempt to redress the negative impact of poverty on individual and schoolwide student achievement, Title I of the ESEA provides additional federal resources targeted to school districts and schools with high concentrations of poverty. The 1994 reauthorization of the ESEA allowed for greater inclusion of ELLs by eliminating a previous law called

Chapter 1 which required that programs distinguish between 'educational deprivation and limited English proficiency' when determining eligibility for programming (Anstrom, 1995). At present, the majority of all ELLs are recipients of Title I, so they are greatly affected by the education reform efforts promoted through Title I legislation. In other words, removing the separation between ELLs and other students in federal education legislation has allowed for new laws to apply to these students as well.

The 1994 ESEA reauthorized and amended Title VII, the *Bilingual Education Act*. This reauthorization emphasized that ELLs must learn English in addition to meeting the same statewide academic content and performance standards as those set for English proficient students. It clarified the benefits of native language development and allowed ELLs to stay in language support programs for more than three years, favoring programs in which students' native language skills were developed as they gained English proficiency (Evans & Hornberger, 2005). In this way, Title VII of 1994 offered support for the expansion of additive or 'strong forms' of bilingual education, such as developmental or dual language programs (Evans & Hornberger, 2005; Wright, 2005).

On one hand, the significance of the 1994 ESEA for language policy is that it offered greater support for learning through the native language. On the other hand, however, its emphasis on standards and assessments in Title I created a space for greater federal involvement in education and imposition of incidental English-only policy. The reauthorization of the ESEA with the *Improving America's Schools Act* laid the foundation for the later passage of *No Child Left Behind*, which supplanted the *Bilingual Education Act* and is the most invasive federal education legislation ever in US history.

No Child Left Behind: The Era of Assessment and Accountability for ELLs

Against a backdrop of a far more culturally and linguistically diverse school population, anti-immigrant backlash and English-only policies, the ESEA was again reauthorized in 2001. Entitled the *No Child Left Behind Act*, the new law builds upon prior federal education legislation yet focuses even more heavily on testing. The law's primary focus is not solely English language learners, but rather its mandates apply to all students. That said, since the passage of the *Bilingual Education Act* in 1968, no federal education policy has as greatly impacted English language learners (ELLs) as *No Child Left Behind* (NCLB).

No Child Left Behind repealed the *Bilingual Education Act* and encourages English-only approaches (Crawford, 2002b; Evans & Hornberger, 2005; Wiley & Wright, 2004). Significantly, the term 'bilingual education' has been eliminated and even the word 'bilingual' entirely erased from the law, causing several significant name changes. Title III of NCLB is now called 'Language Instruction for Limited English Proficient and Immigrant Students' and replaces what was previously Title VII, the *Bilingual Education Act.* NCLB also mandated the renaming of the US Department of Education's 'Office of Bilingual Education and Minority Languages Affairs' (OBEMLA) to the 'Office of English Language Acquisition, Language Enhancement and Academic Achievement for Limited English Proficient Students' (OELA).

At the time that *No Child Left Behind* was passed into law in 2001, I was working in Washington, DC as an educational researcher at what was then called the National Clearinghouse for Bilingual Education (NCBE), which was charged with gathering, analyzing and disseminating research about culturally and linguistically diverse students. In order to continue to receive funding from the US Department of Education, our sole funding source, it was written into the NCLB legislation that the name of the Clearinghouse would need to be changed to the 'National Clearinghouse for English Language Acquisition and Language Instruction Educational Programs' (NCELA), which is the current name.

While NCLB did not outlaw bilingual education outright, it does encourage English-only policies because of the assessment and accountability provisions, a point supported by Wiley and Wright (2004) and Crawford (2002b). Assessment and accountability provisions cut across both Title I and Title III, which are more closely intertwined than ever before. As a condition of receiving federal funding, ELLs must be included within the law's accountability system and make 'adequate yearly progress'. Accordingly, all students must achieve the level of 'proficient' on state assessments by the 2013–2014 school year (US Department of Education, 2001). To ensure all students are assessed, NCLB mandates a participation rate of at least 95% of all students in state assessment systems. As this book describes, standardized tests are being used in most states to meet the accountability requirements of NCLB as a way to demonstrate student progress. Most often, ELLs are included in the same tests as those used to evaluate native English speakers.

The new Titles I and III mandate two types of assessments for students who are ELLs: English language proficiency and academic content (see Figure 2.4). Inclusion in state assessment systems must begin immediately, even if an ELL has been in the United States less than three years – no exemptions are permitted based on time in English instruction

---

No Child Left Behind mandates two types of assessments for ELLs:

- English language proficiency, and

- Academic content (which includes English language arts and math)

Test scores are used to determine if students are making 'adequate yearly progress' so that schools can continue to receive federal funds without sanctions.

Figure 2.4   Assessments for ELLs

(US Department of Education, 2003). Title I Section 1111(b)(7) requires each state to demonstrate that local education agencies will annually assess the English proficiency of all ELLs (measuring students' oral language, reading and writing skills in English). English proficiency assessments are intended to measure the progress an ELL makes in learning English, and implemented at least once a year to all ELL students, including new arrivals; under NCLB, students need to prove they are making progress each year towards becoming proficient in English. English language proficiency assessment is not mandated for non-ELLs, so ELLs are burdened with additional testing when compared to other students. A state must also evaluate the achievement of any ELL in meeting English language arts standards, using assessments in English. States must include all ELLs in their academic content assessments for mathematics and science as well, by providing test accommodations or native language assessments. To meet this mandate, ELLs must take the same tests as native English speakers.

In accordance with the new Title I, a state must now include 'limited English proficient' students (also known as ELLs) into its academic assessment system and assess them in a *valid and reliable manner* that includes:

- Reasonable accommodations.
- To the extent practicable, assessments in the language and form most likely to yield accurate and reliable information on what those students know and can do to determine their mastery of skills in

subjects other than English until they have achieved English language proficiency.

There are further accountability requirements outlined under the new Title III of *No Child Left Behind*, aligned to those in Title I. Each state education association must develop annual measurable achievement objectives to ensure that ELLs make 'adequate yearly progress' in their development and attainment of English proficiency, while meeting rigorous state academic standards in content areas (the same standards as those set for native English speakers). These objectives must reflect:

- The length of time an individual child has been enrolled in a language instruction educational program.
- Increases in the number or percentage of children making progress in learning English and in attaining English proficiency by the end of each school year.
- Adequate yearly progress for ELLs as described in section 1111(b)(2)(B).

The February 2003 draft guidance on Title III, Part II (Standards, Assessment and Accountability) required that each state set measurable achievement objectives by May 2003. In addition, states have since determined adequate yearly progress of ELLs as well as of all other student groups; standards and benchmarks for 'adequate yearly progress' must be the same for ELLs and native English speakers in all content-area subjects.

Growing National Debate Over *No Child Left Behind* and the Assessment of ELLs

As this book goes to press, NCLB is slated for reauthorization in 2008 or 2009, and debates over the assessment of ELLs have begun. In a report published by the Government Accountability Office (GAO) (2006), a non-partisan group that acts as the investigative arm of the US Congress to study federal government programs and expenditures, it was found that states need further support from the US Department of Education in order to develop assessments for ELLs that are valid and reliable. In their evaluation of state assessment and accountability systems, the GAO (2006) found that not only are there problems with test validity and reliability for ELLs, but that in two-thirds of the 48 states studied the percentage of ELLs achieving a score of 'proficient' on a state's language arts and mathematics tests was lower than the state's annual progress goals. One of the main problems with the notion of 'adequate yearly progress' in NCLB is that ELLs, as a group, will by definition always be low performing. When an ELL achieves a level of proficient in their English language proficiency, that student will leave the 'ELL subgroup' and no longer be considered an ELL under NCLB accountability requirements. As such, this group will always be regarded as failing within the current framework, perpetuating a deficit paradigm, or what Ruiz (1984) terms a 'language-as-problem' orientation.[3]

In the first public acknowledgement of problems with the NCLB accountability requirements for ELLs, the US Department of Education's Secretary Spellings responded to the GAO report in a press release announcing a partnership between her office and State Education Associations to 'develop fair and accurate assessments designed for limited English proficient students'. As the press release states, 'Testing is the lynchpin of the *No Child Left Behind Act*, created to bring every child to grade level in reading and math by 2014. The best tools for this effort are valid and reliable content-based assessments in every state' (US Department of Education Press Release, 27 July 2006).

In spite of this acknowledgement of challenges to the validity of tests being used to evaluate ELLs, the US Department of Education has recently decided that ELLs in 18 states must now take English language arts exams (Zehr, 2007). Until 2007 in these states, ELLs participated in alternative assessments rather than the same assessments taken by native English speakers for the purposes of 'adequate yearly progress'. For example, ELLs at the elementary level in New York had participated in English language proficiency tests rather than English language arts tests for the purposes of 'adequate yearly progress'. The federal government decided that this substitution is not permissible, and has required New York and the other 17 states to revise their statewide assessment systems accordingly. In response, Fairfax County, Virginia, which is the 13th largest school district in the United States, has defied the US Department of Education and challenged NCLB by refusing to require its ELLs to participate in the same English tests as those taken by native English speakers (Glod, 2007; Zehr, 2007). While federal officials maintain that all students in a given state must be held to the same standards regardless of their English proficiency, the view of officials in Virginia is best summarized in the following quotation by a member of the Fairfax County School Board:

> 'It is wrong for our students to take a test they are predisposed to fail', said board member Phillip A. Niedzielski-Eichner (Providence). 'We will continue to test their proficiency twice a year and continue to move them forward as quickly as possible. This resolution is not, by any stretch, an attempt to shy away from accountability'. (Glod, 2007: B01)

Virginia is now at the forefront of growing national debate about *No Child Left Behind* and the best way to measure the progress of ELLs.

Discussion

The United States case is unique because it is a country that has a *de facto* language policy rather than an official language. While various efforts to make English the official national language have not achieved their long-term goal, they have succeeded in perpetuating a 'language-as-problem' orientation (Ruiz, 1984) and fed the belief that immigrants do not learn English. They have also promoted the sense that the status of English in this country is in peril, drawing into question US national identity and what it means to be an American in globalizing times. Moreover, the absence of an explicit policy does not mean that no policy exists.

> Even the much vaunted no language policy of many democracies is, in reality, an anti-minority-languages policy, because it delegitimizes such languages by studiously ignoring them, and thereby, not allowing them to be placed on the agenda of supportable general values. (Fishman, 2001: 454)

This certainly applies to the United States, where, as found in this chapter, recent Census data show how immigrants rapidly learn English. Immigrant families typically lose their language by the second or third generation as a result of prolonged linguistic contact with the majority language – English. Yet recent immigration patterns have resulted in a steady flow of new arrivals to the United States who are non-native speakers of English, ensuring that there are always significant numbers of people in the United States who speak other languages. In response, the high status of English has been asserted time and again in US history by those who see it as a threatened language. English is thus the unofficial official language of the United States, where its dominance has been repeatedly demonstrated in accordance with the ebb and flow of immigration waves.

This chapter has looked historically at the treatment of languages other than English in US schools and federal education policy for ELLs, locating recent policy within a context of rapid population change. Although neither packaged nor presented to the public as such, *No Child Left Behind* is in actuality a language policy that is radically impacting language education in schools, and that will have lasting effects on minority languages and their speakers. It differs from policies like the *Bilingual Education Act* during the Civil Rights period of the 1960s and onward, which focused on educational equity and were more tolerant of the use of languages other than English in schooling. Like federal education policy that preceded it, NCLB is a reflection of the federal government's response to a changing society and it has become a means to suppress languages other than English in this country.

Testing is the foundation of *No Child Left Behind*. Termed its lynchpin by the current Secretary of Education, accountability efforts have led to a new instance of testing as *de facto* language policy in American education. English language learners are now showered with tests from the moment they enter school. As this book shows, tests determine many aspects of language education and choices made in schools about which language(s) to use in instruction. An immediate effect of NCLB testing policy is that ELLs are overwhelmingly failing the tests, labeled as deficient and low-performing, and barred from advancement. This chapter also documented the history of the testing movement in the United States, showing how it has contributed to the marginalization of minorities. In this way, testing is repeating its historical use as a sorting mechanism, using rhetoric of science and neutrality to systematically discriminate against immigrant students who are English learners and promote the status of English and its speakers.

Chapter Summary

- Historically, immigrants have entered US schools during alternating periods of relative tolerance or restriction of the languages they speak, depending on the sociopolitical context surrounding schooling at the time. The use of minority languages was restricted after the United States entered World War I, and later tolerated during the Civil Rights Movement of the 1960s. The current period is one of restriction.
- A wide array of program models exists for English language learners which either promote English monolingualism or bilingualism. The United States is extremely linguistically diverse, though immigrants to this country typically lose their language and shift to English by the third generation.
- In the past, standardized testing has been used for gatekeeping purposes in spite of testing bias against racial, ethnic, and language minorities in the United States.
- *No Child Left Behind* is current federal education policy, and mandates the assessment of ELLs in English proficiency and academic content. This law is believed to encourage English-only approaches, and differs from previous education laws for its emphasis on outcomes and accountability.

Chapter 3
The New York Case: The Local Implementation of a National Policy

This book is largely based upon research that was conducted in New York City, and details how national testing policies in the United States, and *No Child Left Behind* in particular, impact the education of English language learners at the local level. Each state has interpreted and implemented NCLB in different ways, creating their own standards, assessments, and testing policies to meet the law's accountability requirements, and each operating within its own complex framework of local legislation and language policies.[4] Within each state, school systems interpret the state's demands, leading to differences at the local level as well as at the state level.

This chapter offers an overview of educational policies and legislation that guide the education of ELLs in New York, and details how the state and city have interpreted the assessment and accountability mandates of *No Child Left Behind.* This chapter is organized into the following sections: (1) Legislation and Policies for the Provision of Services to ELLs & The Recent Decline of Bilingual Education Programs in New York City, (2) The Tests that Count for ELLs in New York High Schools, (3) Public Debates over Testing in New York City, and (4) The Research. New York City offers a unique context for the exploration of testing and language education policy, due to its great racial, ethnic and linguistic diversity. The first section of this chapter offers an overview of local legislation and policies impacting the education of English language learners, and highlights New York's strong historical support for bilingual education programming. In spite of this history, however, this section shows how bilingual education enrollment has decreased while English-only programs have increased since the passage of *No Child Left Behind.* The second section describes city and state testing policies for English learners, with particular attention to the statewide high school exit exams called the Regents, which all students must pass in order to receive a high school diploma. These testing policies reflect the state's interpretation of federal mandates. This chapter then details the study this book is based upon, explaining the research methodology that was used, project design and data analysis. While *No Child Left Behind* will eventually be terminated with changing political tides in Washington, the legacy of this law will remain locally in places like New York for many years to come. The language education policies generated in the law's wake and its emphasis on high-stakes testing will have a lasting impact on English language learners.

Legislation and Policies for the Provision of Services to ELLs and the Recent Decline of Bilingual Education Programs in New York City

Although New York City has a strong history of supporting bilingual education, this has begun to change since the passage of *No Child Left Behind*. New York City is one of the most multilingual cities of the world (García & Fishman, 2002). 'English has never been, and cannot be considered today, New York's vernacular' (García, 2002: 4). The New York City Department of Education (2006a, 2006b) reports that the current total school enrollment is 1,055,986 children, of whom 42% speak a language other than English at home and 13.8% are ELLs. The study this book is based upon examines the implementation of recent policy regarding assessment and high school graduation in an effort to increase understanding of the national issues delineated in the preceding chapters as they play out in New York City.

There are currently 37,810 ELLs enrolled in New York City high schools (New York City Department of Education, 2006b). Of these, the vast majority are 'newly enrolled ELLs', meaning that there are many new immigrants attending city high schools. Of the different city boroughs, the New York City Department of Education (2002) reports that 16.7% of all ELLs attend school in Manhattan, 22.1% in the Bronx, 23% in Brooklyn and 27.8% in Queens.[5] Spanish is by far the predominant language, spoken by 66.1% of all ELLs, followed by Chinese (10.5%), Russian (2.7%), Urdu (2.6%), Bengali (2.5%), Haitian (2.3%), Arabic (1.8%), Korean (1.6%) and Albanian (1.2%). In total, approximately 140 different languages are spoken by ELLs in New York City schools (New York City Department of Education, 2002). This linguistic diversity creates situations where as many as 50 languages are spoken in one school, posing unique challenges and needs which educators must address.

In addition to the federal legislation detailed in the preceding chapter, there is also city and state legislation pertaining to the provision of language support services for ELLs with which schools must comply. The

ASPIRA Consent Decree of 1974 is an agreement between the New York City Board of Education and ASPIRA of New York, a nonprofit organization focusing on the education of Latino youth. The *ASPIRA Consent Decree* mandated the provision of quality bilingual education programs for students 'whose English language deficiency prevents them from effectively participating in the learning process and who can more effectively participate in Spanish' (cited in Rappaport, 2002: 100). This ruling favored and promoted transitional bilingual education programs, which the law required be provided in schools where 20 or more ELLs are native speakers of the same minority language. While the *ASPIRA Consent Decree* has been challenged over the years with changes in the New York City public schools and new leadership (Reyes, 2006), this model has remained the predominant form of bilingual education in the city since the law was passed.

In the wake of the *Lau v. Nichols* case of 1974, the Office for Civil Rights of the US Department of Education was the oversight body responsible for implementation of the ruling. The *Lau Plan of 1977* is an agreement between the New York City Board of Education and the Office for Civil Rights for students 'whose limited English language ability prevents them from effectively participating in the learning process and whose home language is other than English or Spanish' (cited in New York City Department of Education, 2002). In other words, this law ensured that ELLs who speak languages other than Spanish, which was the primary focus of the *ASPIRA Consent Decree*, also receive language support services.

State mandated increase in English instruction

In anticipation of the assessment mandates of *No Child Left Behind*, New York State increased the minimum amount of English instruction that ELLs receive just prior to the law's passage. The New York State Commissioner of Education's Part 154 establishes the following:

> Standards for the use of funds made available by the Legislature to provide financial assistance to school districts having pupils of limited English proficiency. In accordance with the provisions of Part 154, each school district receiving such funds shall provide a program of bilingual education or English as a second language (ESL) for pupils identified as having limited English proficiency. (New York City Department of Education, 2002)

Under Part 154, school districts must identify and serve ELLs. Supporting the *ASPIRA Consent Decree*, a bilingual education program is mandated in schools where there are 20 or more ELLs who all speak the same language.

If there are insufficient numbers of ELLs for a bilingual program, then a 'free-standing' ESL program is provided (New York State Department of Education, Office of Bilingual Education, 2002). Under state and city regulations, high school ELLs in a bilingual program are required to receive ESL and English language arts instruction, native language arts instruction, and social studies, science, and math instruction in their native language and in English using ESL methods.

In 1999, the Commissioner's Part 154 increased the minimum amount of English instruction high school ELLs are required to receive to at least two periods of English class per day. Before 1999, ELLs at all grades and levels of English proficiency were entitled to just one period of ESL per day. After 1999, it was mandated that ELLs in high school at the beginning levels of English proficiency receive three periods of ESL per day, and two periods per day at the intermediate levels. Under the new Part 154, it was mandated that ELLs at the advanced levels receive one period of ESL a day taught by an ESL teacher and also a period of English language arts taught by a certified English teacher (New York State Department of Education, 1999a). The amount of English instruction increased for ELLs with the belief that 'if they were to be prepared to pass English language arts Regents exams, and all the other Regents exams, then they needed a more intense English as a Second Language program' (C. Perez-Hogan, personal communication, 23 June, 2004). At the state level, this is a significant indication that new testing requirements are equated with more English instruction while native language instruction is not being emphasized.

The decrease in bilingual education enrollment since the passage of NCLB

In 2002, it was reported that almost equal numbers of high school ELLs were enrolled in bilingual education as ESL programs; the New York City Department of Education (2002) reported that 17,301 high school ELLs received bilingual education, while 17,318 received a 'free standing' English as a Second Language (ESL) program. Bilingual Education programs in the city existed for the following languages in 2002 (in order of greatest number of programs to least): Spanish, Chinese, Haitian Creole, Russian, Korean, French, Bengali, Arabic, Polish, Urdu, Punjabi and Albanian.

Interestingly, although New York has not officially adopted a new language policy, the number of ELL students enrolled in bilingual education programs has dramatically decreased in the past four years alone while the numbers in ESL programs has steadily increased. This change can be seen in the K-12 enrollment data presented in Table 3.1 and Figure 3.1 below.

Table 3.1 Program enrollment of New York City ELLs by school year, 2002–2006

Program Model	*Year*			
	2002–2003	*2003–2004*	*2004–2005*	*2005–2006*
Transitional bilingual education	37.4%	32.0%	29.8%	27.9%
Dual language	2.3%	2.8%	2.6%	3.2%
Total bilingual education	39.7%	34.8%	32.4%	31.1%
ESL	53.4%	59.7%	65.7%	66.8%
Incomplete information	6.9%	5.5%	1.8%	2.1%
Total	100.0%	100.0%	100.0%	100.0%

Source: New York City Department of Education, 2006b: 23

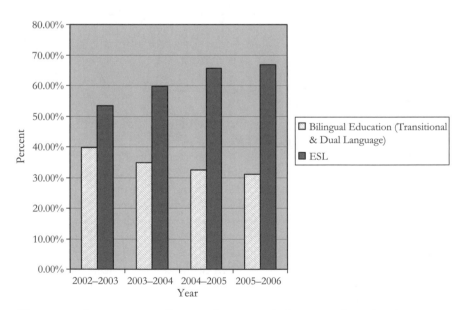

Figure 3.1 Program enrollment of New York City ELLs by school year, 2002–2006

As shown in Table 3.1, data from the New York City Department of Education (2006b) show that in the 2002–2003 school year 39.7% of all ELLs were enrolled in some form of bilingual education (either transitional bilingual education or dual language), and 53.4% were in ESL programs. However, by the 2005–2006 school year, only 31.1% of ELLs were enrolled in bilingual programs while 66.8% were in ESL programs (New York City Department of Education, 2006b).

In June 2006, I had the opportunity to attend a meeting with the Office of English Language Learners of the New York City Department of Education, in which these data were first shared publicly. When I asked why bilingual education enrollment had recently decreased, an administrator from that office responded by saying that the accountability requirements of *No Child Left Behind* are affecting bilingual education programs, so that New York City is 'under the same pressures as everyone else, so what is happening here is the same as what you see happening everywhere, nationally, to bilingual programs' (administrator, New York City Department of Education, meeting notes, 22 June, 2006). This is very strong proof of the argument in this book that *No Child Left Behind* is, in effect, a language policy that is promoting English rather than bilingual education.

The Tests that Count for ELLs in New York High Schools

In compliance with state standards as well as the recent federal *No Child Left Behind* legislation, there are now numerous city and statewide assessments that high school English language learners must take. Recognizing the implications of NCLB just prior to the law's passage, New York raised standards at the secondary level by requiring all high school students, including ELLs, to pass high school exit exams. In addition, tests of English proficiency are now required. For each of these tests, high-stakes decisions such as grade promotion, graduation or placement into specialized programs are based on an individual student's performance.

The Division of Assessment and Accountability of the New York City Department of Education (2003a) reports that new assessments were adopted in the 2002–2003 school year to identify students eligible for language support programs, and to measure ELLs' progress in developing English language proficiency. A newly revised version of the Language Assessment Battery (LAB) is required for new entrants into high school whose home language is other than English, in order to identify students who are entitled to Bilingual/ESL programs. In addition, the New York State Education Department recently adopted the New York State English as a Second Language Achievement Test (NYSESLAT) to measure students' progress in developing English proficiency, as a result of *No Child Left Behind* mandates which state that ELLs must make 'adequate yearly progress' in their development and attainment of English proficiency. This exam was administered for the first time in the Spring of 2003 (New York City Department of Education, 2003a). While these examinations are important, the highest stakes exams at the secondary level are the Regents, described below.

The highest-stakes tests in New York high schools: The Regents exams

In addition to the testing requirements delineated above, all high school ELLs are required to participate in the New York State Regents Testing Program as well, the requirement that is the primary focus of this research. The purpose of the Regents exams is to assess students' performance in various subject areas as required by New York State for high school graduation. Prior to a new mandate in 2000, high school students had the option of receiving either a 'Local Diploma' or a 'Regents Diploma'. In order to receive a Local Diploma, students needed to take a set of Regents Competency Tests (RCTs), which were tests of basic skills, instead of the Regents examinations. By contrast, students in college-track programs who sought a Regents Diploma were required to take a set of Regents exams.

Graduation standards have been raised since then, and all students except those with disabilities must now pass the more rigorous Regents exams in order to graduate – including ELLs. The two diplomas available at present are a 'Regents Diploma' or an 'Advanced Regents Diploma'. To receive a Regents Diploma, students must pass each of the following examinations: the English Regents Exam, one Math Regents Exam,[6] the Global History and Geography Regents Exam, the US History and Government Regents Exam, and one Science Regents Exam (New York State Department of Education, Office of Curriculum, Instruction, and Assessment, 2003a). These are currently the minimum exam requirements in order to earn a high school diploma. While students must pass these five Regents exams for a Regents Diploma, students seeking an Advanced Regents Diploma must pass eight Regents exams (New York State Department of Education, Office of Elementary, Middle, Secondary and Continuing Education, 2000). As a way to increase passing rates, students who take and fail a Regents examination twice are eligible to take a component retest of the exam, which permits students to retake certain portions of the exam that they failed rather than retake the entire exam multiple times (New York State Department of Education, Office of Curriculum, Instruction, and Assessment, 2003b). The Regents exams themselves are described in the next chapter of this book, Chapter 4, which offers examples of items from the tests and a detailed analysis of the linguistic challenges they pose.

The scores that New York City high school students receive on their Regents exams is a primary measure used for citywide accountability to the state. Schools receive a schoolwide accountability score determined by the state to show they have made adequate yearly progress (AYP) under *No Child Left Behind*, and if schools do not meet their AYP goals, they risk being placed on the Schools Under Registration Review (SURR) list. Likewise, statewide scores on the Regents are reported to the US Department of Education for accountability purposes under *No Child Left Behind*, so that the state can continue to receive federal funding without sanctions.

Unlike the majority of states in the United States, New York is one of only eight states permitting students to respond in their native language on translated assessments for content-area subjects (Stansfield & Rivera, 2002; Sullivan *et al.*, 2005). Translated editions of the Regents Examinations in all core areas required for graduation other than English are available in Spanish, Korean, Chinese, Haitian Creole and Russian (New York State Department of Education Bilingual/ESL Network, 2003). Permitted accommodations for ELLs taking Regents examinations in subjects other than English or foreign languages include the following: the use of bilingual glossaries, oral translations of tests and extended test time (New York State Department of Education, 1999b). Bilingual glossaries are available for the following languages: Arabic, Bengali, Bosnian, Burmese, Chinese, Haitian Creole, Korean, Polish, Russian, Serbo-Croatian, Spanish and Vietnamese. Bilingual glossaries were developed for Math, US History and Government, Global History and Geography, Living Environment, Earth Science (New York State Department of Education, Office of Curriculum, Instruction, and Assessment 2003a). However, bilingual glossaries are not available for each subject area in every language. For example, Math is the only subject for which there is bilingual glossary in Bengali, Burmese, or Vietnamese.

As mentioned above, the English Regents examination, a two-day six-hour exam, is now required for all students to graduate from New York City high schools – including ELLs.

All students who first entered ninth grade in September 1996 or there after – including LEP students, regardless of when they first entered a New York State school, must pass the comprehensive Regents examination in

English to receive a diploma. (New York State Department of Education, 1999b: 1)

In other words, even an English language learner who has just arrived in the United States must participate in all core Regents exams, including the English Regents.

Performance by English language learners on the Regents exams

Performance by ELLs on the Regents exams to date has lagged far behind that of English proficient students. According to the New York City Department of Education (2005), just 33.2% of ELLs passed the English Regents exam in 2005, as compared to a pass rate of 77.9% of all students taking the English Regents exam in the same year. For the Math A Regents exam, the ELL citywide pass rate in 2005 was 55.5%, as compared to an overall pass rate of 81.5%. I have compiled the Regents pass rates data from 2002 to 2005 into Table 3.2 and Figures 3.2 and 3.3 below.

Based on the data above, the percentage of ELLs passing the English Regents exam is, on average, 47 percentage points below the pass rate by all students. On the Math A Regents Exam, the ELL pass rate is on average 25 percentage points below the overall pass rate. It is interesting to note that the ELL pass rates increased from 2002 to 2003; pass rates increased for all students during that time frame, but based on my research the increase for ELLs on the English Regents can best be explained by their teachers

Table 3.2 Comparison of ELL pass rates to overall pass rates on English and math A Regents exams, by year

Exam	Year	*Overall pass rate*	*ELL pass rate*	*ELL differential*
English Regents	2002	74.2%	17.4%	−56.8%
	2003	75.2%	32.5%	−42.7
	2004	80.7%	36.2%	−44.5%
	2005	77.9%	33.2%	−44.7%
Math A Regents	2002	50.8%	28.4%	−22.4%
	2003	59.5%	36.3%	−23.2%
	2004	86.9%	58.1%	−28.8%
	2005	81.5%	55.5%	−26.0%

Sources: New York City Department of Education, Division of Assessment and Accountability (2003b, 2004a, 2005)

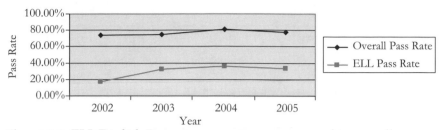

Figure 3.2 ELL English Regents pass rates, as compared to overall pass rates, by year

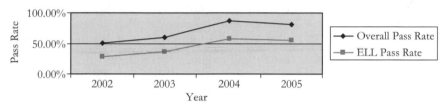

Figure 3.3 ELL math A Regents pass rates, as compared to overall pass rates, by year

becoming more accustomed to the tests themselves in that year, and thus more students who were better prepared were included.

Increase in ELL dropout rate

Poor performance on the Regents corresponds to an increase in dropout rates since it was mandated that ELLs be included in these exams as a requirement for high school graduation. At 30.5%, the dropout rate for ELLs is the highest of any student group in New York City (New York City Department of Education, 2004b). The New York City Department of Education compiled four-year longitudinal data for ELLs in the Class of 2003 (these students were typically entering ninth graders during the 1999–2000 school year). Just 31.6% of ELLs successfully graduated by August 2003, 37.9% were still enrolled and scheduled to continue into a fifth year of high school in September 2003, and 30.5% were dropouts. This is compared to 'English proficient' students, of whom 54.4% successfully graduated, 25.5% were still enrolled, and 20.1% were dropouts (New York City Department of Education, 2004b).

Dropout rates for all students are higher than they were in 1999, and the New York City Independent Budget Office (2004) reports that these

Table 3.3 Dropout Rates Rise Faster for ELLs Post-Testing Mandates, 1999–2002

Year	*1999*		*2000*		*2001*		*2002*	
Student group	ELL	Non-ELL	ELL	Non-ELL	ELL	Non-ELL	ELL	Non-ELL
Dropout rate	21.2%	16.2%	30.6%	19.3%	31.7%	20.4%	31.5%	20.3%

Source: New York City Independent Budget Office (2004)

dropout rates have risen even more rapidly for ELLs. Table 3.3 shows the dropout rates for ELLs as compared to non-ELL students.

As shown in Table 3.3, 21.2% of ELLs in the class of 1999 dropped out of high school as compared to 16.2% of the general student body. In the class of 2002, 31.5% of ELLs dropped out as compared to 20.3% of the general student body. In other words, while the dropout rate for the overall class has increased by about four percentage points, the dropout rate for ELLs has increased far more, by about ten percentage points. The dropout rate among ELLs has almost doubled in the years since it was required that they also be included in Regents examinations as a requirement for high school graduation. This increase occurred after a decade of decline in dropout rates among ELLs, in the years prior to the mandate that they be included in the Regents exams (Del Valle, 2002).

Public Debates Over Testing in New York City

The topic of testing has become increasingly contentious in New York, frequently reported in the local media and often at the center of the political stage. The Regents exams were the cause of controversy in June 2003, when a new version of the Math A Regents exam was introduced. Many teachers and students throughout the state complained that the test was exceedingly difficult, and noted that the pass rate was far lower than it had been on the previous version (Arenson, 2003a). State Commissioner Mills then decided to nullify the results of the June 2003 Math A Regents for juniors and seniors, in the midst of debate, and seniors who had passed their math courses but failed the exam were eventually allowed to graduate (Arenson, 2003b).

In February 2004, New York City Mayor Bloomberg and Schools Chancellor Joel Klein placed testing in newspaper headlines again by adopting a third grade retention policy amidst a sea of controversy, whereby any third grade students failing the citywide exams in reading and math were retained in grade. The mayor and chancellor, who fired any members of the school board opposing this policy, believe it is a necessary step to end social promotion.[7] There are also political benefits of the policy for the mayor and chancellor. Given that fourth grade scores are the ones reported to the state and federal government for accountability under *No Child Left Behind*, the third grade retention policy removed poor performing students from the fourth grade exam, thereby increasing citywide scores.

The mayor and chancellor have adopted the same retention policy for fifth graders in 2005 and seventh graders in 2006. In the summer of 2006, students who failed the exams were permitted to attend summer school programs focused on test preparation with the hope that their scores on the exams would increase enough for these students to be promoted. More than half of the 13,751 third, fifth and seventh graders who failed the exams and attended such programs were retained in grade anyway, because their scores did not increase enough. Opponents of the policies cite research arguing that major educational decisions should not be based solely on one test score, and that students retained in grade are far more prone to eventual school failure (Advocates for Children, 2004).

In response to pressure from advocates, the policies were amended in 2004 such that ELLs can be exempt from the elementary exams if they have been in US schools three years or less; however, this was reversed in 2006. Since the passage of *No Child Left Behind*, New York had been requiring ELLs at the elementary level to take the New York State ESL Achievement Test (NYSESLAT) for their first three years of participation in statewide testing, in lieu of the English Language Arts exam taken by English proficient students. However, the US Department of Education has recently ruled that this practice is out of compliance with NCLB, which mandates the participation of ELLs in statewide assessments after one year in the United States. As a result, New York state must now require all ELLs at the elementary level, from the moment they arrive in the United States, to take the same English Language Arts exam as that taken by native English speakers (Herszenhorn, 2006a, 2006b; Zehr, 2006a, 2006b). This practice took effect in January, 2007. The state leadership has in essence extended the high school Regents policy of full inclusion to the elementary level.

Public debates about the inclusion of ELLs in Regents exams

The issue of including ELLs in high-stakes testing has gained increased attention in recent years, particularly among advocates for their education. On 15 October, 2003, individuals (including teachers of ELLs, academics, parents and ELL students) and advocacy organizations (such as South Asian Youth Action, Advocates for Children and the New York Immigration Coalition), testified at a public hearing in New York City before

New York State Commissioner Mills and the Board of Regents on the negative effects of including ELLs in Regents exams. A primary purpose for testimonials was to change legislation, allowing schools to be permitted waivers from participation in the Regents exams or receive approval for alternatives (New York State Assembly Standing Committee on Education, 2003). The Puerto Rican Legal Defense and Education Fund recently filed a lawsuit against the state on behalf of ELLs, claiming 'disparate impact' of the Regents exams on this student population, though that case is still pending.

The problem of 'push-outs' and the increase in numbers of immigrant youths leaving school to pursue a Graduate Equivalency Diploma (GED) have also recently received greater attention in New York and elsewhere across the nation, as further side-effects of high-stakes testing. 'Push-outs' are defined as students who leave school involuntarily, even though they have a legal right to remain. In 2001, 55,015 students were discharged from New York City high schools; this number is higher than the schoolwide dropout rate for that year, which was 14,549. Advocates for Children & Office of Public Advocate Betsy Gotbaum (2002) report that a significant number of these students were 'push-outs', because there was no process for their discharge, they were not informed of their rights to stay in school until the age of 21, and they were not offered educational support services. They report that the incentives for push-outs relate to recent accountability measures, in that encouraging low-performing students to leave school increases overall test performance and masks high dropout rates. Immigrant students are particularly vulnerable to becoming push-outs, as they are disproportionately at-risk – they are more likely to remain in school beyond the traditional four years and their performance on tests is typically lower (Advocates for Children & Office of Public Advocate Betsy Gotbaum, 2002). On 19 June, 2004 the New York City Department of Education settled a lawsuit filed by Advocates for Children against three city high schools for forcing students out, resolving that schools have a legal obligation to allow students to work towards their high school graduation until the age of 21 and to inform students of this right (Lewin, 2004).

Enrollment in GED programs by youths under the age of 21 has dramatically increased in New York City in recent years, from 24,466 in 2002 to 37,010 in 2003 (New York State Department of Education, as cited in Campanile, 2004). This reflects a national increase, as teenagers accounted for 49% of those earning a GED in 2002, up from 33% a decade earlier (Arenson, 2004). According to Arenson (2004: 3), '[r]ecent immigrants with weak English are frequently discouraged from enrolling in high school and pointed toward GED programs'. This is confirmed in focus group research that was conducted in New York City, where ELL students reported being 'encouraged' by school staff to pursue a GED instead of a high school diploma (Advocates for Children & The New York Immigration Coalition, 2002). The increase in GED enrollment in New York City is explained in the following passage:

> Students who are unable to pass Regents exams no longer have the middle option of attaining a local, non-Regents diploma, or graduating from an alternative school that uses portfolio assessments as graduation measures. Today they either have to pass the Regents or get a GED. (Advocates for Children & Office of Public Advocate Betsy Gotbaum, 2002: 3)

In GED programs in New York, students obtain a high school equivalency diploma by passing the Tests of General Educational Development, which are administered by the American Council on Education in Washington, DC. In this way, they are able to circumvent passing the five core Regents exams that are now required in order to graduate from city high schools. However, analyses of the economic rate of return for education show that students receiving a GED typically earn less than students with a traditional high school diploma, such that there is no statistical difference in earnings between students who receive a GED and high school dropouts (Cameron & Heckman, 1993).

In 2004, New York State Assemblyman Peter Rivera proposed a bill that would allow immigrant students in the United States for five years or less to follow an alternative route for high school graduation, so they would no longer have to take the English Regents exam (Gormley, 2004). In addition, the New York Immigration Coalition organized a protest rally and news event at City Hall on 16 June, 2004, the day that students began the June Regents exams, to state their opposition to how Regents exams have a harmful impact on the education of immigrant children in New York City high schools (Davila, 2004). As stated at the outset, this study of New York City offers an example of how the national emphasis on testing plays out within a local context, just when it becomes possible to weigh the effects of *No Child Left Behind*.

The Research

In order to study the standardized testing of ELLs from a language policy perspective, the research this book is based upon involved qualitative fieldwork in ten New York City high schools serving ELLs. To date, little research has been devoted to the inclusion of ELLs in high-stakes testing in the United States, particularly with regard to the language policy implications of this practice. Quantitative data indicate how ELLs perform on standardized tests when compared to other students. However, studies such as these do not tell the human stories about how schools and individuals within them negotiate federal education reforms based on standards, and specifically high-stakes standardized tests that are inclusive of ELLs. While a few qualitative studies do exist, there is in general a wide gap in research on this topic. The purpose of this research was to fill this gap in existing research by exploring how the reality of high-stakes testing is lived in schools serving ELLs.

Two principal questions guided this research:

(1) In what ways have reforms emphasizing high-stakes tests influenced the instructional practices and the learning experiences of ELLs in high school?
(2) What are the implications of the focus on assessment for language planning and policy?

To explore these questions, data were collected over the entire 2003–2004 academic year (for a more detailed description of the methodology, see Menken, 2005).

Methodology

The first research question consists of two parts: the first part explores how high-stakes testing influences instructional practices, and the focus of this question is on teachers and their teaching; the second part examines how high-stakes testing influences the learning experiences of ELLs, and the focus of this question is on students. Both parts of the first research question 'seek to understand the lived experiences of individuals and their intentions within their "lifeworld," [answering] the question, "What is it like to have a certain experience?"' (Crabtree & Miller, 1992: 24). Answering this question entails qualitative interviews, as a way to learn about experiences through the human stories told by the people most directly affected. It also involves classroom observations, offering a glimpse into school life. Federal, state and district educational policymakers were informally interviewed as well, and relevant literature, policy documents and student performance data were reviewed to provide background data. The second research question is entirely theoretical. This question applies findings from the fieldwork to explore the language planning and policy implications of high-stakes assessment.

Accordingly, the data consisted of: (A) interviews; (B) observations; (C) state, district and school policy documents; (D) standardized test scores; and (E) graduation, promotion/retention and dropout data. The findings from this research draw most heavily on the interview data that were collected. A combination of in-depth individual interviews and group interviews of students, teachers, and federal, state, district and school administrators provide primary data. The main data sources are New York City teachers who are preparing high school ELLs for the Regents exams, high school administrators who oversee programming for ELLs, and high school ELL students.

A total of 128 participants were interviewed, as follows: 61 ELL students, 19 administrators (including school principals, assistant principals and ESL or foreign language coordinators),[8] 44 teachers, and four guidance counselors were interviewed in-depth for the purposes of this research study. Interview protocols for individual and group interviews were employed across each school site included in this study and a protocol was also used for classroom observations. Different protocols were used for educators (teachers and administrators) and students, as well as for classroom observations. Interviews were semi-structured (Mishler, 1986; LeCompte & Preissle, 1993). The purpose of interviews with teachers and administrators was to learn their perceptions of how the testing emphasis has impacted them, their instruction and their students – with particular attention to language. Interviews with ELL students asked about their experiences with different high-stakes exams, their opinions about the tests, how they feel in school and how testing impacts their futures. Classroom observations offered a way to contextualize the data gathered from interviews with students, teachers and administrators.

Project design

This study involved qualitative research in ten high schools across the boroughs of New York City.[9] As shown in Figure 3.4 below, the research followed a 'pyramid design', whereby schools were studied to varying degrees of depth in order to make this a manageable project. One high school was studied in greatest depth over the entire 2003–2004 academic year, as a focal site for intensive ethnography. Three 'second tier' schools were selected where the following was conducted: (1) two or more site visits, (2) interviews with administrators, teachers and students, and (3) classroom observations. A remaining set of six 'third tier' schools were visited once or more, and interviews were conducted with at least one administrator and two teachers at each. In this way, findings from the intensive study of the first school were investigated in a broader sample of schools.

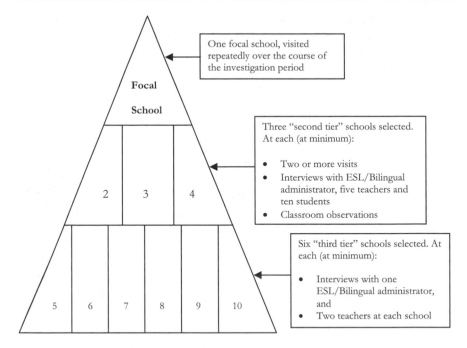

Figure 3.4 Pyramid project design

Participants

Table 2.3 in Chapter 2 showed the different program models for ELLs in the United States. In New York City high schools, the program models for ELLs include: pull-out ESL, sheltered content, transitional bilingual education and dual language. In addition, all high school students must fulfill a foreign language requirement and typically do so by studying a language for one period (about 45 minutes) each day. ELLs who attend schools where their home language is offered as a foreign language to native English speakers can often enroll in native language arts classes (e.g. where Spanish is taught to native speakers of Spanish) or, in cases where there are not enough native speakers of that language to create a separate class, simply enroll in foreign language classes where students are a mixture of native English speakers and native speakers of the language being taught.

Figure 3.4 lists the participants in this study at each school site. Due to the variety of program models for ELLs in New York City schools, there are several different types of high school teachers who work with

ELLs: ESL teachers, bilingual content teachers (who teach subjects such as math, science and social studies bilingually), native language arts teachers (foreign language teachers who teach languages such as Spanish or Bengali to native speakers of those languages), English language arts teachers, sheltered content teachers (who teach subjects such as math, science and social studies using ESL pedagogy to make content accessible) and English monolingual teachers of all subjects who have ELLs in their classrooms. I ensured a representative group of teachers was interviewed at each 'tier' of schools. Efforts were also made to interview a diverse group of students, according to such characteristics as their native language and level of English proficiency.

Site selection and sampling

This research project is a case study, whereby New York City provides an example of how the national emphasis on high-stakes testing is implemented at the local level, even though New York City is vast and complex, with hundreds of high schools in the city. As Yin (1984) explains, the boundary of cases extends from the individual to the nation, and is not monolithic. Miles and Huberman justify this approach in the following:

> We argue in this book, with much recent practice to support us, that multiple cases offer the researcher an even deeper understanding of processes and outcomes of cases ... (Miles & Huberman, 1994: 26)

In planning this research project, a great deal of attention was paid to site selection, sampling and the challenges of multi-case implementation. A 'purposeful sample' is defined as 'typical of the population in which we are interested, assuming that errors of judgment in the selection will tend to counterbalance one another' (Judd *et al.*, 1991: 136). In this case, my concern was to choose schools that, when taken together, are typical of schools serving English language learners in New York City. A different process was used to select the focal school than was used for the other nine schools selected for participation in this study. The high school selected as the focal site currently serves a total of 5000 students, and offers bilingual education and ESL classes to a combination of Latino, Asian, African and Eastern European students. This school was hand-selected to be the focal site because it serves a diverse population of ELLs. Also, this school had managed to raise its test scores for ELLs on the Regents exams, when scores in earlier years had been far below the city average. Of students tested, 81.3% had met the graduation requirement on the English Regents, and 79.5% had met the graduation requirement on the Math Regents (New York City Department of Education, 2003b).

In order to select a purposeful sample for the nine remaining high schools, such characteristics as the following were considered for each school: location by borough, percentage of ELLs, language groups represented, socioeconomic status, test scores, language program offered for ELLs (i.e. ESL or bilingual) and school size. To do so, I gathered data that were available from the New York City Department of Education about each of the different city high schools and compiled the information. These data indicated that a total of 135 high schools were serving ELLs in New York City when I started data collection.

It was then necessary to narrow the sample from all 135 high schools serving ELLs to nine for inclusion in this study. What Kuzel (1992) terms 'criterion sampling' (after Patton, 1990) is the first strategy that was employed to narrow the sample. Because ELLs are the focus of this study, only high schools with a student population of 15% ELLs or greater were selected. I determined that 47 schools serve an ELL population of 15% or higher. Next, nine of the 47 high schools serving an ELL population of 15% or more were selected on a stratified random sample basis and balanced by the characteristics mentioned above (e.g. location, language program offered, etc.).

Each of the ten schools ultimately included in this study is described in Table 3.4. The schools included in this study are dispersed across the city boroughs, representing a wide range in terms of size, student population, educational programming for ELLs, test scores and other performance indicators, percentage ELLs and language groups represented. Of the high schools studied, three are located in the Bronx, three are in Manhattan, three are in Queens, and one is in Brooklyn. The types of schools studied are also dispersed across the boroughs; for example, at least one large high school was studied in each borough with the exception of Staten Island, which at the time did not have any high schools meeting the requirement that 15% of the total population be comprised by ELLs.

Data analysis

For data analysis, interviews were recorded in the form of fieldnotes and audio recordings that were transcribed. Following the guidance of LeCompte and Preissle (1993), and Miles and Huberman (1994), I first reviewed fieldnotes and other data and noted categories or patterns as they emerged. In later stages of analysis, the codes were revised to create 'taxonomies' that show how certain groups of terms might be connected to each other. As data were analyzed, I kept a record of each time a certain

Table 3.4 Summary of the ten schools included in this study

| | School ID number | # Students | Student population | | | | | Language groups represented | Language program | Regents pass rates after 4 years high school (schoolwide) | | Class size | Free lunch eligible[11] |
			ELL	White	Black	Hispanic	Asian + Other			English	Math		
Tier 1	School #1	4600	15%	4%	33%	59%	6%	Mostly Spanish, some Eastern European, African, Asian	ESL, Spanish Bilingual, Advanced Placement (AP) Spanish	80%	70%	34	91%
Tier 2	School #2	4440	19%	4%	24%	68%	4%	Spanish, Eastern European, African, Asian	ESL, Spanish Bilingual	56%	52%	34+	85%
	School #3	225	100%	5%	31%	60%	4%	Spanish, African, Asian, Eastern European, M. Eastern	Sheltered ESL	N/A	N/A	15	89%
	School #4	4000	15%	16%	15%	51%	18%	Mostly Spanish and Bengali, then other Asian, E. European, African	ESL, Sheltered content, some Spanish Bilingual, Bengali Native Language Arts (NLA)	78%	66%	34	60%

(Continued)

Table 3.4 (Continued)

| School ID number | # Students | ELL | Student population | | | | | Language groups represented | Language program | Regents pass rates after 4 years high school (schoolwide) | | Class size | Free lunch eligible[1] |
			White	Black	Hispanic	Asian + Other				English	Math		
School #5	70	86%	1%	1%	1%	97%	Chinese	ESL, Chinese Bilingual, Chinese NLA, Chinese Foreign Language (FL)	N/A	N/A	17–25	N/A
School #6	4300	34%	5%	8%	60%	27%	Mostly Spanish, Chinese and Korean, +20 other languages	ESL; Chinese Bilingual, Spanish Bilingual, Korean NLA	68%	60%	34	34%
School #7	340	100%	0%	0%	100%	0%	Spanish	Spanish Bilingual, AP Spanish	46%	67%	20–30	73%

Tier 3

(Continued)

Table 3.4 (Continued)

	School ID number	# Students	ELL	White	Black	Hispanic	Asian + Other	Language groups represented	Language program	English	Math	Class size	Free lunch eligible[11]
					Student population					Regents pass rates after 4 years high school (schoolwide)			
Tier 3	School #8	1718	45%	2%	16%	38%	45%	Chinese, Spanish, some Bengali and others	Chinese and Spanish Bilingual, ESL	55%	57%	34	83%
	School #9	3800	25%	18%	8%	45%	28%	Spanish, Chinese and over 100 languages total	Spanish and Chinese Bilingual, Spanish, Chinese and Korean FL; ESL	70%	66%	30	30%
	School #10	3200	15%	23%	33%	19%	26%	Haitian Creole, Chinese, with Spanish and others	Partial Haitian Creole and Chinese Bilingual, ESL	84%	79%	34	39%

Sources: Information gathered at school sites and New York City Department of Education, Division of Assessment and Accountability (2004a)[10]

code was used, to identify prevalent themes. In this way, the findings reported in this book reflect the themes that arose most frequently in interviews. For example, the topic of the importance of the tests, test anxiety, and test stories of running out of time arose 89 times in interviews with educators and students; for this reason, this theme is examined in Chapter 5.

Discussion

Within the national context of testing policies under *No Child Left Behind*, on one hand New York is quite accommodating of English language learners because it is part of a small minority of states offering test translations for these students. On the other hand, however, New York has high school exit exams that all students, including ELLs, must pass. These exams carry very high stakes, as they are used to measure adequate yearly progress under NCLB and to determine whether a student will receive a high school diploma. In response to new pressures placed on ELLs to pass these tests, New York State increased the minimum amount of English that ELLs are to receive, in order to prepare them for the tests. In this way, the state has responded to testing pressures by adopting an incidental language policy promoting English.

Due to its great cultural and linguistic diversity, New York City offers a rich context in which to explore the impact of NCLB testing policies and accountability mandates on ELLs. Furthermore, New York City offers an example of how testing policy shapes language policy in a state that has not been affected by the anti-bilingual education ballot measures passed elsewhere, such as in California, Arizona and Massachusetts. In fact, New York City has a long history of favoring bilingual education, since the passage of the *ASPIRA Consent Decree* in 1974. Yet it appears that the city is moving towards English-only, even without anti-bilingual education mandates. Although the city has not explicitly adopted a new language policy, the numbers of students enrolled in bilingual education programs has decreased significantly since the passage of NCLB, while the numbers of students enrolled in English-only programs has increased.

As described in this chapter, ELL students in New York City are disproportionately failing the statewide exams, with passing rates that are typically 47 percentage points below English-proficient students on the English Regents exam and 25 percentage points below other students on the Math Regents. At the high school level, low passing rates are associated with an increase in ELL high school dropout rates and cases of at-risk students being 'pushed out' of high school by education officials against their will. In addition, the youth enrollment in Graduate Equivalency Diploma programs has dramatically increased in recent years, because they offer a way for students to circumvent the Regents exam requirements. Unfortunately, however, GED programs do not offer the same economic advantages of a high school diploma in the long run.

This book shares the findings of qualitative research I conducted in ten New York City high schools to explore how Regents exams are affecting the instructional practices and learning experiences of ELLs, and thereby shaping language education policies. This chapter details how the research was conducted. In this way, these research findings provide one example of an issue that is national in scope; although New York is unique and has interpreted NCLB in its own way, *No Child Left Behind* is affecting classroom practices and language policies in schools across the United States. Therefore, while this book primarily details what is happening in New York, throughout the book information and research findings are shared from other states as well. It is my hope that the readers of this book will take away a deeper understanding of the ways that testing is impacting English language learners in school.

Chapter Summary

- New York has historically been favorable towards bilingual education, as transitional bilingual education programs have been mandated for ELLs in New York since 1974.
- However, since the passage of *No Child Left Behind* in 2001, bilingual programs have decreased in number while English-only ESL programming has increased. Similarly, recent state policy has increased the amount of English instruction for ELLs. This supports the argument in this book that NCLB is a *de facto* English-only language education policy.
- ELLs are now required to pass five Regents examinations to graduate from high school and meet NCLB testing mandates. Yet ELLs typically score far below native English speakers on these exams. Low ELL passing rates on statewide tests have been linked to ELLs leaving school by dropping out or attending alternate degree programs.
- A qualitative study was conducted for this book in ten New York City high schools serving ELLs, to explore how the national emphasis on high-stakes testing impacts the instructional practices and learning experiences of ELLs in school, and to examine new language education policy in the wake of testing mandates.

Part 2

Standardized Tests in Daily School Life

Chapter 4

Tongue-Tied: The Linguistic Challenges that Standardized Tests Pose for English Language Learners

In implementation of *No Child Left Behind*, serious difficulties have arisen from the law's assessment and accountability mandates because most states are using standardized test scores as a way to prove to the federal government that students are progressing in the ways the law requires. The main problem with this approach is the fact that most ELLs are taking tests in English that were never intended for them. At the time that *No Child Left Behind* was passed into law, most states already had statewide assessments in place. So, in order to comply with the mandate that ELLs also be evaluated, states simply began including these students into the same tests already being taken by native English speakers. Yet the fit is awkward at best, as most states rely on tests that are in English only for the evaluation of content-area knowledge. Research indicates that any assessment of an English language learner's content-area knowledge administered in English is likely to be greatly influenced by the student's English language proficiency, and that testing done in English is first and foremost an English language proficiency exam (Council of Great City Schools/National Clearinghouse for English Language Acquisition, 2002; García & Menken, 2006; Menken, 2000). There also continues to be cultural and linguistic complexity in test items that are further sources of measurement errors, and have yet to be properly addressed in the assessments being used for high-stakes decisionmaking (Abedi & Dietal, 2004; Abedi *et al.*, 2004; Solano-Flores & Trumball, 2003).

These problems are further compounded by the fact that modern exams are highly linguistically complex. Assessments in the late 20th century focused on reading comprehension, primarily requiring students to answer multiple-choice questions. Although ELLs never did particularly well on this type of exam, these tests required receptive language skills which are more easily acquired by a language learner than productive skills. As the testing industry has evolved into a focus on 'performance-based assessments', students taking new exams are required to both engage with multiple literacies and produce language in complex ways that take far longer to acquire (García & Menken, 2006). As a result of all of these issues combined, language proficiency is now inextricably linked to the test score a student attains, making it nearly impossible to yield a reliable and valid score when an exam like this is taken by an English language learner.

In order to understand the issues of involving ELLs in tests used for high-stakes decisionmaking, and particularly to determine high school graduation, it is necessary to be familiar with the tests currently being implemented. This chapter provides a detailed exploration of actual tests, looking at test items from New York, California and Texas, the states with the largest numbers of ELLs in the United States (Padolsky, 2005). The chapter is therefore divided into the following sections: (1) Challenges of English Language Arts Exams, (2) Challenges of Mathematics Exams and (3) Test Translation and Accommodation Issues. The first section of this chapter offers examples from recent English language arts tests administered to high school students in New York and California, and the second section examines recent Math exam questions from New York and Texas, providing a linguistic analysis of different test items. By analyzing actual tests and their content, it is possible to understand why they may pose challenges specific to an English language learner that would not be experienced the same way by a student proficient in English. Chapters 2 and 3 of this book indicate that the achievement gap between ELLs and other students on statewide assessments is wide in New York and elsewhere in the United States, typically by 20–50 percentage points (Abedi & Dietal, 2004; Center on Education Policy, 2005). This chapter will show how all of the tests, including math, are linguistically challenging, which explains why the language proficiency of ELLs typically impedes upon their performance.

Across the United States, ELLs are being included into tests that were originally intended for native English speakers, by using test accommodations such as extended time or test translations that intend to make the test scores an ELL attains comparable to a native English speaker's scores. The third section of this chapter counters the myth that the testing accommodations being used are sufficient to truly 'level the playing field' for these students. It shows how the test scores that ELLs attain are not actually comparable to those of native English speakers, drawing into question their use for making high-stakes decisions.

Challenges of English Language Arts Exams: Examples from New York and California

In addition to tests of content such as math and science, states and districts are now requiring ELLs to pass the same English language arts exams taken by native English speakers to meet the accountability requirements of *No Child Left Behind* and, at the secondary level, as a gatekeeper to decide whether these students will graduate from high school. These practices raise concerns with regard to the validity, reliability, and fairness of the inclusion of this student population (Heubert & Hauser, 1999). The reality is that English language learners typically perform worse than other students on standardized tests, and this has serious consequences for them. Research shows that English language learners consistently score far below native English speakers on wide-scale assessments, in language arts as well as in content-area subjects, and across grade levels (Escamilla *et al.*, 2003; Valenzuela, 2005). Not surprisingly, it is the English proficiency level of ELLs which negatively impacts their performance on English language arts exams (Uebelacker, 2005).

New York's English Regents exams

As stated previously, high school students in New York must pass each of the following examinations in order to receive a high school diploma: the English Regents Exam, one Math Regents Exam, two Social Studies Regents Exams and one Science Regents Exam (New York State Department of Education, Office of Curriculum, Instruction, and Assessment, 2003a). In addition to being a graduation requirement, the scores that high school students receive on their Regents exams is the primary measure used for citywide accountability to the state. Likewise, statewide scores on the Regents are reported to the US Department of Education for accountability purposes, so that the state can continue to receive federal funding without sanctions. As such, the stakes attached to these tests are high for students and educators.

The English Regents exam is demanding for any student, and particularly so for ELLs for obvious reasons – their limited proficiency in the English language is a barrier that keeps many students from passing. Even an English language learner who has only just arrived in the United States must participate in the English Regents exam to graduate. Furthermore, *No Child Left Behind* mandates that the participation rate in statewide assessments must be at least 95% of all students, including ELLs, which pushes schools to test all of their students so that they can meet the law's 'adequate yearly progress' targets – even when they serve large numbers of new arrivals. This contradicts research by Cummins (2000) and Thomas and

Collier (1997), who state that it takes ELLs at the very least five years to acquire the academic language in English needed to perform to the level of native English speakers on assessments.

Offered twice per year, the English Regents exam is a long test that is divided into two three-hour sessions taken over two consecutive days. ELLs are permitted extended time and the use of a bilingual dictionary. The basic format of the English Regents is as follows:

Session One
Part A (Task 1): Listening – Listen to a passage, write an essay and answer multiple-choice questions based on the passage.
Part B (Task 2): Reading – Read a text and corresponding graphic (e.g. map, graphic organizer, chart, etc.); write a persuasive essay (e.g. a speech, letter, etc.) and answer multiple-choice questions using both documents.

Session Two
Part A (Task 3): Literature – Read two different passages from differing genres of literature (usually a poem and either an essay or an excerpt from a work of literature); answer multiple-choice questions and write an essay that ties both texts together around a set theme.
Part B (Task 4): Critical Lens – Read a quotation; write an essay based on two works of literature the student has read which must be used to agree or disagree with the quotation.

These tasks are described in greater detail below, using examples taken from actual exams.

In the listening part, Task 1, students listen to a passage that can be on a variety of topics (such as science, politics, economics, history or anthropology). In the English Regents that was administered 27 January 2003, the listening passage in the 'directions for teachers' booklet was two single-spaced pages in length, lasting about ten minutes when read aloud by the teacher proctoring the exam. Exam Proctors are directed to read the passage twice. These are the directions that were read aloud to students by the exam proctor are shown in Figure 4.1.

Below is the first paragraph of the listening passage that was read aloud to students (out of a total of nine paragraphs):

What, then, is this vote that we are hearing so much about just now [in 1908], so much more than people have heard in discussion at least, for a great many years? I think we may give the vote a threefold description. We may describe the vote as, first of all, a symbol, secondly, a safeguard, and thirdly, an instrument. It is a symbol of freedom, a symbol of citizenship, a symbol of liberty. It is a safeguard of all those liberties which

> Look at page 2 of your examination booklet and follow along while I read the **Overview** and **The Situation**.
>
> **Overview:**
> For this part of the test, you will listen to a speech about the struggle of women to obtain voting rights in England, answer some multiple-choice questions, and write a response based on the situation described below. You will hear the speech twice. You may take notes on the next page anytime you wish during the readings.
>
> **The Situation:**
> For a social studies unit on the history of voting rights, your teacher has asked each student to prepare a report on an issue related to the struggle for voting rights in another country. You have decided to do your report on the social conditions that led women in England to seek the right to vote. In preparation for writing your report, listen to a speech delivered in 1908 by Emmeline Pankhurst. Then use relevant information from the speech to write your report.
>
> Now I will read the passage aloud to you for the first time.

Figure 4.1 English Regents, direction for teachers (New York State Department of Education, 2003)

it symbolises. And in these later years it has come to be regarded more than anything else as an instrument, something with which you can get a great many more things than our forefathers who fought for the vote ever realised as possible to get with it. It seems to me that such a thing is worth fighting for, and women to-day are fighting very strenuously in order to get it…. (English Regents, Direction for Teachers, New York State Department of Education, 2003)

As students listen to the passage, they must take notes to be able to successfully answer the multiple-choice questions and write the essay later. An example of a multiple-choice question based on the passage is shown in Figure 4.2. For the essay portion of Task 1, students were asked to write a report for their social studies class in which they discuss the social conditions in England that led women there to seek the right to vote.

In this particular example, it is clear that the English Regents demand a high level of English proficiency, as students are required to understand the oral speech of a British woman from 1908. Cummins (1992) writes about the importance of language being context-embedded for ELLs to be able to decipher meaning, yet this passage is not contextualized for current ELL students as no pictures or other visual cues are offered, and it is unlikely

> 1 The speaker refers to "our forefathers who fought
>   for the vote" in order to emphasize the
>   (1) freedom of her ancestors
>   (2) peaceful nature of women
>   (3) value of the vote
>   (4) responsibilities of citizens

Figure 4.2 English Regents exam (New York State Department of Education, 2003: 4)

students are familiar with life in early twentieth century England. Similarly, the listening part of the June 2004 English Regents was about the role of 'griots' in West African society. In this case, ELL students who do not know that a *griot* is a West African storyteller must possess enough English ability to not only understand the main points of the listening passage, but also to be able to glean a definition of the *griot*. To do so is demanding for all students, most of whom probably did not know the term *griot*, but particularly so for ELLs who have the added challenge of negotiating the complexities of comprehending a second language.

In Task 2 (Reading), the text is usually non-fiction, and students must read and decipher both an essay and corresponding graphic. The example below is an excerpt from Task 2 in the June 2004 English Regents, which was two and a half pages long and about global warming. For this task, there were 16 paragraphs altogether in an essay of 1475 words.

> Measuring the warming that has already taken place is relatively simple; the trick is unraveling the causes and projecting what will happen over the next century. To do that, IPCC scientists fed a wide range of scenarios involving varying estimates of population and economic growth, changes in technology and other factors into computers. That process gave them 35 estimates, ranging from 6 billion to 35 billion tons, of how much excess carbon dioxide will enter the atmosphere. Then they loaded these estimates into the even larger, more powerful computer programs that attempt to model the planet's climate. Because no one climate model is considered definitive, they used seven different versions, which yielded 235 independent predictions of global temperature increase. That's where the range of 2.5°F to 10.4°F comes from … (English Regents, New York State Department of Education, 2004a: 7)

There is a map presented with this reading passage that depicts the consequences of global warming. The excerpt is followed by ten multiple-choice questions for students to complete that check their reading comprehension and understanding of the content of the passage. In addition, for the essay they must use both documents (the reading passage and map) to write a letter to their local newspaper explaining global warming and how it may affect humans. In addition to being able to comprehend the scientific language and content of the reading passage, and decipher the corresponding map, ELLs must show their understanding through their persuasive writing ability.

Below is an excerpt from an interview with an English teacher at one of the schools in this study, which brings to life some of the issues mentioned above. In this excerpt, the teacher first compares the new English Regents to the old version of the exam, and then discusses the challenges of the January 2004 exam for ELLs (the author's voice is italicized):

> *How would you describe your teaching strategies and the curriculum now, as compared to before the new testing requirements of 2000?*
> Ms. S: The old test had multiple-choice questions. This test has them too, but it doesn't count for as much for the grade. Now you have four essays, double the amount of essays from the first test. The old exam directions were, like, a paragraph and now they're three-quarters a page long. So the old test was more simple and straightforward. The directions for this exam are very repetitive so they say the same thing over which is confusing for students. Just this past test [January 2004] was difficult for our ELLs. They didn't know the words. Part 2 gave them an article on teen curfews and I happened to have proctored a classroom for ELLs, and so many students didn't know what the word 'curfew' was. That word was not translated, and that word was not in their English-Spanish dictionary … Look, their entire success for that part of the test depended on that word.
> (Ms S., English Teacher, School #6, interview notes)

In the quotation above, the teacher makes three main points that were echoed in other interviews across school sites. First, the directions alone are complicated and difficult for ELLs to understand. Second, the English Regents exam involves a great deal of essay writing, and ELLs typically develop receptive skills more rapidly than the productive skills needed to write an essay in academic English (Cummins, 1992; García & Menken, 2006). And third, the vocabulary used in the English Regents exam (and others) is sophisticated and often culturally complex, making it difficult for ELLs to comprehend; this is because the exam was intended to assess native English speakers after 11 years of schooling.

In Task 3 (Literature) of the English Regents given in January 2004, students read a poem called 'High School Senior' from *The Wellspring* by

Sharon Olds (2001) and also a two and a half page passage (single-spaced) of *Just Beyond the Firelight*, a novel by Robert Walker (1988), called 'Excavating Rachael's Room'. The following is an excerpt from the passage by Walker (1988):

> ... With her eighteenth birthday near, Rachael has moved to Boston, leaving her room and the cleaning of it to us ... The dogs peer into the darkness from around our legs and look up at us. The room – well – undulates. It stands as a shrine to questionable taste, a paean to the worst of American consumerism. The last few echoes of Def Leppard and Twisted Sister are barely audible ... And there's Barbie. And Barbie's clothes. And Barbie's camper ... Twister – The Game That Ties You Up In Knots. (English Regents Exam, New York State Department of Education, 2004a: 3)

While the language of this passage is in modern English, which would typically be accessible to ELLs who have developed basic communicative competence[12] in English, this test item involves challenging vocabulary and many cultural references to Americana that an English language learner might not know (e.g. 'Barbie' and 'Twister').

After reading the two passages and answering the multiple-choice questions about them, students are required to do the following:

> Your Task: After you have read both passages and answered the multiple-choice questions, write a unified essay about life's transitions as revealed in the passages. In your essay, use ideas from *both* passages to establish a controlling idea about life's transitions. Using evidence from *each* passage, develop your controlling idea and show how the author uses specific literary elements or techniques to convey that idea. (Directions, English Regents Exam, New York State Department of Education, 2004a: 2)

ELLs taking this exam must not only be able to comprehend the two reading passages, but completing Task 3 successfully involves the ability to identify and analyze literary devices, and to compare and contrast them.

Task 4 (The Critical Lens) is cited repeatedly across school sites as one of the most difficult parts of the English Regents for ELLs to complete successfully. Below are the directions and the quotation from the Critical Lens in the English Regents administered in January 2004:

> **Your Task:**
> Write a critical essay in which you discuss *two* works of literature you have read from the particular perspective of the statement that is provided for you in the **Critical Lens**. In your essay, provide a valid interpretation of the statement, agree *or* disagree with the statement as

you have interpreted it, and support your opinion using specific references to appropriate literary elements from the two works. You may use scrap paper to plan your response. Write your essay in Part B, beginning page 9 of the essay booklet.

Critical Lens:
'Things can happen in some cities° and the tale of them will be interesting: the same story laid in another city° would be ridiculous'. – *Frank Norris McTeague: A Story of San Francisco: Authoritative Text, Contexts, Criticism*, 1997

°For the purpose of writing your critical essay, you may interpret the word 'cities' to mean locations and the word 'city' to mean location. (English Regents Exam, New York State Department of Education, 2004: 8)

Task 4 requires that the students decipher and interpret the quotation they are provided, decide if they agree or disagree with the quotation as they interpret it, and make their argument in an essay using two works of literature to support their viewpoint. This task is challenging for all students, but particularly so for a student in the midst of learning the English language.

An interview with an ESL teacher clarifies the difficulty of the critical lens in the following, when explaining how complex an abstract quotation can be for ELL students:

> ... Day two was really tough. In my class I try to get students interested talking about a theme that interests them like 'love', and then I teach them how to use stories [read in the class] to do Tasks 3 and 4. But then what they get from me in the classroom is well-instructed and structured so they get a good understanding of what they need to do. But then what happens is the Regents will come up with a quote that they have to, like, it's not tricky but, like, it throws them off ... So when I teach them about love for example the quote I gave was, 'Love can conquer any obstacle including death' ... They analyze the quote I gave them, which is a straight sentence and not very abstract, and they can do that. But something like this, [points to the exam] what do they make out of this?
> (Mr L, ESL teacher, Focal School, interview notes)

In this interview, Mr 'L' offers an explanation that was repeated by other teachers as well: the challenge of the critical lens for an English language learner is that the quotation is usually abstract, and in second language acquisition literal language is typically mastered before the subtlety of abstract language is learned.

In total, students must write four essays in order to complete the English Regents exam. A rubric by the New York State Department of Education is provided for grading the essay portions of the exam. There are five 'qualities' the rubric measures, which are as follows: Meaning, Development, Organization, Language Use and Conventions (Scoring Rubric, English Regents, New York State Department of Education, 2004a). For each of these qualities, students receive a score, so writing ability greatly impacts a student's overall score.

California's High School Exit Exam in English Language Arts

Like New York and approximately half of the United States, California also requires a high school exit exam. In that state, the California High School Exit Examination (CAHSEE) has two parts – Math and English Language Arts – and all students must pass both in order to receive a high school diploma. The exam is designed to directly align to California's academic content standards in English Language Arts and Mathematics. The English Language Arts part is four hours and 30 minutes in length, taken over two days. There are a total of 79 multiple-choice questions and one essay. ELLs are permitted test accommodations which match what the students 'regularly use in the classroom', such as being tested in a separate room with other ELLs, additional supervised breaks, extra time, the use of bilingual glossaries or allowing students to hear a translated version of the test directions and to ask clarifying questions in their primary language (California Department of Education, 2004). ELLs must take the CAHSEE English Language Arts (ELA) exam in tenth grade with all students (California Department of Education, 2005b). As mentioned above, this usually is not enough time for an ELL to acquire English; however, ELLs must take the exam regardless of the length of time that they have been in the United States, in accordance with both state and federal education policy.

The English language arts questions of the CAHSEE are organized into the following strands: Word Analysis, Reading Comprehension, Literary Response, Writing Strategies, Writing Conventions, and Writing Applications. The test items in the first three strands are in the reading section of the exam, and the test items in the latter three strands are in the writing section. For the CAHSEE, students must read fiction and non-fictional pieces, ranging from poetry to an essay, such as a recent one on 'seining for minnows'. Test items released in 2005 show that students were required to read a passage of 580 words from *Wouldn't Take Nothing for My Journey Now* by Maya Angelou, and then answer multiple-choice questions such as the following:

2. Which sentence below is an example of a simile?
A I will have set no clock …
B I do not want to know my name …

C We need hours of aimless wandering ...
D A day away acts as a spring tonic.
(California Department of Education, 2005a)

To answer this question, students must know what a simile is and have understood the passage. Like New York's English Regents exam, the CAHSEE demands that students are able to analyze literature and that they are familiar with literary terminology; this exam differs from the Regents in that this is mainly done through multiple-choice questions rather than essay writing. In the following example, students are required to read a passage of 1154 words about the musings of a boy who must move from his hometown when his father receives a job promotion, and then answer questions such as:

18. Read this sentence from the selection.

> ... I know that somewhere there are parents telling their children about a town filled with oak trees, a place where you can get the best milkshake in the world...

What makes the preceding statement ironic?
A the fact that, like the narrator, other children are worried about moving
B the fact that, like the people in the narrator's neighborhood, most people enjoy their homes
C the fact that, like the narrator's father, parents often get promotions
D the fact that, like the narrator's home, every house has its stories
(California Department of Education, 2005a; reprinted with permission of CDE Press, Sacramento, CA)

None of the answers to this test item are a perfect fit; as is often the case with standardized tests, the test taker must use his or her judgment to select the correct answer. Yet an English language learner, particularly one who has recently arrived in the United States, typically does not have the experience with the language that is required to judge which option 'sounds best'.

For the Writing Strategies and Conventions strands, students are given a rough draft of an essay which may contain errors in grammar, punctuation, sentence structure and organization. The following is an excerpt from an essay entitled 'Appreciate the Forgotten', and a corresponding question.

... (7) Susan Hibbard's invention didn't transform the world, but it did make a difference for other women inventors. (8) She took old turkey feathers and bound them together to make the first feather duster... (11) Eventually, Hibbard won the patent for her invention. (12) Soon afterward, women were gaining confidence in their ideas and feeling happy about their right to patent them...

134. Which is the BEST way to revise the sentence labeled 12?
A Women were soon being granted more patents because of their confidence in their ideas.
B Gaining confidence in their ideas and their right to patent were other women of the day.
C Soon, women were gaining confidence in their ideas and confidence in their right to patent them.
D Her fight helped other women gain confidence in their ideas and their right to patent them.
(California Department of Education, 2005a; reprinted with permission of CDE Press, Sacramento, CA)

In this example, students must both understand the content of what they have read and also have grammar skills and writing style in English to revise the sentence in the way the test writers intended. It is particularly challenging to know whether C or D is the best answer, as the difference is subtle. Similarly, students must answer cloze response questions or edit underlined portions of sentences in accordance with writing conventions and grammatical accuracy, as in the following:

139. The Alaskan rivers are clear and sparkling in summer however, they are frozen in winter.
A in summer, however they are frozen in winter.
B in summer; however, they are frozen in winter.
C summer: however they are frozen in winter.
D Leave as is.

164. The committee had _____ last meeting on Tuesday.
A it's
B its
C there
D they're
(California Department of Education, 2005a)

Knowledge of Standard Academic American English writing conventions and grammatical accuracy are necessary skills for answering these test items correctly.

Clearly, the language proficiency required by the preceding English language arts exams and others being used nationally are, by definition, challenging for English language learners. The linguistic challenges of the items delineated above place ELLs at a disadvantage when their test scores are compared to native English speakers and used for high-stakes decisionmaking. June 2006 marked the first time that graduating seniors in California were required to pass the high school exit exam to receive a diploma. Although the CAHSEE is generally believed to be more of a basic skills test than the English Regents, which was originally designed to evaluate college readiness, CAHSEE statewide failure rates are high and approximately 50,000 seniors had not passed by March 2006 (Kabbany, 2006). At least half of all ELLs have not passed the exam (Rumberger, 2006). Arturo Gonzalez, a partner with Morrison Foerster, one of California's largest law firms, is currently placing a lawsuit against the State Board of Education on behalf of failing seniors. So far, the California Court of Appeals has upheld the controversial CAHSEE, but the attorneys representing the group of California students who brought the lawsuit have requested review by the California Supreme Court (Hull, 2006).

Challenges of Mathematics Exams in New York and Texas

The importance of language in mathematics has often been downplayed, such that math is viewed as independent of language proficiency because it involves numeracy (Dale & Cuevas, 1992). A careful analysis of math exams currently being implemented in states across the United States, however, quickly dispels this myth. In fact, like other registers of English, the language register of mathematics includes unique vocabulary, syntax, semantic properties (truth conditions), and discourse for the communication of math ideas (Halliday, 1975). In their study of high school exit exams implemented in 26 states, the Center on Education Policy (2005) found that the percentage of ELLs who pass the math portion on the first try is 30–40 percentage points lower than overall pass rates. As the authors of this study point out, this raises the possibility that many ELLs will be denied a high school diploma based on their test performance.

Math Regents exams in New York

Most ELLs in New York take the Mathematics A Regents exam, which assesses basic math knowledge required for graduation.[13] This exam is highly literacy-based, and in this way differs from the older exam that was used (the Regents Competency Test or RCT). The Math A exam is three hours long, and divided into four parts. Part I is comprised of multiple-choice questions which require computation. The exams administered in January and June, 2004 had 30 multiple-choice questions in Part I. Each question is worth two credits, making a maximum total of 60 credits for that section, and no partial credit for an answer is possible in this part. Part I is the most heavily weighted, as the maximum total of credits for the entire exam is 84 credits.

Some of the questions in Part I are traditional math problems, as in the following:

1 If $2(x + 3) = x + 10$, then x equals

(1) 14   (3) 5

(2) 7   (4) 4

(Math A Regents Exam, New York State Department of Education, 2004c: 2)

Others are text-based problems, whereby students must decipher the written text in order to show their knowledge of math terminology or to extract the computations required for answering the question. The following are examples of text-based questions and word problems from Part I of the Math A Regents:

4 Which statement about quadrilaterals is true?
(1) All quadrilaterals have four right angles.
(2) All quadrilaterals have equal sides.
(3) All quadrilaterals have four sides.
(4) All quadrilaterals are parallelograms.

15 Which statement is the converse of 'If the sum of two angles is 180°, then the angles are supplementary'?
(1) If two angles are supplementary, then their sum is 180°.
(2) If the sum of two angles is not 180°, then the angles are not supplementary.
(3) If two angles are not supplementary, then their sum is not 180°.
(4) If the sum of two angles is not 180°, then the angles are supplementary.
(Math A Regents Exam, New York State Department of Education, 2004c: 2–3)

As can be seen in these examples, the linguistic demands of the Math A Regents include reading comprehension, the ability to understand the syntax used in the phrasing of math questions, knowledge of math-specific vocabulary, as well as computational ability.

Part II of the Math A Regents not only demands the same skills as in Part I, but also requires that students display how they arrive at their answer. In this part of the exam, each question is worth two points. It is possible for students to receive partial credit, so the New York State Department of Education gives teachers a scoring key for use in grading the exam. Below are the directions for Part II (Figure 4.3), and a question taken from the Math A Regents exam as an example.

Part II

Answer all questions in this part. Each correct answer will receive 2 credits. Clearly indicate the necessary steps, including appropriate formula substitutions, diagrams, graphs, charts, etc. For all questions in this part, a correct numerical answer with no work shown will receive only 1 credit. [10]

33 Bob and Latoya both drove to a baseball game at a college stadium. Bob lives 70 miles from the stadium and Latoya lives 60 miles from it, as shown in the accompanying diagram. Bob drove at a rate of 50 miles per hour, and Latoya drove at a rate of 40 miles per hour. If they both left home at the same time, who got to the stadium first?

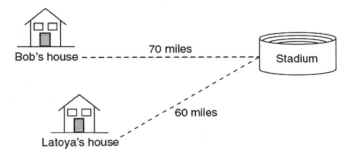

Figure 4.3 Math A Regents Exam, New York State Department of Education, 2004c: 11

The directions given to teachers guiding them on how to score this particular question, with the point allocation for responses, are as follows:

(33) **[2]** Bob, and appropriate work is shown, such as using the distance formula to calculate the two travel times or setting up a proportion.
[1] Appropriate work is shown, but one computational or conceptual error is made, but an appropriate answer is found.
or
[1] Appropriate work is shown, but no answer or an incorrect answer is found.
[0] Bob, but no work or inappropriate work is shown.
or
[0] A zero response is completely incorrect, irrelevant, or incoherent or is a correct response that was obtained by an obviously incorrect procedure. (Mathematics A Scoring Key for Teachers, New York State Department of Education, 2004c: 3)

These directions show the answer that would yield two credits, one credit or zero credits, respectively. As can be seen in this example, the ability to display the process for attaining the correct answer is as important as the answer itself.

The following excerpt is taken from an interview with the Assistant Principal of Mathematics at School #4 in this research study, where he explains the linguistic challenges of the Math A Regents exam and how this differs from the previous RCT basic skills test:

> *It was mandated ELLs be included in the Regents in 2001. When you stand back and look at this, how are the standardized tests and particularly the Regents affecting your ELL students?*
> AP: Well in 2001 they started the Math A. ELLs had always been included in the RCT, but those two exams are very different in structure. It was calculations, but Math A is more reading. Before you could pull it out and regardless of language just do the math...
> *What specifically are the challenges of the Math A Regents for ELLs?*
> AP: They have to read and comprehend effectively in English, because it's not purely mathematical the way it's presented. They don't necessarily come out and ask you 'Find the area of the rectangle whose length is *2l* and whose width is *4w*'. They don't do that. They give you a whole story. Find the area of the garden [laughs]! The whole nine yards, you know?! What's the shape of the garden, the color. A garden? What's a garden?! (Math Assistant Principal, School #4, interview transcript)

As explained in this quotation, students can become confused about the math they need to apply when language prevents them from understanding what they are being asked to do. What the assistant principal makes clear in this quotation is that the Math A Regents exam is not only a measure of content knowledge, but rather it is also a measure of language proficiency.

In Parts III and IV of the Math A Regents exam, a student's ability to explain the steps for arriving at the correct answer are even more important than in Part II (see Figure 4.4). For this test item, students will receive full credit if they give the correct answer and explain appropriately how they arrived at their answer; a correct answer without an explanation only receives half credit. Like the preceding example, this test question includes a visual aid which is very helpful to an English learner. Yet on top of being able to do the actual computations the exam demands, it is critical that ELL students are able to understand the language used in mathematics questions with regard to their specific vocabulary, syntax, semantics and communicative discourse. As recognized by Halliday (1975), these aspects of 'math register' differ significantly from other registers of the English

Part IV

Answer all questions in this part. Each correct answer will receive 4 credits. Clearly indicate the necessary steps, including appropriate formula substitutions, diagrams, graphs, charts, etc. For all questions in this part, a correct numerical answer with no work shown will receive only 1 credit. [8]

38 In the accompanying diagram, the base of a 15-foot ladder rests on the ground 4 feet from a 6-foot fence.

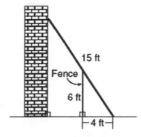

a If the ladder touches the top of the fence and the side of a building, what angle, to the *nearest degree*, does the ladder make with the ground?

b Using the angle found in part *a*, determine how far the top of the ladder reaches up the side of the building, to the *nearest foot*.

Figure 4.4 Math A Regents Exam, New York State Department of Education, 2004c: 2)

language (or other languages). As the examples above show, in the movement over time from traditional assessments based on computation to performance-based assessments, a student's ability to show how they arrive at an answer has become increasingly important. Showing the process for attaining an answer involves language to explain the steps involved. As such, an ELL student must not only be able to comprehend the math register, they must be able to produce it as well.

The linguistic challenges of the Math A Regents are further clarified in the following passage, taken from a focus group interview in New York City with ELL students in the 11th grade. 'S1' is a girl who is a native speaker of Spanish and 'S2' is a boy who is a native speaker of Bengali.

You said Math is the most difficult [Regents]. Are there difficult questions that the Math Regents ask? Can you give an example?
S2: When they put numbers into words, like 'bigger than'/'smaller than'. They use words to try to confuse you. If it comes before or after, when they put in words it's more confusing than when they put in numbers ...

S1: 'Bigger than 50', 'smaller than' a number. Sometimes they try to confuse you, like

S2: So what's something bigger than 50 and smaller than a number, and they have some conditions you have to apply. They don't give any numbers, they only put words!

S1: [nods] So you gotta find out which number is that. So it's a lot of thinking and more questions you gotta answer. And you don't have a lot of time.

(Focus group interview, 11th grade students, Focal School #1, interview transcript)

In this interview, these English language learners show the challenges they must face when taking the Math A Regents because the exam is so heavily reliant on language. While the Math A Regents intends to assess a student's content knowledge in math, it is also a language proficiency exam.

Texas assessment of knowledge and skills in mathematics

In second place after California, Texas has the largest English language learner population in the United States (Padolsky, 2005). The Texas Assessment of Knowledge and Skills (TAKS) exams are required in Math, English Language Arts, Social Studies and Science for both grades 10 and 11; the grade 10 exams are used to meet requirements of *No Child Left Behind* and the grade 11 exams are used to determine graduation (Center on Education Policy, 2005). Like the use of Regents exams in New York, public universities and community colleges in Texas also use high school exit exam scores for admissions purposes. Taken together, the stakes of the TAKS exam are extremely high.

There are no native language versions of the TAKS, nor are other accommodations or test modifications permitted, such as the use of a bilingual dictionary and/or the simplification or translation of directions (García, 2003). The only special treatment for ELLs is that they are permitted a one-time postponement of the exam if they have a low level of English language proficiency (as determined by a different test), and have been in the United States less than a year. The Center on Education Policy (2005) reports that while the overall cumulative pass rate on the TAKS was 89% for all students, it was only 54% for ELLs. In the meantime, dropout rates in Texas have increased in recent years for minority students, most of whom are language minorities and/or of low socioeconomic status, and twice as likely as white students to drop out of school (Valencia & Villarreal, 2005). Likewise, the ELL dropout rate in Texas has increased (Ruiz de Velasco, 2005).

The TAKS consists of multiple-choice, short-answer and writing prompt or essay questions. The TAKS math exam covers ten objectives; the first five objectives pertain to material learned by students in that state's Algebra I course, and objectives six through eight involve material learned in the state's Geometry course. Objective nine consists of percents, proportions, probability and statistics and objective ten involves math processes and tools (Texas Education Agency, Student Assessment Division, 2004). For the July 2004 Math portion of the TAKS, 40 test questions out of a total of 60 (two-thirds of the entire test) involved solving word problems of two sentences or more. The following are test items from the July 2004 TAKS exam:

10 The land area of Texas is about 50,000 square miles smaller than twice the land area of California. If x represents the land area of California, which expression can be used to determine the land area of Texas?

F $50,000 - 2x$

G $\dfrac{x - 50,000}{2}$

H $\dfrac{x}{2} - 50,000$

J $2x - 50,000$

29 The net profit, p, that a company makes from the production of widgets is represented by the equation $p = 2.5n - 25,000$, where n is the number of widgets the company sells. Which is the best interpretation of this information?

A The company has made a profit of $25,000.

B The company needs to sell more than 10,000 widgets before it makes a profit.

C The company's profit needs to be more than $25,000.

D The company has sold more than 10,000 of its widgets.

(Texas Education Agency, 2004; reprinted with permission of Pearson Publishing, Austin, TX)

All of the test items on the Math portion of the TAKS were in multiple-choice format. Questions 10 and 29 are typical of word problems on this exam. For the reasons discussed previously, word problems such as these pose great challenges for English language learners who must decode the language in order to determine the calculations needed to solve the problem. In these examples, students must be able to negotiate terminology and phrases such as 'twice the land area', 'net profit' and 'widgets' to select mathematical formulas which most accurately reflect the English that they have read; this is not easy for any math student, and particularly difficult for an English learner.

The two questions below are also recent test items from the TAKS, both providing an image that goes with the question:

23 Start with a 1-unit-by-1-unit unshaded square. In each iteration, the following steps occur for the smallest unshaded squares resulting from the previous iteration.
Step 1: Divide the square into a 3-by-3 grid of squares
Step 2: Shade only the center square of this 3-by-3

What fraction of the 1-unit-by-1-unit square is shaded after the second iteration?

A 4/9
B 7/9
C 17/81
D 64/73

38 The 12-foot-long bed of a dump truck loaded with debris must rise to an angle of 30° before the debris will spill out. Approximately how high must the front of the bed rise for the debris to spill out?

Dump Truck

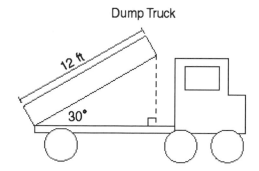

F 1.7 ft
G 18 ft
H 10.4 ft
J 6 ft
(Texas Education Agency, 2004; reprinted with permission of Pearson Publishing, Austin, TX)

On the July 2004 TAKS, 28 of the 60 mathematics test items contained some sort of chart, table, or picture that might provide some context for an English language learner. Question 38 was chosen to share here because it offers one of the most helpful visual cues of all, as it shows a picture of a dump truck which will aid a student unfamiliar with terms like 'dump truck' and even 'debris'. By contrast, question 23 also provides a visual cue, but in this case the image is far less helpful. The directions for question 23 are very complicated, requiring that students understand the directions and, as indicated by the term 'iteration', that they repeat the steps to solve the problem correctly. The image helps, but is clearly not enough scaffolding to indicate to an ELL for whom the language is incomprehensible what calculations are needed to solve the problem. While images attached to test questions are certainly helpful to English learners, the amount of help they provide varies and an image is rarely enough to entirely remove linguistic barriers from test items.

Given that the TAKS exam is only available in English, a student who is not yet proficient in English will be at a great disadvantage on this math exam when compared to a native English speaker. Even though TAKS questions are in multiple-choice format, unlike the Regents exam which requires that students explain how they arrived at the answer, the TAKS is clearly a language proficiency test as well as a test of math content due to the linguistic demands of the test questions.

In the ways highlighted in this chapter, the exams currently being used in compliance with *No Child Left Behind* and for other high-stakes decisionmaking (like high school graduation) are linguistically complex, which is a major part of the reason that ELLs usually do not perform as well as native English speakers. A significant portion of the challenge, as explained above, is that the language of the exams is typically what Cummins (1992) terms 'context-reduced' (e.g. written text without pictures or other visual cues). When a test item does offer a visual cue, it is often not enough to contextualize the language to the point that it is comprehensible. Standardized testing that is linguistically complex in the ways outlined above cannot yield valid and reliable scores for ELLs. As shall be detailed in Chapters 5 and 6, the linguistic challenges of the exams and the fact that ELLs are disproportionately likely to fail has had a domino effect into the classroom, dramatically impacting the instruction and educational experiences of ELLs in high school.

Test Translation and Accommodation Issues

In an attempt to address the issues of language and test performance, many states, while including ELL students in English-medium standardized assessments, have instituted testing accommodations or modifications intended to 'level the playing field'. However, these have raised a new set of policy and psychometric challenges, and have failed to make scores attained by an English language learner truly comparable to a score attained by a native English speaker. For instance, each state has its own definition of an English language learner, causing disparity in policies regarding when and how they will be included, whether or not their scores are reported, and if they make 'adequate yearly progress' (Abedi & Dietal, 2004; Holmes *et al.*, 2000). At the same time, there is further variance in the types of accommodations permitted by states, if any.

As identified in a comprehensive study of state policies by Rivera and Stansfield (2000), accommodations can be classified into four main types:

(1) *Presentation* – permits repetition, explanation, test translations into students' native languages, or test administration by an ESL/bilingual specialist.
(2) *Response* – allows a student to dictate his/her answers, and to respond in his/her native language.
(3) *Setting* – includes individual or small group administration of the test, or administration in a separate location.
(4) *Timing/scheduling* – allows for additional time to complete the test or extra breaks during administration. (Rivera & Stansfield, 2000)

Studies of state regulations indicate that the most common types of accommodations fall into the categories of *timing/scheduling* and *setting* accommodations, which do not specifically address the linguistic needs of ELLs (Holmes *et al.*, 2000; Rivera & Stansfield, 2000). Rivera and Stansfield (2000) point out how these accommodations were actually designed for students in special education programs, and not ELLs. *Presentation* and *response* accommodations can address ELLs' linguistic needs, but these are less commonly permitted. In specific, 34 states permit some type of accommodations and, of these, 22 allow non-linguistic accommodations that may help students feel more comfortable during an exam but do not actually support them linguistically (Stansfield & Rivera, 2002). In fact, research conducted by Pennock-Roman and Rivera (2006), where they compiled the literature on the different types of testing accommodations for ELLs, indicates that most of the accommodations currently being used fail to reduce the achievement gap between English proficient students and English language learners. While accommodations are intended to make test content more accessible to ELLs, research indicates that the types of accommodations most commonly permitted by states are mismatched to the needs of this population of students.

While very little research exists regarding the effectiveness of accommodations, a few studies have been conducted in this area. Noting that language has been the cause for large achievement differences by ELLs and non-ELL students on standardized math exams, Abedi and Lord (2001) investigated the importance of language on math word problems. Items from the National Assessment of Educational Progress (NAEP) math exam were administered to 1174 eighth grade students, along with parallel items modified to reduce their linguistic complexity. They found that linguistic modification resulted in significant differences in math performance, and students in low-level and average math classes, ELLs and low socioeconomic status students benefited greatly. Additional research has shown that the only accommodation that narrows the gap between ELL and non-ELL students is linguistic modification of questions with excessive language demands. Other accommodations such as providing extra time, using a glossary of key terms on the test, or reducing the language complexity of the test questions increase scores for ELL and non-ELL students alike, and therefore do not narrow the gap between these groups (Abedi, 2001; Abedi et al., 2004).

As a way to reduce the interference of language in the measurement accuracy of content-area assessments, some states and districts use native language versions of the tests offered to assess content knowledge (Elmore & Rothman, 1999). New York is one of a small minority of states nationwide that permit the use of native language assessments (Rivera & Stansfield, 2000). Specifically, 14 states allow translated or bilingual tests, but only eight of these permit students to respond in their native language (Stansfield & Rivera, 2002). Of the eight states permitting translations, however, just five of these actually provide the translations they permit – making the use of translations very rare (Sullivan et al., 2005).

Furthermore, research points to two main problems in the use of native language assessments: validity challenges and mismatch with language of instruction or language variety (Abedi et al., 2004). With regard to validity, the challenge is that maintaining construct equivalence is difficult when the test is either translated directly from one language to another or when tests in two languages are developed. Some languages such as Spanish have several different varieties, so the language variety a student speaks needs to be matched to the language variety of the test in order to avoid validity problems. In addition, native language versions of tests are only useful when students can best demonstrate content knowledge in that language, usually because they have received content instruction in their native language. If they have received instruction in English, they may not be familiar with content-specific vocabulary and the accommodation will be ineffective (Abedi *et al.*, 2004). Based on these research findings, Abedi *et al.* (2004) instead suggest that native language assessments of content should only be administered to students who receive content-area instruction in that language or to students who have been educated in that language and just arrived in the United States.

In research on one state's assessment system, the Colorado Student Assessment Program (CSAP), Escamilla *et al.* (2003) found that scores by Latinos taking the exam in Spanish were equivalent to, and sometimes higher, than the scores of Latinos taking the exam in English. Scores by all Latinos, however, were far lower than scores for all third and fourth graders in the state. This indicates that while native language versions of the CSAP may offer some help, the wide achievement gap remains. In their analysis of 14 experimental studies of test accommodations for ELLs, Pennock-Roman and Rivera (2006) support findings by Abedi *et al.* (2004) and perhaps offer some further explanation of the findings by Escamilla *et al.* (2003). Specifically, they conclude that native language accommodations appear promising, but only for students who possess native language literacy skills, receive classroom instruction and exams in their native language and have low levels of proficiency in English (Pennock-Roman & Rivera, 2006).

Regents exam translations in New York

Test translation is the primary test accommodation schools in New York provide to non-native speakers of English, making it is an interesting state in which to analyze testing policy and ELLs given this accommodation is so rarely permitted nationally. In New York, there are translated versions of the Regents Examinations in all core areas required for high school graduation other than English and foreign language. In specific, Math, Science and Social Studies Regents are available in Spanish, Korean, Chinese, Haitian Creole and Russian (New York State Department of Education, 2003a). In my research in New York City high schools, the existence of translations was found to be helpful to students and important as a way to justify and maintain bilingual education programs in the five languages into which Regents are translated. At the same time, however, test translations do not truly 'level the playing field' for ELLs by producing test scores comparable to those they would receive if they were native English speakers taking the exams in English; language remains a threat to test validity even when the test is provided in a student's native language. Furthermore, translations are only offered in five of the 140 or more different languages spoken by ELLs in New York City; there is a significant population of students speaking languages in which translations are not provided, comprising approximately 20% of ELLs in New York City public schools. These students obviously cannot benefit from the use of translations, making the gap even wider for these students between the test scores they attain and what they truly know and are able to do.

A key issue is that students must write their test responses entirely in English or in their native language, as mixing languages in test responses will lower a student's score. Yet students in bilingual programs usually receive instruction in both English and their native language, with different amounts of each language being used. Language allocation in instruction by bilingual high school teachers is very complex and varies widely, which results in some teachers using more English in daily instruction than others, who use more of the students' native language; my observations in ten New York City high schools reflect the entirety of this spectrum of language use in instruction. A fundamental validity threat in the use of translations is that the language of instruction must be matched to the language of an assessment (Abedi *et al.*, 2004). Where instruction is bilingual, test questions and responses should therefore also be bilingual to yield valid data; however, this is not permitted. Further compounding these issues, there are disparities at different school sites as to how the test translations are actually implemented, if at all. While some students receive copies of both exams (in English and also in their native language) and choose the one for which they will write their responses, other students receive only one copy (in English or their native language). In some cases, teachers decide for students if translations will be used, while in others students decide for themselves the language in which they will be tested.

Translations provide only limited help when students do not possess a high level of content-specific vocabulary in their first language. Most secondary ELLs in New York receive content-area instruction entirely or predominantly in English, which means they typically do not learn the vocabulary needed to perform well on a translated Regents examination. Like in the English versions, translated Regents exams demand a high level of literacy and also knowledge of the vocabulary, syntax, semantics and communicative discourse specific to each subject or discipline. Students in bilingual education programs usually do not receive instruction solely in their native language, but rather receive instruction in both their native language and English, which causes a mismatch between the language of instruction and the language of the exam. If ELL students have received instruction in English, they may not be familiar with content-specific vocabulary and the accommodation will be ineffective (Abedi *et al.*, 2004).

To offer an example, below is question 24 from the January 2004 Living Environment (Biology) Regents Examination in English, along with the translated versions in Spanish, Haitian Creole, and Chinese:

[English Version]
24 Leaves of green plants contain openings known as stomates, which are opened and closed by specialized cells allowing for gas exchange between the leaf and the outside environment. Which phrase best represents the net flow of gases involved in photosynthesis into and out of the leaf through thee openings on a sunny day?
(1) carbon dioxide moves in; oxygen moves out
(2) carbon dioxide and oxygen move in; ozone moves out
(3) oxygen moves in; nitrogen moves out
(4) water and ozone move in; carbon dioxide moves out

[Spanish Version]
24 Las hojas de las plantas verdes contienen aberturas
conocidas como estomas. Ciertas células especializadas abren y cierran estos estomas, lo cual permite un intercambio gaseoso entre la hoja y el medio ambiente exterior. ¿Cuál frase representa mejor el flujo neto de los gases involucrados en la fotosíntesis, los cuales entran y salen de la hoja por medio de estos estomas, durante un día soleado?
(1) entra dióxido de carbono; sale oxígeno
(2) entran dióxido de carbono y oxígeno; sale ozono
(3) entra oxígeno; sale nitrógeno
(4) entran agua y ozono; sale dióxido de carbono

[Haitian Creole Version]
24 Fèy plant vèt genyen ouvèti ki rele stomat. Se selil espesyalize ki ouvri stomat yo epi ki fèmen yo. Sa pèmèt genyen echanj gaz ant fèy la ak anviwonman an. Kilès nan fraz sa yo ki pi byen dekri mouvman antre soti gaz ki gen rapò ak fotosentèz ouvèti nan fèy la pandan yon jounen solèy?
(1) diyoksid kabòn antre; oksijèn soti
(2) diyoksid kabòn ak oksijèn antre; ozòn soti
(3) oksijèn antre; azòt soti
(4) dlo ak ozòn antre; diyoksid kabòn soti

[Chinese Version]

24 綠色植物的葉子含有稱為「氣孔」的開口，
這些氣孔由專門的細胞開、關，以實現葉子
與外部環境之間的氣體交換。下列哪句話最
恰當地表示在一個晴天的光合作用過程中透
過這些開口進出葉子的氣體的淨流向？

(1) 二氧化碳流入；氧氣流出
(2) 二氧化碳和氧氣流入；臭氧流出
(3) 氧氣流入；氮氣流出
(4) 水和臭氧流入；二氧化碳流出

(Living Environment Regents Exam, New York State Department of Education, 2004b: 4)

In this question, two science vocabulary terms key to answering correctly are 'stomates' and 'photosynthesis' ('estomas' and 'fotosíntesis' in Spanish, 'stomat' and 'fotosentèz' in Haitian Creole, etc.). The first part of the question offers a definition of 'stomates', yet gleaning the definition is complicated whichever the language medium because the question demands a high level of literacy, the ability to draw meaning from complex syntax that differs from that of everyday spoken language, and also knowledge of science vocabulary (e.g. 'specialized cells', 'gas exchange'). Furthermore, the student needs to know what 'photosynthesis' is, as it seems that it is a student's understanding of this concept that test writers want to assess in question 24. If a student is to answer this question correctly on a translated exam, s/he must possess strong literacy skills and understand complex syntax, science-specific vocabulary, as well as the concept of photosynthesis in her/his native language.

One-third of all secondary ELLs in New York City have been in the United States for longer than five years, and most long-term ELLs are more comfortable reading and writing in English because they have typically received all or most of their instruction in English since their arrival (Menken & Kleyn, 2007). This is either because they were enrolled in English-only programs, or because they were enrolled in 'weak' forms of bilingual education, where instruction was primarily in English. Even new arrivals often feel unprepared to take an exam in their native language, when they have taken a Regents test preparation course taught mostly or entirely in English. The following quotations, by ELLs who have received instruction primarily or only in English while in the United States, explain why Regents exam translations are often not an effective test accommodation for these students:

> For Global History Regents, [exam proctors] ask if any of us, for ESL students, they ask if we need a copy in our native language. But I didn't say it, I don't find it helpful. Because I don't know my language anymore, everything I learned has been in English. I never take anything in bilingual, all my classes are in English ...
> (12th grade ELL, native speaker of Chinese, interview transcript)

> *Would it help you if [the Regents] were in your language?*
> S1: ...But I feel okay about [taking Regents in English] because I'm studying in English. My language has different words and the meanings are different than the English. They change the language, it could be different for this. The meaning, you know, to write these things I don't know how to write them in my language because I studied them in English.
> (11th grade ELL, native speaker of Bulgarian, Focal School #1, focus group interview transcript)

In these examples, translated Regents exams would be inappropriate because the courses the students have taken to prepare for the exams have been in English only. As these students explain, ELLs might also not know the academic register in their native language, even if they are able to communicate proficiently in the spoken register. While intuitively it might seem to make sense to give any ELL student an exam in their native language, if they have learned and studied the material covered on a content-area Regents examination (such as the Living Environment Regents) entirely in English or even partly in English, then it is likely language will still pose an interference to a true assessment of that student's content knowledge.

Language as a threat to a content test's validity, even on the translated versions, is an issue faced by ELLs in bilingual programs as well as by those in English-only programs. Schools vary widely in how they define bilingual education, so that schools and often teachers have their own language allocation policies. As such, bilingual content-area teachers typically use both English and the student's native language in instruction to varying degrees. The complexities this creates when students take Regents exams, on which students can only respond in one language, is a point that was made repeatedly in interviews, and explained in the following interview with a bilingual math teacher:

> *You said before that ELLs aren't doing well on the Math A Regents. Why?*
> **Mr H:** Language would be the main reason. They don't have a good background in English.

But isn't the exam in Spanish?
Mr H: True, but I don't teach it in Spanish, I teach it in Spanish and English. The book is in English that they're using.
Why do you think that is?
Mr H: I think that we're trying to get them strong in the language and give more exposure in English to try to get them to read the problems in English. But at the same time, going back and forth, I go back and forth. For example, I have them read a verbal problem in English and have them read it, then convert it to an algebraic expression. We'll read it in English, translate to Spanish, and then do it.
(Mr H, Spanish bilingual math teacher, Focal School #1, interview notes)

At the schools in this study with bilingual programs, most of which are transitional programs where English is favored in instruction, the vast majority of bilingual teachers go 'back and forth' between languages during instruction. Native language usage is limited by the fact that all or most of the materials to prepare students for the Regents exams, such as course textbooks, are only available in English. Yet a student's native language is often used orally, for instance to translate or explain key concepts. In this way, a mismatch is created between instruction that is *bi*lingual, and testing that is *mono*lingual. The way this mismatch influences instruction is explored further in Chapter 6.

This point is further clarified when a bilingual Math assistant principal analyzes a question in Spanish from the Math A Regents exam:

Could you describe the greatest challenges of the Math Regents for ELLs with specific examples?
Ms A: [She brings out a copy of the June 2003 Math A Regents Spanish translation and looks at it, pointing to examples] ... [W]e tend to emphasize the concepts in English so if you say 'propriedad numerica' versus 'numerical property' it may be confusing for me unless the teacher says 'propriedad numerica' for me all the time. Maybe the teacher is using another word. In class we say the words in English and Spanish but we try to emphasize the vocabulary in English. And really this one, number 32 [points to another example]. You say all these words in Spanish and then it says 'Bridge Street', 'Harvard Street'. You're talking about streets and you're saying 'calle' in the paragraph and then you say 'Bridge Street'. As a bilingual child I might not know you are talking about the names of streets ... How could you get it right? You have to extract the math from the reading.
(Ms A, Math Assistant Principal, School #2, interview notes)

The use of 'Harvard Street' in the Spanish version of this Math Regents exam shows the awkwardness often found in the language of test translations, which tend to be direct or word-for-word translations, and the confusion this can cause. This topic was frequently mentioned in interviews when participants discussed test translations. For instance, a bilingual math teacher at Focal School #1 offered a similar example from an exam question which stated in English, 'Multiply $(5xy^2)$ and $(5x)$'. However, the Spanish version stated, 'Multiplique $(5xy^2)$ y $(5x)$'. The use of 'y' in the Spanish version instead of 'and' confused many of his students, who thought that 'y' was another symbol in the algebraic formula (Mr J., Spanish bilingual math teacher, Focal School #1, interview notes). Furthermore, by comparing the Spanish vocabulary in the questions ('propriedad numerica') to the English vocabulary often used in instruction ('numerical property'), the Math assistant principal here points out the problems of mismatch between language usage in class versus language usage in the Regents exams.

There is often a similar mismatch between the ways many ELLs use language in their daily lives and how it is used in the exam. For example, many students speak a non-standard variety of English or their native language, while the exam is written in the standard. Similarly, many students practice codeswitching, which is defined by Spolsky (1998) as changing from language to language within the same utterance. However, as discussed above, when a student is given a Regents exam he or she must still answer the questions on the exam using just one language code (such that responses are entirely in standard English or entirely in a standard version of the native language). This challenge is discussed by a Spanish bilingual social studies teacher in the following excerpt:

> So [students] can tell me some things about the totalitarian government in Spanish but not in English, that's what I mean. Last year they told me was, a problem they had with bilingual students for the Regents was they were using both languages for the essay part. They'd write one sentence in English and one in Spanish because they weren't exactly sure how to say it in English. And that's what I'm trying to steer them away from. It affects their grade, they won't get the same grade if they're writing in both languages ... I try to prevent them from mixing both languages in their writing, which some of them do – either codeswitching or writing everything in 'Spanglish', is what I would call it. Many find it very difficult to use only one language.
>
> (Ms I, Spanish bilingual social studies teacher, Focal School #1, interview transcript)

As the teacher indicates, codeswitching in responses lowers a student's test score. Yet for students learning in bilingual classrooms and living in bi- or multilingual communities, as is the case of many young New Yorkers, codeswitching is part of daily communication (García *et al.*, 2001).

The excerpt below offers students' voices to further clarify several of the complexities described above that arise when test translations are offered. The quotation is from a focus group with four ELL students in the tenth grade. 'S1', 'S3' and 'S4'are native speakers of Spanish who have taken bilingual classes, while 'S2' is a native speaker of Urdu who has received all of her instruction in English.

[To the Spanish speakers] Will you or did you take the Regents in Spanish or English?
S1: In math they give you both, but you got to fill that one. You got to do that in one. I will take it in English. They give it to me in class in English so I won't understand a lot of it in Spanish. It's so difficult that I can't do it in Spanish.
S4: The translation they do is hard to understand, the Spanish to English, you can't understand the words. They give two booklets.
S3: They were supposed to say centimeter and they said inches instead. They change the words in the translation. Sometimes they leave out the words.
... **S2:** [to other students] It's easy for you. For the Spanish students there are more opportunities because it doesn't come in Urdu. We're just left out [laughs]. They could take any exam in Spanish except the English, but we have to do it in English even though we don't understand. I took the Science Regents and I had only been here two months, just new to this country. And in my country I didn't study in an English school!
(10th Grade ELLs, Focal School #1, focus group notes)

The students in this passage raise several issues that were also raised in interviews across school sites. First, as discussed previously, this excerpt shows the challenges ELLs face when the language of instruction and/or their daily language usage is not aligned to the language of the exam. Secondly, as 'S3' points out, there are often basic errors or simple mistranslations in the translated versions. For example, there was a mistranslation in question 15 of the Math A Regents administered in January 2004, where the Spanish version mistakenly used the word *converso* (converse) instead of *inverso* (inverse). I observed the day this exam was being graded, and on the blackboard at School #2 it said: '*Bilingual papers Part I #15 correct answer is #1 or #2'. According to teachers there, errors on the translated versions such as these are common (observations of grading Math A Regents, School #2, fieldnotes).

In the preceding interview transcript, 'S2' raises another issue that is extremely important pertaining to students who speak languages that are not offered in Regents translations. S2 is a native speaker of Urdu and, although Urdu speakers are a significant population in New York City high schools, content-area Regents exams are not translated into her language; in fact, there are more Urdu speakers than there are Haitian Creole speakers, yet content-area Regents exams are offered in Haitian Creole (New York City Department of Education, 2002). As stated above, Regents exams in subjects other than English and foreign language are translated into five of the languages spoken by ELLs, but approximately 20% of ELLs speak other languages. This means that there are many ELLs who are placed at an unfair disadvantage when compared to other ELLs, because they are unable to benefit from exam translations. This topic is discussed further in Chapter 8, because this testing policy has essentially created a hierarchy among speakers of different languages in which students who speak languages not recognized by the Regents are the most disadvantaged. This limitation and the others mentioned in this section seriously threaten the validity of scores students receive when taking translated versions of the Regents.

That said, it is important to state explicitly that Regents exam translations do benefit ELL students in New York. For example, S3 in the preceding interview transcript uses Spanish translations to help her when she is unable to understand a test item in English. From the data collected, the students most likely to benefit from translations are those with high levels of native language literacy who possess content-specific vocabulary in their native language, such as recent arrivals who have received a comparable high school education in their home country. At the same time, we cannot rely on translations or any other accommodation to erase the disadvantages ELLs face when taking standardized tests.

Discussion

This chapter has shown how all of the exams demand language and literacy ability, posing new challenges specific to students who are English language learners. English language arts exams involve literary terminology and essay writing, and were intended to evaluate the English language proficiency of native English speakers. By definition, English language learners will not perform well on such tests of English. Yet this does not mean that these students are failing to progress in the ways they should towards learning the English language; we know from years of research that it takes at least five to seven years, and often even eleven years, for a student to acquire a second language to the level of a native speaker as measured on a standardized test (Cummins, 2000; Shohamy, 2001; Thomas & Collier, 1997). This does not indicate that the student or those who educate them are failing; it simply means the students are following a normal process of language learning. Furthermore, in mandating that ELLs pass such exams in order to graduate from high school, states have in essence made English proficiency mandatory.

Content-area exams in math, science, and social studies are also linguistically complex, as they involve reading comprehension, the ability to understand the specialized syntax used in the phrasing of questions, and knowledge of content-specific vocabulary. Because of this, it is impossible just to measure a student's understanding of the content without language posing a threat to the test's validity. For example, the math tests currently being used in New York and Texas are tests of both math content and language proficiency, because content and language are inextricably linked; it is very difficult for test developers to truly separate content from language. As a result, the test score an ELL receives on a math exam is impacted by their language proficiency, which is why ELLs in New York and elsewhere do not perform as well on math tests as native English speakers. This does not mean the students are not learning math, but simply is a reflection of the fact that they are simultaneously acquiring English.

In addition, while exam translations are found to be very helpful for ELLs, they cannot fully 'level the playing field' as they are intended to do. The translations are linguistically complex and provide only limited help when students do not possess a high level of literacy and content-specific vocabulary in their native language. Furthermore, translations only work well if the language of instruction matches the language of the exam; when ELLs are taught mostly or entirely in English (as most are in New York City, where ESL and transitional bilingual programs are the predominant models at the secondary level), students will not know all of the vocabulary and syntax they need for a test in their native language. As a result, even though translations help, they still are not enough to make an ELL's test score comparable to a native English speaker's test score.

The trouble is that in the United States at present test scores are being used for high-stakes decisions such as high school graduation, and to evaluate if a school should continue to receive federal funding without sanctions. Assessments are invaluable, for instance by offering teachers information about where their students need the most support, and by giving students feedback on their progress. However, the practice of using a standardized test score as the decisive factor in high-stakes decisionmaking is questionable at best.

Many have argued that when making high-stakes decisions standardized tests should at least be balanced by alternative assessment measures, like portfolios, which have greater possibility for validity when they are sensitive to both the academic and language growth of ELLs (August & Hakuta, 1997; Cummins, 2000; Northeast Islands Regional Educational LAB, 1999). In addition to test accommodations, certain states also have alternate assessments for ELLs in place. Some states are currently exploring the use of portfolio assessment on a wide scale to measure the educational progress of these students (Northeast Islands Regional Educational LAB, 1999). In the meantime, as states continue the debatable practice of high-stakes testing, it is particularly important to critique it, because the scores students receive within the era of *No Child Left Behind* so deeply affect their lives. This topic is the focus of the next chapter, in which we turn our attention to the experiences of ELL students.

Chapter Summary

- Analysis of English language arts exams from New York and California show that language usage in these tests is very challenging for an English language learner.
- Similarly, linguistic analysis of Math tests from Texas and New York shows that these tests are also challenging for ELLs as they involve a great deal of language. Tests of other subjects, such as Science and Social Studies, are equally linguistically complex.
- Accommodations such as translations are used to reduce the interference of language on tests. While accommodations offer some help to English language learners, they are not enough to completely erase the effects language proficiency will have on the test scores an English language learner attains. Translations are most effective for students with strong native language literacy skills who receive instruction on the test subject in their native language.
- The linguistic complexity of standardized tests and the lack of sufficient accommodations explain why English language learners typically do not perform as well as native English speakers on such tests. For this reason, the validity of their scores is questionable. As a result, standardized tests administered to English language learners are not a valid basis for high-stakes decision making.

Chapter 5

The Ones Left Behind: How High-Stakes Tests Impact the Lives and Schooling Experiences of ELL Students

In spite of the issues that surround the assessment of ELLs outlined in previous chapters of this book, most states in the United States are now administering standardized tests, and using the results to make crucial decisions about individual students (Blank *et al.*, 1999). As stated previously, ELLs are particularly vulnerable to high-stakes decisions based on test results; tests are used to determine high school graduation, grade promotion and the placement of ELLs into tracked or remedial education programs (Heubert & Hauser, 1999). The supporters of high-stakes testing and the accountability mandates of *No Child Left Behind* argue that these policies will improve the education of poor and minority students and reduce the achievement gap, while opponents of these policies argue instead that their effects are punitive for these students and in fact reduce the quality of education they receive. This chapter explores how high-stakes testing affects ELL students, by hearing their voices and learning from them about the positive and negative outcomes of testing.

In specific, the sections of this chapter are as follows: (1) The Human Stories Behind Test Data; (2) Retake, Retake, Retake; (3) Prolonged Time in School and Extended Schooling; (4) Testing as an Incentive to Leave School: 'Return to Home Country', GED, and Dropping Out; (5) Challenges for New Arrivals and Students with Limited Literacy/Interrupted Formal Schooling; (6) The Thrill of Victory and the Agony of Defeat. While high-stakes testing has generated a great deal of interest in recent years, there remains limited research in this area – particularly with regard to its impact on English language learners. The first section of this chapter shares data from interviews with high school students in New York City, who discuss their experiences with testing. One of the realities of high-stakes testing for ELLs is that the students must frequently retake the exams in order to pass, due to the challenges they pose. The second section of the chapter examines this reality, and describes which exams the students and teachers feel are most challenging. Related to this, the length of time that ELLs are in high school is often prolonged because of the testing requirements, as shown in the third section.

A serious unintended consequence of high-stakes testing in New York and elsewhere is that it creates an incentive for students to leave school, either to return to their country of origin, to leave traditional schooling to pursue an alternative diploma, or to drop out – this is described in the fourth part. The chapter continues to show how older ELLs, particularly those who arrive in the United States in high school and students with interrupted formal education have the greatest incentives to leave school, as these students are the least likely of all ELLs to pass the graduation requirements in New York. Testing places enormous pressure on ELLs, as examined in the sixth section of this chapter, which negatively impacts their self-esteem when they fail but has a positive impact when they pass.

Amrein and Berliner (2002) note a number of the unintended consequences of high-stakes testing for student academic performance, in their study of testing data from 28 states. They found high-stakes testing to be associated with:

- Increased dropout rates, decreased graduation rates, and higher rates of younger individuals taking the Graduate Equivalency Diploma (GED) exams;
- Higher numbers of low performing students being retained in grade before pivotal testing years to ensure their preparedness; and,
- High numbers of suspensions and expulsions of low performing students before testing days. (Amrein & Berliner, 2002: 2–3)

These findings support many of the concerns raised by educators and educational researchers with regard to negative outcomes of high-stakes testing for all students, and particularly ELLs.

A major critique of test-based accountability systems increasingly visible in the literature is that the tests fail language minority youth. Valenzuela (2005) and McNeil and Valenzuela (2000) find support for many of the findings above in their exploration of the impact of high-stakes testing in Texas. Praised by politicians and gaining national recognition for raising educational quality, these authors find instead that 'Texas-style accountability', the model upon which *No Child Left Behind* is based, reduces the quality and quantity of education offered, and has the most damaging effects on poor and minority youth. While scores have increased on statewide tests overall, the vast majority of students failing these high-stakes exams are

African-Americans, Latinos, and English language learners (ELLs). Valenzuela (1999) makes the argument that educational policy in the United States serves to subtract from students their linguistic, cultural, and community-based identities, instead of building on these aspects of diversity as assets. Her more recent work explicitly links the accountability system in Texas to her notion of 'subtractive' education, arguing that high-stakes testing is the most detrimental current educational policy for Latinos and ELLs (Valenzuela, 2002, 2005).

Many states are now implementing high school exit exams that also serve to meet the accountability requirements of *No Child Left Behind*, as described in Chapter 4 of this book. According to a study by the Center on Education Policy conducted by Sullivan *et al.* (2005), 20 states are using high school exit exams to also meet NCLB high school requirements and they predict that 87% of ELLs will have to pass high school exit exams in the near future. As they write:

> Almost all states with exit requirements have an implicit requirement that students should know English in order to graduate from high school. Consistent with this, ELLs must generally pass state exit exams in reading/language arts in English. (Sullivan *et al.*, 2005: 87)

In this way, these authors draw a link between testing policy and language policy that promotes English; having English-only testing as a graduation requirement is tantamount to English-only policy.

On the other side of the testing debate, however, supporters of *No Child Left Behind* accountability mandates state that the law is critical for closing the achievement gap among students according to race, class and ethnicity.

> 'There is a battle raging for the soul of American education', noted Kati Haycock, Director of The Education Trust. 'In our work around the country, we often hear local educators talk about the progress they are seeing *as a result of* the new accountability. These education leaders are especially concerned with the messages communicated by those opposed to accountability. Too often, the critics imply that students from low-income families and students of color simply cannot be expected to be taught to high levels'. (Education Trust, 2003: 1)

Leaders of the Education Trust argue that the law has brought the needs of low-performing students into the public spotlight, causing greater attention to be paid to these students then before. The findings presented below indicate that while attention towards these students has indeed increased, much of that attention has been negative.

The Human Stories Behind Test Data

To explore these issues in greater depth, it is helpful to turn now to findings from the research I conducted in New York City. Within the current climate of accountability in public education in the United States, high-stakes tests have generated a great deal of quantitative data about students in the form of test scores. In contrast to this data, the findings reported in this chapter tell some of the human stories behind the testing movement and thereby begin to fill a gap in existing research. Specifically, the remainder of this chapter examines how the inclusion of ELLs in Regents exams affects these students at the ten schools included in this study. While this research took place in New York City, the findings reported here offer a local example of a much larger national issue.

In New York City and elsewhere across the United States, the majority of ELLs do not perform as well as native English speakers on the standardized tests being used for accountability purposes under *No Child Left Behind*, as detailed in Chapter 3. Because of the traditionally poorer performance by ELLs on Regents exams and because the tests are attached to the attainment of a high school diploma, these findings show that English language learners are greatly impacted by the exams every day. For an English language learner in high school, high-stakes standardized exams are therefore a major part of their introduction and enculturation to the United States, given that they are such a defining force in students' daily educational experiences.

What follows are students' voices in a transcript which encapsulates the issues delineated above and frames the testing debate as it pertains to ELLs. The students in this focus group are seniors enrolled in an English Regents preparation course for ELLs, who range in age from 18 to 20 years old. All of the students in this group have failed the English Regents at least once and yet they have passed their other Regents exams and completed all necessary coursework for graduation; as a result, the exam is the main reason they attend school each day. 'S1' is from Paraguay, 'S4' is from the Dominican Republic and 'S5' is from Honduras. As referenced in this excerpt, a score of 55 is the minimum needed to pass the English Regents exam.

> *Is that true for the other students also, that your main reason for being here is the English Regents? [Students nod in agreement]*
> ... **S4:** The main problem for me is that we have to learn, like, the English that people here they know since they grow up, things like that. We got the English like second language you know, and it's difficult for us and even they say we have to pass the Regents with 55. That's the main

problem. I'm not born here, and even when people they born here even they can't pass. So what do they expect for us? Like that, with three years living here for the first time, it's not right.

S1: And then mostly because there's a lot of students who came from Dominican Republic and other countries, they are taking here, and they know they have to take the English Regents. And the problem is that they don't know too much English, and they have to learn, they have to, to work a lot to take the Regents. That's the problem here.

S4: … [M]y friends in DR they graduated in 2002. So I don't feel good too, oh, like, still in high school. I'm still in high school! All the teachers went to me, like, 'Oh, you should have finished in your country because here it's going to be two years. You're going to be left back, left behind like two years'. And it's true. That's what's going on right now … I was close, I was close twice. 50 and then, no three times, 49, then 50, and then 51. And now I get the worst report I get a 45. You see? What, I'm going backwards now? You see? Come on. [Students laugh] …

[Another student had entered the room, and now raises his hand to speak]
Yes, please…

S5: … My sister told me you need to work hard to pass the Regents. It doesn't matter if you're here like two years or a year and half. Just study hard … I take for example my sister. She came here ten years ago, she didn't have nothing, no papers, nothing. She worked hard and now she's going to finish her master's degree at [New York University] in social work. And she says you want to do something you have to work hard. But you need to work hard. You know, like math, I hate math but I passed already, and the only thing left is English Regents. Why I passed? I worked hard, and if you work hard you're going to pass. It doesn't matter if you have one and a half years, you work hard for something you're going to pass.

S4: You can work hard, but if they want they will fail you … You know what? You get a 51 and just for four points they're going to fail you?! Come on, it's your life. It's your life. You're supposed to go to college. I want to do a career, I want to do a career, and you know I want to do a life. And I want to have a family. And for four points they're going to [ruin] my life?! Come on. That's not right.

(Senior ELL students, School #2, focus group interview transcript)

In the preceding interview, 'S4' details his thoughts about his experiences taking the English Regents four different times. In chronological order, his scores were as follows: 49, 50, 51 and 45 (55 is the passing score). Ironically, his scores have not consistently improved as he has acquired English, which he sees as a problem with the exams and unjust. His story exemplifies what is deeply unfair about the inclusion of ELLs in the English Regents, for whom language becomes a barrier to their high school graduation. By contrast, 'S5' supports the idea of setting high standards and requiring ELLs to pass the Regents, and conveys the belief that with hard work this population of students can also succeed. The disagreement between S4 and S5 perfectly depicts the tension surrounding the testing debate, which is between raising standards on one hand and punishing ELLs for their lack of English on the other. The discussion that follows refers back to the points made by the students in this transcript.

Retake, Retake, Retake: The Difficulty of Regents Exams for ELLs

As evident in the experiences of the students in the preceding transcript, ELLs often take Regents exams over and over again, in an effort to increase their scores and pass. Like the students quoted above, I spoke with students in many schools whose sole reason for returning to high school each day was to increase their test scores to the minimum required to pass. Below are two excerpts from interviews showing how prevalent it is for ELLs to retake exams, the first from a student focus group at one school and the second from an interview with an assistant principal at another school:

[Excerpt One:]
['S2' is from Bangladesh, 'S3' is from Guinea and 'S4' is from the Dominican Republic. They are 11th or 12th graders at Focal School #1, and recent arrivals to the United States]
How do you feel about the Regents exams? Are they important? Why or why not?
... **S3:** Some of us started in 11th grade. They put the Regents for everybody, like everybody knows English. But I only been here two years, so I had to take each of the Regents twice before I passed it.
S4: I took biology twice and still haven't passed it. It's really hard.
S2: English Regents is hardest for all of us.
S4: Yeah, it's six hours!
S2: People born here and stuff it's easy for them, but for us it's really hard. The math and stuff isn't hard but the English is.
S3: English is the hardest because most of the kids take English Regents four or five times before they pass – not the regular English kids, but the ESL kids. The first time I failed with a 36, and the second time I passed.

It's not really that easy, man … The Regents also slows us up. If we don't pass in June, I'm 18 and we have to stay here.
(Students in English Regents Preparation class, Focal School #1, focus group interview notes)

[Excerpt Two:]
How are the standardized tests affecting your ELL students, and what are the greatest challenges of the tests for ELLs?
Ms V: … Overall I have about 60% of ELLs meeting the benchmark of 55 and higher on the English Regents. I don't know, I think the schoolwide average is 73 or 78? I'm blanking. But anyway, there are 60% meeting it at any given time. But to graduate, they all must meet it …
(Ms V, Assistant Principal of Instruction, School #9, interview notes)

As shown in Excerpt One, students frequently retake Regents exams, particularly the English Regents. In Excerpt Two, 'Ms V' notes that about 60% of ELLs pass the English Regents at any given time at her school, which means that at least 40% will need to retake the exam to pursue a high school diploma. It is safe to assume that of the 60% of ELLs who passed, a significant number were retaking the exam because they had failed it previously. Retaking is part of exam culture in high schools serving large numbers of ELLs, showing the enormous challenge of the exams and how they define ELL students' experiences in school.

Students and teachers repeatedly refer to the English and Math Regents exams in interviews as the most difficult for ELLs to pass. The statistics that Ms V shares above are actually far higher than citywide performance by ELLs. In fact, just 33.2% of ELLs passed the English Regents exam in 2005, as compared to a pass rate of 80.7% of all students on the English Regents exam in the same year. For the Math A Regents exam, the ELL citywide pass rate in 2005 was 58.1% as compared to an overall pass rate of 81.5% (New York City Department of Education, 2005). In the passage below, students in a focus group discuss the difficulty of the English Regents, and again show the prevalence of ELLs retaking exams across school sites.

Have you taken the Regents? [S1 nods]. Which ones and how many times?
S1: Yes. It's just the English. I passed all of them, all of the others, I just missing the English. I got a 50. One of the things about the Regents is they have to have another one, different for us. The Regents there is now has to be for people born in this country. We have to take a different issue, we don't speak English very well. What happen if I fail it, I will no graduate …
[To S3] Have you taken the Regents?

S3: Two times. I've taken the English Regents, it's my big problem …
So all of you have passed all of the Regents, right? It's just English?
All students: Yes.
And you have all of your credits to graduate?
S2: I have 48, and you need 40 to graduate.
S3: I have 45.
S1: like 50.
(ELLs in 12th grade, School #2, focus group interview transcript)

All of the students quoted in this transcript have completed their requirements for high school graduation except for passing the English Regents exam. Students need 40 course credits to graduate, and all of the students in this group had already exceeded their required credits for graduation at the time of the interview. They will each take the English Regents exam at least twice, and most likely more times, to graduate.

Students are typically very familiar with the different parts of the Regents exams and able to articulate exactly what aspects of the exams are difficult, using vocabulary they have acquired from the exams themselves, as can be seen in the passage that follows:

> ['*S1' is a senior from Yemen, 'S2' is a sophomore from Ecuador, 'S3' is a senior from Peru; all are recent arrivals*]
> *So everyone thinks that the English Regents is the most difficult of all the different Regents? [Students nod in agreement] Did you all pass?*
> **S3:** No.
> **S2:** No.
> **S1:** I mean, why we here? [students laugh]
> *Right, right, okay. And do you know which part is the hardest for you?*
> **S3:** Yeah, the Critical Lens when you have to understand the message or the poem.
> **S1:** The third part of the essay [Task 3]. Sometimes the answer is like compare and contrast something like that. I don't know word exactly what is that. They ask us to compare the poem and the writing that they give us, and tell what's the difference and the similarity …
> **S2:** Listening is hardest. Note taking. Me confunde, es muy rápido.
> (ELLs in English Regents preparation course, School #4, focus group interview transcript)

In this passage, students describe the challenges of the English Regents exams for them because they are ELLs. This passage offers further evidence regarding the prevalence of ELLs retaking exams; each of the passages above are from interviews at different schools, and this theme is true across school sites. Retaking is particularly commonplace at School #4, where students are told they must obtain a score of 65 to pass when the actual passing score is 55. In addition, most ELLs interviewed for this research were found using vocabulary specific to the Regents exams, like the term 'Critical Lens', which is indicative of how central these exams are in the daily lives and schooling experiences of ELLs, a point developed further in Chapter 6.

While students and teachers repeatedly refer to English as the most difficult Regents exam, Math is also seen as particularly challenging for ELLs. While the pass rate of ELLs citywide is higher on the Math Regents than the English Regents, there still remains an achievement gap of over 30 percentage points between ELLs and all students. The challenge of the Math Regents is described in the following passage, by an administrator at School #2 who used to be the Assistant Principal for ESL/foreign language at School #1:

> We conducted a ten-year study at [Focal School #1] on improvements we made on the English Regents. The problem is not English Regents now, but content-area exams. Three or four students didn't graduate in January because of English, but nine or ten didn't graduate because of the Math Regents. Math teachers aren't trained in language teaching and there is a lot of English on the Math test. It's hard to convince people. But content teachers are not qualified, they're trained to develop content. (Mr C, Assistant Principal, School #2, interview notes)

As 'Mr C' notes, because this school made a concerted effort to improve ELL pass rates on the English Regents, they are now left with addressing the wide achievement gap on the Math Regents. The fact that few bilingual math teachers have had training in the education of ELLs is likely a contributing factor to the poor performance by ELLs on the Math A Regents, given the linguistic complexity of the exam. From the data presented in this section, it is clear that retaking Regents exams is widespread across New York City high schools and that the English and Math Regents pose great challenges for ELLs.

Prolonged Time in School and Extended Schooling

High school in the United States is typically four years in length, yet this has actually become atypical for ELLs attending school within a high-stakes testing climate. Barring students from high school graduation until they pass the Regents exams has a number of consequences, which include ELLs attending high school for more years, attending more classes per day, and attending more after-school and tutoring programs than native English speakers. The quotations offered above show how students in New York are prevented from graduation because of their test scores, even when they have successfully completed all of their coursework. Similarly, as clarified further in the section that follows, older ELLs are often required to repeat grades of high school they may have completed in their home country to give them a chance at passing the Regents exams; high school counselors at the schools in this study routinely place new arrivals to high school in ninth grade, even when they are overage and have the necessary credits from their home country to place them in a higher grade. As a result, ELLs systematically stay in school beyond the traditional four years. These findings are consistent with nationwide research, as the Center on Education Policy found that the length of time ELLs must attend school has lengthened across the United States due to testing (Sullivan *et al.*, 2005).

Because of the many challenges ELLs must overcome to pass the Regents exams, they are often encouraged or required to attend longer school days than what is required of native English speakers.

> *I'm curious about something you said. Other schools have said they've also shifted their curricula. How do you do that, are there classes you have to give up?*
>
> **Ms O:** Well let's put it this way, our [ELL] kids go from periods one to twelve around here. We have an extended day program. So you find that, well, I come from another high school where periods were one to eight. This school the periods are one to twelve so they just add an extra class period, they have a long day, they can fit it in. So they don't give up anything, they get what they need. If they need to have a class of something or need to spend two sessions so they can graduate they do.
>
> (Ms O, ESL Assistant Principal, School #4, interview transcript)

As 'Ms O' describes, most students in New York City attend high school for eight periods per day, yet ELLs at her school are often there for 12 periods per day. Many of the larger city high schools are open for 12 or 13 periods per day, with students coming on a rotating schedule to avoid overcrowding. While native English speakers at these schools generally come for just eight periods of the day, ELLs are found to come to school for every period the building is open in an effort to pass the Regents and graduate more quickly. ELLs also attend extended school days at some of the smaller schools, such as School #5 which currently serves fewer than 100 students.

Does your schedule run on an extended day?
Mr Y: Yes, we have a nine period day. This is not officially a p.m. school but kids also stay in the school for tutoring and instruction. We have individual scheduling, and it's a very long day for my kids. We call it really a ten period day ... We have to have extended day to cover everything. We also have zero period first thing in morning, when teachers work one-on-one or in small groups with students.
(Mr Y, principal, School #5, interview transcript)

In this passage, 'Mr Y' explains that his school offers an extended day to cover all the material students need to learn in a limited period of time. Both Mr Y and Ms O explain that ELLs attend Saturday school, after-school and tutoring programs to prepare for the Regents exams. The fact that ELLs often attend more school than native English speakers is not problematic *per se*, what is troubling is that so much of their time in school is focused on test preparation, and that the tests for which they are preparing are not geared towards addressing the needs of ELLs. This is discussed in greater detail in Chapter 6, which analyzes the different approaches high schools take to increase their students' pass rates on the Regents exams.

As a related side-effect of testing policy, in interviews I encountered several cases of ELLs who had been admitted to colleges but were not permitted to attend because they had not fulfilled the high school exit exam requirement. In this excerpt from the data that were collected, a teacher explains the regulations:

How are the standardized tests affecting your ELL students?
Ms R: Those who are seniors are a bundle of nerves. There were some who had passed everything but the Regents. They couldn't matriculate. For CUNY schools you can take nine credits before you matriculate. This one boy was going to the College of Staten Island and they said if you didn't pass you'd have to quit.
(Ms R, ESL Teacher, School #9, interview notes)

As 'Ms R' explains, City University of New York (CUNY) colleges will accept students who have not passed the Regents exams for admission and allow them to take up to three classes, but will not allow them to actually matriculate until they receive a high school diploma. ESL teachers at School #2 also informed me about students who had been admitted to college but could not graduate or matriculate because of the Regents exams: '[student name] got into college and still hasn't passed the Regents yet. He was accepted but he hasn't passed the Regents' (Mr P, ESL Teacher, School #2 focus group interview transcript). This means that a single test score will override an institution of higher education's assessment of a student's college readiness.

Testing as an Incentive to Leave School: 'Return to Home Country', GED and Dropping Out

Of great concern is that because of the challenges that the Regents exams pose for ELLs and their high-stakes consequences, the exams act to push these students to leave school, either of their own volition or with their school's encouragement. The students most likely to leave or be pressured to leave are older ELLs. Students leave school to return to their home country and obtain a high school diploma there, to enter a Graduate Equivalency Diploma (GED) program in the United States, or to drop out of school completely. In this discussion, it is important to keep in mind that the enrollment of students in most urban high schools in the US decreases dramatically by senior year – a problem which is particularly acute in such cities as Los Angeles, Chicago, New York, Houston and Philadelphia. For instance, the population by grade at the focal school studied in New York City is as follows: 1145 ninth graders, 1154 tenth graders, 730 11th graders, and just 479 12th graders (New York City Department of Education, 2004a). Seniors like those quoted in the transcript at the start of this chapter, who have successfully passed their courses and attained the necessary credits for graduation, are actually high achievers in their grade cohort. Of all the students who started school in freshman year with them, they are among a minority who actually made it so far in high school. Yet these students are being barred from high school graduation because of the Regents exams, which act as a final gatekeeper for the select ELL students to have arrived to the point where they are actually eligible for graduation. Many link low graduation rates to testing:

> **Ms K:** ... One big effect of the standardized testing is that they're not graduating!!! Very few are actually graduating!! We get six or seven sections of freshman, and we get three graduating. It's dropping rapidly. (Ms K., ESL coordinator, Focal School #1, interview notes)

In this excerpt, an ESL coordinator discusses how the Regents exams reduce the graduation rates among ELLs at her school.

In gathering data for the purposes of this research, I learned that the moment an English language learner arrives to a high school in New York City, they are often advised by school guidance counselors or teachers that it will most likely take the student longer than the traditional four years to graduate. If that student is older, they are routinely encouraged to return to the country from which they have just arrived to finish high school, as in the following:

Do standardized tests such as the Regents affect you and the school? If so, how?
Mr A: ... It's hardest for students who come here older, let's say a girl who is older, for example 17 or 18. We often suggest to parents that they go back to the home country and they sometimes do it. They go back to their country. Because if you come here at too advanced an age, you're up the creek. There just isn't enough time to get the proficiency you need to pass the English Regents. Forget about the [ELL] subclass. I think you need at least three years here to pass that test. So if you're 17 or 18, you have no chance of graduating with your class because of the English Regents.
(Mr A, school counselor for ELLs, Focal School #1, interview notes)

This is the new reception for ELLs who arrive in the United States during high school; schools are under pressure not to teach those who are hardest to teach, and this limits the opportunities offered to ELLs.

Similarly, older ELL students and others who are struggling in school are often asked to leave school to pursue a GED, even though they have a legal right to remain. This occurs across school sites, as in the two excerpts below from different schools:

Mr N: With this new system *[shows me a policy about legal right for students to remain in school until age 21, which is newly being enforced in the wake of a lawsuit against the Department of Education]*, now the system has changed. We showed them they have the right to be here until 21 ... This is something new that might affect the curriculum within the school. Up through last year we were able to get rid of them. So what we will do now? So you are flunking the Math Regents or taking this class, and we will say, 'Go take a GED'.
(Mr N, bilingual counselor, Focal School #1, interview notes)

You mentioned the Regents preparation course you are teaching now is challenging. Can you give an example?
Ms K: ... I know that they can officially be in the school system past 18, but I don't know how long. But I know that unofficially at this school they start to push students towards other programs. And I'm sure it's for statistical reasons, you know, it doesn't look good if we don't have the graduates. So there we have students, sort of, conference and GED programs are suggested, etcetera. So, yeah, they are approaching that point where they're going to be asked to get everything done in a ridiculously short period of time or to leave.
(Ms K, ESL Teacher, School #4, interview transcript)

In the first excerpt, a guidance counselor at Focal School #1 explains how he encourages older ELLs to leave school and attend a GED program instead. In the second excerpt, 'Ms K' discusses how her school 'unofficially' pushes students into GED programs. Both quotations indicate the pressure on schools to encourage students to leave, because test scores and graduation rates are important factors within the existing system of accountability in New York under *No Child Left Behind*. In these ways, Regents exams are linked to leaving school.

Although some students are encouraged by their schools to leave the traditional high school track and pursue a GED, sometimes others choose to leave:

> *How do you think the standardized tests, the Regents, are affecting your ELL students?*
>
> **Mr B:** I think many of them reach a point where they realize perhaps they're not going to graduate from high school. I think that is a reality. I have a number of older kids in my classroom, 17, 18 or 19 years old. Some who have not gone through formal education, or who are not there, for whatever economic reasons they find themselves. GED. That's the word. '[Mr B], how can I get my GED?' They realize to pass the English Regents at ages 17 or 18 at Level One ESL, let's be real. And that reality check kicks in with them. There's a daily level of frustration, anxiety, fear.
>
> (Mr B, Bilingual Social Studies Teacher, Focal School #1, interview transcript)

In this passage, 'Mr B' explains how the Regents exams are a force that compels students in his bilingual social studies classes to leave school and pursue a GED instead. Again, ELLs and particularly those who arrive in the United States during high school must learn the English language and also cover all of the material on the Regents exams in a very limited amount of time; for many students, the challenges of doing so prove to be too great. Taking a GED allows students to circumvent passing the five core Regents exams that are now required in order to graduate from city high schools. At the same time, however, doing so may limit their future opportunities (Cameron & Heckman, 1993). The enrollment of students under 21 in GED programs in New York City has increased by over 13,000 students within the past five years (New York State Department of Education, as cited in Campanile, 2004).

New research is proving a correlation between high school exit exams and increased dropout rates in the *No Child Left Behind* era. In their national research, Dee and Jacob (2006) report that students in states with high school exit exams are more likely to drop out than students in states without exit exams, while Warren *et al.* (2005) show that rates of high school completion are lower in states with exit exams than in states without them. ELLs in New York City across school sites offered a great deal of anecdotal evidence that there is a relationship between Regents exams and leaving school. The following two excerpts from focus group interviews with ELL students offer examples:

[S1, S3 and S4 are native speakers of Spanish, and S2 speaks Urdu]
S3: There are a lot of people bilingual who are here one semester or two semester but can't pass because of English Regents.
S4: I know a lot of people, like, that came three months ago. They can't pass it because they really don't know the language. Then they have to stay in school longer.
S1: Some people give up trying to learn.
S2: Yeah, they drop out ... My friend's brother was, like, he lived in a village in Pakistan. I knew a little English but he didn't know anything. If you say, 'How are you?' he says, 'okay'. He was here a junior and he couldn't graduate. He was in this school three years and then they ask him to take GED.
(ELLs in 10th and 11th grades, Focal School #1, focus group interview transcript)

I think there are a lot of people out there that drop out of school because of that test, they get older and they gotta drop out. They can't pass the test because sometimes they make it too hard.
(ELL student in English Regents Preparation Class, Focal School #1, interview transcript)

In these two passages, students tell stories about other students they know and describe the incentives created by the Regents exams to leave school and pursue a GED or drop out. The problem with either of these choices is that studies on the economic rate of return for education show that students receiving a GED and students who drop out typically earn less than students with a traditional high school diploma; in fact, research shows no statistical difference in earnings between students who receive a GED and high school dropouts (Cameron & Heckman, 1993).

High-stakes testing in English serves to increase the already high status of this language in the United States, and is linked to the marginalization of ELL students. In their study of the California High School Exit Exams (CAHSEE), Garcia and Gopal discover a wide achievement gap between ELLs and other high school students, and draw the following conclusions:

> In this study, disparate CAHSEE test scores suggested that English language proficiency as a form of cultural capital operated as an exclusionary device, and increased understanding about how high-stakes tests contributed to the reproduction of educational inequalities. (Garcia & Gopal, 2003: 134)

These authors problematize the practice of using high school exit exams as the single criterion for deciding high school graduation, due to how this practice negatively affects an English learner's access to future opportunities.

Challenges for New Arrivals and Students with Limited Literacy/Interrupted Formal Schooling

Passing the Regents examinations required for high school graduation is an arduous task for ELLs who, unlike native English speakers, must acquire the English language at the same time as they learn all of the content covered on the exams. While passing the Regents is challenging for anyone learning the English language, it is particularly so for older students who arrive in the United States during high school and students with limited literacy skills either in their native language or in English. The challenges that older arrivals in high school face were discussed in the section above, as older students are more likely to choose or be encouraged to leave school than younger students. These students often do not have the credits they need to graduate, nor do they have the time while in school to take the classes that will prepare them to pass the different Regents exams.

Students with limited literacy skills either in their native language or in English must cover an inordinate amount in a very short time period. Often, ELLs with very limited literacy are students who have had interrupted formal education; these students are termed 'SIFE' by the New York City Department of Education. There are many SIFE students in New York City schools, though schools are only just beginning to collect data about these students. For instance, School #2 compiled this data for the first time in the 2003–2004 year and found that 104 or 13% of ELLs enrolled in the school are in the SIFE category. Students with limited literacy levels are at a serious disadvantage when taking the Regents exams, as noted below (this quotation is from School #7, which has a large SIFE population):

> *How are students here performing on the English Regents?*
> **Ms S:** . . . This is entering immigrants into high school with no experience, I think to demand they have the same exam [as native English speakers]

is just ludicrous! I'd like to put these examiners in China. And some of these students come with good skills. But a lot of our kids come with literacy issues, I would say most of them. There are varying degrees of literacy issues, we're not allowed to screen [for admission], but we have kids who come here with a third grade reading ability in their own country, and they're failing out … A lot make tremendous strides here, going from a third grade level to seventh grade if they apply themselves.
(Ms S, ESL Teacher, School #7, interview notes)

In this citation, 'Ms S' describes how challenging it is for ELLs who have limited literacy skills to pass the English Regents exams, and the reality is that most are unable to do so. While the students do progress, as she notes, they cannot attain a level of literacy sufficient for achieving a passing score of 55 on the Regents exams; Regents exams do not measure progress, but are rather a measure of attainment of a set bar. These students are particularly likely to stay in high school for prolonged periods, as shown in the following:

Do you serve students here who have had limited formal schooling?
Mr S: About 15% of our student population … These students aren't moving fast enough to graduate, even in six years, so we're looking at a project to speed that up. Kids want to graduate after six years. Seven, some can do it in seven years, but it gets really hard for them.
(Principal, School #3, interview notes)

As 'Mr S' states, it is almost impossible for students with limited schooling to graduate from high school within the traditional four year time period; rather, it takes far longer because language and literacy ability are a major part of what Regents exams actually assess, even on content-area exams such as math. As such, students are greatly hindered if they do not possess the literacy skills needed to pass the Regents exams. For SIFE students, it is particularly problematic that Regents exams only consider if a student passes or not, and that the tests do not measure the progress they make each year, even when these students make great annual gains.

The Thrill of Victory and the Agony of Defeat: Self-Esteem and the Pressure to Perform

A primary theme that repeatedly emerges in interview data with administrators, teachers and students is that high-stakes tests place tremendous pressure on ELLs and failing the exams negatively impacts their self-esteem. As two students note:

> **S3:** I failed the English Regents three times, and I'm here only for the English Regents . . . I have all the credits I need to graduate and passed all the Regents.
> *You have all the credits you need to graduate?*
> **S3:** More. More credits.
> *How do you feel about that?*
> **S3:** Bad. I feel bad because I don't get go to college *[S3 starts to cry]*.
> **S4:** I feel, like, guilty because people they blame it on us, you know, it's your fault.
> (Senior ELL students, School #2, focus group interview transcript)

This citation shows how failing the Regents has a negative effect on a student's self-esteem. This sentiment is supported by teachers and administrators in the following:

> *How are the standardized tests affecting your ELL students?*
> **Ms T:** A lot of them develop a low self-esteem. I've seen a lot of conflict with parents, who blame students for not trying hard enough. But I don't think they realize how difficult it is.
> (Ms T, ESL coordinator, School #4, interview notes)

> *How are the standardized tests affecting your ELL students?*
> **Mr X:** I think it's extremely demanding to a point of demoralizing to the students and disregards the needs of students. Even in ESL One they ask students to study poetry when they can't get around in the city, that's what we're dealing with. The whole approach to Regents testing is elitist, it's a value judgment.
> (Mr X, ESL Teacher/Chinese Bilingual Teacher, School #8, interview notes)

As can be seen here, when teachers and administrators were asked about how testing affects their ELL students in interviews, they often mentioned students' self-confidence in their responses. In these quotations, the ESL teacher and coordinator indicate that students often feel ashamed about their inability to pass Regents exams, which weighs upon their self-esteem.

With regard to the pressure the Regents exams place on students, the following quotations bring this issue to life:

> *Is standardized testing, and particularly the Regents, affecting your students? If so, how?*
> **Mr R:** There is greater pressure on students to learn English as quickly as possible, and teachers to help them learn, because although many

students can take the exam in their native language, many are not suffi-
ciently literate in their language ...
Ms N: Knowing they have to take this test puts a lot of anxiety on the
kids. They may be confident, but I think deep down they don't think
they're going to pass it.
(Regents teachers, School #3, focus group interview transcript)

[S1 and S3 are from China, S2 is from Bosnia]
Are the exams difficult or easy? Why? Which of the different Regents exams is
the most difficult for you?
S1: ... How can I take Global Regents if I don't even have three years
experience? The school says if you don't pass it you can't graduate. And
my mom was getting me pressure like, okay, if you don't pass it I will get
mad at you. I have a lot of pressure.
S2: Too much pressure.
S3: Yeah.
(11th grade ELLs, School #4, focus group interview transcript)

From these quotations, it becomes clear that high-stakes testing places great
pressure on ELLs and their teachers to speed up the process of English language acquisition; this is part of new language acquisition policy whereby
English acquisition is promoted through standardized testing. Yet from
second language acquisition research we know that it typically takes an
English language learner at least five to seven years to acquire the academic
language in English needed to perform to the level of native English speakers on assessments (Cummins, 2000; Thomas & Collier, 1997).

Representing the other side of the testing debate, testing has great meaning for ELLs and those who educate them when students are able to
succeed in passing the standardized tests administered by their district or
state – in spite of the odds. The following quotation is a continuation of the
focus group transcript cited above, in which 'S2', a girl from Bosnia, shares
her opinion:

The Regents exams are the same tests that native speakers of English take. Do
you think it's fair you have to take all the Regents?
S2: I don't know about English Regents, but other ones yes. It's fair
because other kids. You cannot say, 'Oh look, they not gonna to do it'.
Like English, the original English people they were born here. They
gonna say, 'Look, they have an opportunity, they cannot do it'. Like, you
know, we want to show we can do it, like, if we go to college you need
something to prove you are ready for it. So I think for me, yeah. We
should take.

In this passage, 'S2' makes the point that although she questions having to take the English Regents exams, she feels that passing other content-area exams is an accomplishment which proves to native English speakers that ELLs know the content needed for college and are able to achieve to high standards. This is a similar point that was made during an interview with the principal of School #7, a small alternative high school serving Latino students who are recent immigrants. At this new school, scores on the English Regents increased after the first year of operation to above the city-wide average for ELLs. Although he generally opposes high-stakes testing, the principal explained that having higher scores on the English Regents has validated the school's existence in the eyes of other school administrators in the city, and this validation was a catalyst in the regional superintendent's decision to fund expansion of the school.

Discussion

Requiring students to rush their process of English language acquisition is part of new language acquisition policy whereby standardized tests implicitly promote English. Yet, ELLs have a greater distance to travel in high school than do native speakers of English, because they must acquire the English language and also learn all of the material covered on high-stakes exams. ELLs are included in all Regents exams from the moment they arrive in high school, regardless of when they arrive or their level of language or literacy ability. As can be seen in the data presented in this chapter, this places enormous pressure on ELLs and their teachers and is, for many students, simply an impossible task. As heard from students and educators above, failing the Regents exams causes most students to stay in high school longer and prevents them from continuing on to other opportunities such as college. And, it creates a push for students to leave school to pursue a GED, leave the United States, or simply drop out of school entirely. The ELLs facing the greatest challenges on standardized graduation exams are older students who arrive in the United States during high school, and those ELLs who have limited literacy skills either in their native language and/or in English. At the same time, however, including ELLs in the same exams as those taken by native English speakers offers validation to students, educators, and the programs that serve them. Though validation is an important benefit of testing, such benefits are outweighed by the negative effects of testing that were so frequently reported in interviews; high-stakes testing is an issue of social equity for ELL students when its results are inequitable.

Heubert states the following in his discussion of the disparate impact of high-stakes testing:

> We should therefore be concerned, to put it mildly, that students of color, students with disabilities, English language learners, and low-income students are failing some demanding state graduation tests at rates as high as 60 to 90 percent. And these failure rates would be even higher if they included the many students who drop out or are retained in grade before they even take the graduation exams. (Heubert, 2002: 3)

Because high-stakes testing has been found to have a harmful impact on certain groups, he recommends that policymakers avoid those policies that have the most deleterious consequences: grade retention, placement of students into low-track classes, and requiring students to pass graduation or promotion tests (without ensuring that schools have provided students the opportunity to learn the skills and knowledge that the tests measure).

Chapter Summary

- High-stakes testing has an enormous impact on the daily lives of ELLs in school, and students feel a great deal of pressure to learn English as quickly as possible and improve their test scores. Students report that the English Regents is the most difficult exam, and show how testing impacts their self-esteem.
- Due to the difficulty of the exams, many students repeatedly retake and fail the tests, prolonging the length of time they are in high school. This includes students who have completed all of the other requirements for high school graduation, and come to school daily just to attend Regents preparation courses in hopes of passing. Similarly, many students attend an extended school day to prepare.
- Because of the testing, many students are unable to graduate from high school – including those who have already been admitted to college or other institutions of higher education. This limits students' future opportunities.
- Testing creates an incentive for ELLs to drop out of high school or seek an alternative diploma; ELLs currently have the highest dropout rate of all students in New York City. Students are being encouraged by school administrators to leave school and even to return to their home country, particularly older students who are unlikely to pass.

Chapter 6

'Teaching to the Test' as Language Policy: The Focus on Test Preparation in Curriculum and Instruction for ELLs

Because of the consequences of standardized tests being used in compliance with *No Child Left Behind*, educators of English language learners across the United States are now focused on preparing their students to pass the tests that count (Amrein & Berliner, 2002; McNeil & Valenzuela, 2000; Valenzuela, 2002, 2005; Wright, 2002). When exams are linked to high-stakes consequences in the ways detailed in this book, they by definition greatly impact students' educational experiences and future opportunities. Due to the importance of these exams for ELLs and those who educate them, educators in New York and elsewhere across the United States are under strong pressure to 'teach to the test', and closely align the education of English language learners to the exams by focusing instruction on test content and skills or, more explicitly, by devoting class time to teaching test items and test-taking strategies.

New York City offers a particularly unique context for exploring the connection between testing and language policy within the US context. When compared with other school districts, New York City has had a long history of supporting bilingual education. However, recent state mandates have increased the minimum amount of English instruction secondary ELLs receive in order to prepare these students to pass English Regents exams; embedded within these state mandates is top-down language policy emphasizing English, which was galvanized by the demands of NCLB.

High-stakes tests have become *de facto* language education policy, shaping the content that schools teach, how it is taught, by whom it is taught, and in what language(s) it is taught. In schools serving language minority students, 'teaching to the test' necessarily involves changes to school language use, with teachers and school administrators becoming the primary language policymakers. Ricento and Hornberger (1996) describe the processes involved in language planning and policy as an onion that must be unpeeled, because a role is played at each level of educational systems in deciding and promoting language policies. This imagery perfectly depicts the creation of language policy in US public schools within a high-stakes testing climate. In the absence of official language education policy in the United States, individuals at the state, district, school and classroom level each affect changes in their local contexts. This means that a top-down language policy like *No Child Left Behind* is interpreted and negotiated by the individuals at every layer of the educational system – often in contradictory ways. This chapter details what actually happens within schools responding to high-stakes testing, showing how bottom-up language policies are created in response to top-down policy, and how testing policy transforms into language policy.

Specifically, this chapter is divided into the following two large sections: (1) How Teachers and Schools Transform Testing Policy into Language Policy and (2) Alignment of Curriculum and Teaching to the Test. Because New York City is one of just five states which currently use test translations (Sullivan *et al.*, 2005), this leaves a bit more space open for language policy interpretation than what is found elsewhere. While English-only testing has been found to result in English-only instruction, particularly in states such as California and Massachusetts which also have recently adopted anti-bilingual education legislation (Alamillo & Viramontes, 2000; Gàndara, 2000; García, 2003; Gutiérrez *et al.*, 2002), testing in New York has a more polarizing effect on choices about the language medium of instruction. As described in the first section of this chapter, teachers and schools decipher the demands of the exams and then decide whether courses are best taught in a student's native language or English, and how native language is used in the classroom, if at all. While most schools and teachers were found to have increased the amount of English used in instruction to prepare students for the high school exit exams, particularly the English Regents, one school and several teachers were found to have increased native language instruction instead.

This chapter details in the second section the wide range of ways that educators prepare ELLs for the exams and the many changes they have made to curricula and teaching, drawing primarily on data from interviews conducted with teachers and administrators. They explain how English as a second language instruction has become similar to English language arts classes taken by native English speakers, and that such classes mainly cover the material on the tests. Many of the practices described in this section actually undermine the quality of instruction ELLs receive, as an unplanned byproduct of the testing focus.

Critics of the uses of standardized tests for high-stakes accountability point to numerous unintended negative effects, including the placement of greater emphasis on certain subjects and skills at the expense of other areas that are not included in the test, as discussed below. How negative effects are produced is clarified in the following passage:

> ... in most cases the instruments and technology have not been up to the demands that have been placed on them by high-stakes accountability. Assessment systems that are useful monitors lose much of their dependability and credibility for that purpose when high stakes are attached to them. The unintended negative effects of the high-stakes accountability uses often outweigh the intended positive effects. (Linn, 2000: 14)

This quote clarifies how unintended consequences arise when high stakes are attached to test results.

How Teachers and Schools Transform Testing Policy into Language Policy

Educators in New York City frequently used the term 'teaching to the test' in my conversations with them. Some define it as involving direct, explicit test preparation strategies, such as using past exam questions during class time to practice. Others define it as using strategies that are less direct, such as emphasizing the skills and content that the exams require during instruction in a more general way. Under a definition that includes both direct and indirect instructional strategies that actively prepare students for high-stakes tests, the vast majority of educators of ELLs who participated in this study teach to the test. This trend is troubling, as it so often disregards research and practices proven effective in the education of ELLs, and occurs at the expense of broader learning.

As stated above, 'teaching to the test' results in changes to language policy at the classroom level. In the schools participating in the research I conducted in New York, language policies changed in schools after it was decided that ELLs would be included in the state's high-stakes tests. Schools shifted their policies in different ways, yet all of the changes described in this section were done in the name of Regents testing. In this way, the link between testing and language policy is clear: exams in essence determine language policy in schools.

Increases in the amount of English offered

In response to the pressure of Regents exams, schools and teachers in this study were found to have changed how much instruction students receive either in English or in their native language. To some extent these changes have been influenced by New York State mandates; as explained in Chapter 3, the Commissioner's Part 154 was passed in 1999, and increased the minimum amount of English instruction high school ELLs are required to receive. Before then, ELLs at all grades and levels of English proficiency were entitled to just one period of ESL per day. After 1999, it was mandated that ELLs in high school at the beginning levels of English proficiency receive three periods of ESL per day, and two periods per day at the intermediate levels. And, Part 154 required that ELLs at the advanced levels receive one period of ESL a day taught by an ESL teacher and also a period of English language arts taught by a certified English teacher (New York State Department of Education, 1999a). The amount of English instruction increased to prepare ELLs to pass the English Regents and other exams. This mandate is significant because by increasing the minimum amount of English instruction that ELLs are to receive, the state has implicitly acknowledged that embedded within the Regents exams is an incidental language policy promoting English.

In the quotation below, an assistant principal describes the impact of Part 154 after 1999:

> *How would you describe the school's curriculum and programming for ELLs now, as compared to before the new testing requirements of 2000?*
> **Ms V:** [nods vigorously] ... They didn't have to take the English Regents before 1999. Alright, before '99 it was three periods beginning, two intermediate, and one advanced. After '99 what changed was they gave a second period no one had – advanced and transitional levels now had two ...
> *I want to go back to something you said. Advanced students are now doing two periods of English here?*
> **Ms V:** That's a state mandate. New York is ahead of the game with NCLB [No Child Left Behind] ... If you're going to say that these students must take the Regents then they need another period of instructional support, so it was mandated and that's good.
> (Ms V, Assistant Principal Supervision, School #9, interview notes)

As 'Ms V' explains, Part 154 caused some schools to increase the number of English instructional periods they offered advanced ESL students to meet the demands of high-stakes testing. In practice, the new mandates under Part 154 proved to be most significant for advanced ELLs. All ten schools included in this research serve a population of at least 15% ELLs, and most had already been offering their beginning and intermediate students two periods or more of ESL each day. What changed was that the advanced ESL students receive more English instruction, as they now must take a period of English language arts class taught by a certified English teacher in addition to ESL.

What is particularly interesting is that some schools have gone above and beyond the mandated amount of English that ELLs are to receive under Part 154. For example, School #4 has increased how much English is offered to ELLs, in an effort to increase their scores on the Regents. In Chapter Five, the administrators at School #4 were quoted explaining how ELLs there attend an extended school schedule, often twelve periods per day. The passage below is taken from an interview with an assistant principal at this school, who describes how their extended day is used to offer students more English instruction and the rationale for doing so:

> *About the Regents, do standardized tests, in particular the Regents, affect you and your school and ELL students? And if so, how?*
>
> **Ms O:** ... It has affected, it has affected the way we program, the classes we offer and it's affected the strategies and the methodology we use. What we have done to address it, we've done it in several ways. We now have a class expressly for the cohort of 2004, strictly devoted to those students ... And now there is a distinct goal which is they must pass the Regents, so the focus of your lessons has to be the ELA [English language arts] standards. You have to be very aware and methodical in your teaching and in your strategies. And teaching, aligning what you are doing to standards and curriculum so they will pass the Regents. You know it's a definite, definitive focus ...
>
> *So are students getting more ESL now than they were before?*
>
> **Ms O:** In this building they are, this building they are. They exceed the mandated amount of minutes in this building ...
>
> (Ms O, ESL/Bilingual Assistant Principal, School #4, interview transcript)

In this quotation, 'Ms O' makes several key points relevant to the focus of this chapter. They added ESL courses at her school when they realized ELLs there were not performing as well as native English speakers on the Regents exams. Changes to their ESL programming and curricula resulted from pressure on the school to have a positive annual yearly progress report for city and state accountability under *No Child Left Behind*, which is based on Regents scores. To do this, as she describes, they have added English Regents preparation courses to an ELL student's school day; ELLs are required to enroll in a double-period English Regents preparation course that meets daily before they take the test. Furthermore, Saturday Regents preparation classes are essentially mandatory, and the school has added a writing course for ELLs. Ms O also mentions how the Regents exams have caused changes in the content, curriculum, and pedagogy of ESL classes, which is a point addressed in greater detail below. Like most schools in this sample, testing promotes English at this school, and high-stakes testing has resulted in an increase in the quantity of English instruction ELL students receive.

Increases in native language instruction

Focal School #1 offers a unique contrasting example, where the school has increased how much instruction ELLs receive in their native language as a strategy to help improve their performance on the English Regents exams. This finding is very significant because this school has made these changes within a testing context which, as described above, implicitly promotes English; the school has thereby found a way to promote native language maintenance and development in spite of the current high-stakes testing climate. At this school, they discovered that the skills on the Advanced Placement (AP) Spanish exam and in the national curriculum for the AP courses are similar to the skills demanded on the English Regents exam. The school began requiring Latino ELLs to enroll in courses on Spanish as a Native Language at the lower levels, and AP Spanish at the more advanced levels. Doing so feels subversive, as the AP Spanish courses were originally intended to evaluate native English speakers learning Spanish as a foreign language, and passing AP exams awards these students with college or university credits for foreign language study. In other words, this school is using one gatekeeping test for an entirely different gatekeeping purpose, and promoting native language development in the process.

The assistant principal from School #1 was instrumental in implementing this approach, and was hired by School #2 to replicate the Spanish program there. We had many interviews during the year I was collecting data, and he explains the reasoning behind the Spanish program in the following:

> **Mr C:** At [Focal School #1], when I arrived there were only nine kids registered for AP Spanish literature, that's ridiculous! And 49 for AP Spanish language. Our goal now is everyone takes AP literature because that's the English Regents, you pass one you'll pass the other. Over 90 kids took AP language, we moved most into AP literature where they got fours and fives [three or higher is passing] ... [T]hey're preparing for it for four years, from the beginning. They are preparing, they have four years to prepare for that test. Teachers said, 'Oh my God, it looks like the English Regents!' ... Then we re-did their curriculum for foreign language, the whole outlook. It was mandatory that at the end of the term kids must analyze a radio program. You know what I'm really doing is Regents, Task 1.

Am I teaching to the test? Absolutely. Am I doing it covertly? Absolutely. (Mr C, Assistant Principal, School #2 (formerly Assistant Principal of School #1), interview notes)

The program that 'Mr C' implemented funnels Latino students into AP Spanish after they have completed four terms of Spanish Native language arts courses. According to Mr C, schools were not demanding a high level of Spanish literacy from their Latino ELL students, resulting in low English Regents scores. In addition, the skills and format of the AP Spanish exams are similar to those of the English Regents, so preparing students in their native language for the AP Spanish exam prepares them for the English Regents. They also added an English Regents preparation course that was offered entirely in Spanish.

The approach taken by this school proved to be so successful in improving the performance of ELLs on the English Regents, increasing their pass rates by 50 percentage points, that it is now being implemented in schools across the region where it is located. While it may seem counterintuitive to increase Spanish instruction as a way to improve English performance on a standardized test, it is consistent with bilingual education research which shows that developing literacy in a student's first language helps them develop literacy in their second language, because literacy skills transfer (Cummins, 1992, 2000). With regard to language policy, School #1 decided to promote a bilingual language policy emphasizing Spanish language instruction, even though the requirement that students pass the English Regents exam would seem to promote an English-only policy and is interpreted as such elsewhere. This school has found a way to preserve native language instruction within a context that implicitly promotes English only.

The tension between bilingual education and monolingual testing

At the classroom level, bilingual teachers of content-area subjects such as math, science and social studies were found to adopt language policies favoring English or students' native languages, in order to align their instruction to the Regents exams. Although the majority of schools in this sample have increased the quantity of English instruction students receive on a daily basis, the existence of test translations has ensured that some minority language instruction still occurs. While translations help many students understand test items, they also affect the language of instruction in bilingual classrooms because most bilingual educators use language strategically in their classrooms as a test preparation strategy; this is one side-effect of testing in the United States that has not yet been documented. Many bilingual content teachers allow testing to decide which language they will use in instruction and the language policy a teacher adopts is often related to whether a test translation is used or not. Research argues that the language of an exam must be aligned to the language of instruction for the exam results to be valid (Abedi *et al.*, 2004). However, as the following examples highlight, doing so often promotes monolingual language policy, and undermines the implementation of a program that is truly bilingual.

In cases where their students will take exam translations, teachers often match their language of instruction to the language of the exam and offer instruction solely in the students' native language.

> *Do standardized tests such as the Regents affect you and the school? If so, how?*
> **Mr B:** The whole system is geared towards numbers and percent. In all honesty I don't see myself as an English teacher, and I'll explain to you what I mean by that. We are forced to teach certain concepts, which is cool, about American History and as a result of that we have to get as many of our kids as possible to pass the Regents exams. It's about numbers, it's about percentages, and I'm cool for that. However, because my students take that Regents exam in Spanish, that's the way I basically teach most of my class – in Spanish.
> (Mr B, Bilingual US History teacher, Focal School #1, interview transcript)

In this passage, 'Mr B' explains that because most of his students take the Regents exam in Spanish then teaching them English is not a priority for him; rather, he has adopted a language policy in his classroom which is aligned to a Regents exam which is offered in Spanish. While Mr B does occasionally use some English in his instruction, the following is an example of a teacher who only uses the students' native language (Chinese) in instruction because of the Regents exams:

> *So when you said you do lessons that prepare students for the Regents, can you give an example of lessons or tell a story about that?*
> **Mr W:** ... So the majority of my students will actually be taking the Living Environment [Science] Regents in Chinese. Because I'm pretty strapped for time, I have to teach the most amount of content area within the time I do have, which means I have to teach in Chinese. If I teach it in English it will probably take longer because they might not understand everything I said – to ensure they have everything concept-wise. Because after all, I'm a Biology teacher, I'm not an English teacher. So I'm responsible for them understanding the biological concepts, that's my first

objective ... So I have to instruct fully in Chinese. That's how it affects me teaching it [science].
If they didn't have Science Regents, if they didn't exist, would you teach more English?
Mr W: Yes, definitely ...
(Mr W, Chinese Bilingual Science (Biology) teacher, School #5, interview transcript)

'Mr W' explains above how the language policy in his classroom is shaped by the Regents, and he teaches only in Chinese. The school where he teaches offers a dual-language program whereby both English and Chinese are meant to be emphasized equally. This example shows the tension often created between the *de facto* language policy of standardized tests and a school's language policy. In this case, the Regents outweigh the school's bilingual policy because of the high stakes of the exams, as Mr W explains. The result of this is that he offers monolingual instruction in Chinese rather than bilingual instruction.

Where ELLs are concerned, 'teaching to the test' is deeply intertwined with language policy. As noted by Mr W, 'teaching to the test' for an ELL population involves aligning the language of instruction to the language of the exam as a strategy that will help students pass. This point is reiterated in the following passage, where 'Ms I' describes having just learned from her supervisor that her students can receive a Social Studies exam in either English or Spanish, but not both:

> I was told they only get one test booklet by my supervisor. I wanted to know how much I had to structure my classes towards the [Social Studies] Regents in Spanish or in English. Do I teach in English to prepare for English Regents, or in Spanish to prepare for Spanish Regents?
> (Ms I, Spanish Bilingual Social Studies teacher, Focal School #1, interview transcript)

This excerpt shows how a school's policy regarding the use of translations dictates the language policy of this teacher's classroom. As Ms I explains, if her students are required to take the Social Studies Regents exam in English then she will teach social studies in English to prepare them for the exam. But if they will take the exam in Spanish, she will teach in that language instead. Clearly, there is a direct connection between testing and language policy in bilingual classrooms, and pressure on bilingual teachers to teach monolingually (in one or the other language, but not both).

More commonly, educators at the classroom level interpret the demands of testing by emphasizing English in instruction at the expense of native language. What is interesting about analyzing testing from a language policy perspective is that the policies the tests produce are often contradictory – even within the same school. While the Social Studies teacher quoted above, Mr B, teaches almost entirely in Spanish, the math teachers at his school are taking an entirely different approach. From my interviews and classroom observations, I found that all of the bilingual math teachers at this school have adopted a policy whereby English serves the role of the official, written language while Spanish is only used orally. I learned that this language policy has been promulgated by the assistant principal for math, as shown in the following excerpt:

> **Mr J:** In here they want you to do like that. The AP [assistant principal] doesn't want you to just teach Spanish, she wants English there somehow. Sometimes she goes to the class and says to me, 'You have to speak more English' ...
> **Ms L:** She told me after my first observation, she said 'Use more English.'
> (Mr J and Ms L, Spanish Bilingual Math Teachers, Focal School #1, interview transcript)

These two bilingual teachers explain that the assistant principal requires that they use as much English as possible, which accounts for their approach in giving written material to students in English, and then translating it orally into Spanish.

I asked the assistant principal herself about her policy of promoting more English than native language, and her explanation was as follows:

> *How much Spanish is used in bilingual Math classes?*
> **Ms S:** ... It has nothing to do with a bias against bilingual or ESL, nothing at all like that ... But the English Regents exam that's in English, they have to do it in English. They have to pass them to get a high school diploma. I think now colleges know there's a language requirement to graduate, except to go to one of the colleges with a bilingual program, so it's in their interest.
> (Ms S, Math Assistant Principal, Focal School #1, interview transcript)

As per this quote, 'Ms S' emphasizes learning English because it is the language needed to pass the English Regents exam and graduate from high school. So, she aligns language policy in math class to the demands of the English Regents exam.

Bilingual teachers of content-area subjects are caught between preparing students for Regents exams that are monolingual and meeting the goals of bilingual education. A primary tenet of bilingual education programs is that both language and content be taught simultaneously

(Baker, 2001; Brisk, 2005; Cummins, 2000). Returning to the cases of the teachers teaching soling through the minority language, the problem with this approach is that the policy at both of these schools is for content courses to be taught in both English and the minority language (Spanish or Chinese) to ensure that students receive enough English instruction in the school day. While many bilingual programs do offer instruction solely through the minority language in certain subjects, with instruction through the majority language in other subjects, this is not the language policy at either of these schools. Although matching the language of instruction to the language of the exam increases the validity of a student's test score, it places bilingual teachers in a bind created by a disjuncture between testing that is *mono*lingual and instruction that is *bi*lingual.

This is another example of the conflict created by the *de facto* language policy of the Regents exams and a school's language policy. The trouble is that it is typically not a clear and cohesive schoolwide language policy that decides instruction will be in one language or the other; rather, language policies are being created by tests in ad hoc, uncoordinated, and often competing ways – without regard for theory or effective practices in bilingual education. As shown above, teachers resolve this tension on an individual basis either by emphasizing one language or the other in instruction; in the New York case, where there are exam translations, testing has resulted in a polarizing of bilingual instruction whereby teachers are pressured to favor one language or another. Something is sacrificed in either case, creating a 'no-win' situation for bilingual teachers: when teachers use only one language in instruction, their students do not learn the second; and, when teachers use both languages, this is likely to negatively affect their students' test scores.

Before concluding this section, it is necessary to acknowledge other factors that affect language allocation in bilingual content classes – in particular, the absence of materials in minority languages and the shortage of bilingual teachers. For example, there is a Math A curriculum used citywide which prepares students for the Math A Regents exam, yet the textbook and corresponding materials are only available in English. Similarly, the four science labs and test preparation materials required to prepare for the Living Environment Regents exam are only available in English. There is a shortage of Spanish materials, and an even greater shortage of materials in other minority languages. There is a large Haitian population at School #10 and a large Bengali population at School #4. While these schools offer bilingual education on paper, in actuality they do not because they have not been able to hire the teachers needed to staff a bilingual program, and minority language materials are scarce. In combination with the pressure of standardized testing, and individual language ideologies, factors such as these play an enormous role in shaping language policies in school.

Alignment of Curriculum and Teaching to the Tests

Some of the most observable changes in schools catalyzed by the national testing emphasis have been to school curricula and instruction, where what is taught is now closely aligned to the tests in order to prepare students to pass. Haugen (1972) provides one of the earliest theoretical frameworks for language planning and policy, in which he identifies status and corpus planning as two primary goals. Cooper (1989) adds *acquisition planning* to these as a third goal, acknowledging the power of schooling in language planning and referring to language teaching as an object of policymaking. For Spolsky (2004: 9), language policy encompasses all of the 'language practices, beliefs and management of a community or polity'. The ways that language practices and language teaching have changed in classrooms to prepare ELL students for high-stakes exams, as detailed below, are interpreted here as language policymaking. The examples below offer further support for the idea of testing policy as *de facto* language policy.

Teachers and school administrators report that the material covered in their classes focuses on what is covered in the exams. In all ten schools that were studied for this research, the curriculum for ELLs is closely aligned to the Regents exams and teachers employ a wide range of strategies in the classroom to prepare their students for the tests. Yet these changes are often inappropriate for ELLs, particularly in ESL classes.

When ESL becomes English language arts: Changes to the ESL curriculum

For ELLs in New York City, preparation for the English Regents typically starts at the beginning levels of ESL class and the ESL curriculum often looks similar to that of English language arts for native English speakers, where literary analysis rather than communicative competence is the new focus. The English Regents exam is extremely challenging for ELLs; the English proficiency level of ELLs negatively impacts their performance on English language arts exams (Uebelacker, 2005). In New York City, it is primarily ESL teachers who are now responsible for preparing ELLs to pass the English Regents exam, which has caused major changes to ESL at the classroom level. In the passages that follow, this chapter shares findings which show the ways in which schools have aligned their curricula to the tests, and the effects this has on teaching and learning.

In addition to extending the Advanced Placement Spanish program at School #1 after it was mandated that English language learners take the English Regents, Regents preparation has been incorporated into every level of ESL instruction. For example, ESL Level One (beginning) through ESL Level Eight (advanced) at the focal school requires students to listen to a dialogue, paraphrase what they heard, use a graphic organizer related to the dialogue, and write about it. Students must demonstrate their attainment of these benchmarks as part of their course grade and grade promotion. These skills mirror those demanded by the English Regents exam; listening, paraphrasing and notetaking are required in Task 1 of the English Regents and using graphic organizers is required in Task 2. This is explained in the following passage, taken from an interview with the school's ESL coordinator:

> **Ms K:** ... [B]ut the Regents, we're teaching to the test. Our whole curriculum is designed to teach skills they need to pass that test. We're looking at the Regents because that's the test they have to pass to graduate ...
> *What is teaching to the test?*
> **Ms K:** From the very start we're teaching things that are on the test. I guess there are different ways you can define it. On one hand, we redesigned our whole curriculum by defining what skills will be on the test ... When the new Regents came, we just looked to see what else we needed, and see we covered all the skills on it. For example, notetaking really hadn't been a priority until then at all. And we discovered students really didn't know how to take notes. This has now become a big part of lessons with me now, and now notetaking and listening is a skill in the new curriculum.
> (Ms K, ESL Coordinator, Focal School #1, interview notes)

This interview excerpt explains why high-stakes exams have such a strong influence on curriculum and teaching in New York and elsewhere, and how this plays out in actual practice. As this administrator explains, the decision to include ELLs in the English Regents caused her school to change the content of ESL classes in ways that explicitly prepare students to pass the exams. All ESL courses at the focal school prepare ELLs to pass the English Regents exam from the very beginning of their high school career, regardless of a student's level of English proficiency when they arrive. This point is echoed elsewhere, as the majority of the schools in this sample begin Regents preparation as early as possible.

School #3, however, was the only school in all ten studied that offers an opposing example. In the passage below, the school principal shares his school's rationale for limiting Regents preparation to only eleventh or twelfth grades, and not earlier. This principal's school is small, serving 225 ELLs who are new arrivals to the United States, and is very high-performing, employing a demanding portfolio process to determine grade promotion and high school graduation. As the principal states:

> **Mr S:** The minute the Regents get shifted to tenth grade, it would affect how those teachers are teachers. They want to give them all the subjects and [Regents] undermines the language development we want to do. We're looking really closely at what other schools are doing. As a result, most are more homogeneous and doing direct instruction, where teachers do more talking and students less ...
> *What would you do if there weren't Regents?*
> **Mr S:** I think we would have much more. Our curriculum wouldn't shift into just coverage of content and we would take more time with each subject area, and have a more rigorous portfolio project.
> (Mr S, Principal, School #3, interview transcript)

'Mr S' acknowledges how the current focus on testing alters curriculum and instruction, and explains how this is in direct conflict with the high-quality model they had developed to successfully meet the needs of English language learners. In this way, the need to prepare students for high-stakes tests comes into conflict with this school's effective programming for ELLs.[14]

Changes to instruction

For this research, I observed hours of explicit test preparation in classrooms where this occurs every day. Teachers often gave students questions from prior exams to practice and used an English Regents preparation guide as a primary course text (Mr T, English Regents Preparation teacher, Focal School #1, interview notes). Beginning ESL students who have just arrived from other countries are placed immediately into English Regents preparation courses, which are advanced, before they have learned any basic fundamentals of the English language. The following quotation offers an example:

> *What sorts of things do you do in the English Regents class you mentioned, and how do you 'teach to the test' like you said?*
> **Ms T:** You can't say in this school you're teaching to the test because you're supposed to say that you have all these wonderful lesson plans that take into account techniques of the test, rather than 'I'm teaching to

the test'. But, that's the only way, giving them old tests, old exams to practice . . . Juniors that just came to this country, let's say we're supposed to place them in Levels One or Two. Well, we can't do that. We have to place them right away in Regents prep class. See how I'm saying it's unfair for them to be in a situation like this?
(Ms T, ESL coordinator, School #4, interview notes)

This quotation offers an example of how ESL curricula have changed to focus on testing, emphasizing 'drill-and-kill' approaches which require that students spend many hours practicing exam questions in order to prepare for the tests. In addition, this quotation mentions how ELLs with low levels of English proficiency must engage in explicit test preparation which bars them from attending a beginning ESL class because of their need to pass the test and graduate. While doing so may improve these students' chances of passing the Regents exams, the practice is problematic because it prevents them from receiving pedagogy appropriate for their level of language proficiency.

Teachers are pressured to align their teaching to the English Regents and are found doing so in schools across New York City. One such example is provided in the following quotation, in which an ESL teacher describes her teaching:

Do standardized tests like the Regents affect you and your instruction? And if so, how?
Ms K: . . . In many ways there are days when I feel like an English teacher and not an ESL teacher. I'm teaching literary terminology and I'm teaching, sort of, formulas for writing in exam essays. That's something very different that I didn't anticipate I would have as an ESL teacher. It's just on a daily basis it definitely influences what I do. It's in the back of my mind, along with ESL standards are English standards and the Regents requirements. So every lesson I'm planning I'm thinking towards those ends. So I'm always conscious, does this relate to Part One of the Regents? Does this relate to Part Two of the Regents? How does this relate to Part Three? . . . So, actually, this whole unit was planned around different parts of the Regents.
(Ms K, ESL Teacher, School #4, interview transcript)

This quotation shares how one teacher 'teaches to the test' in response to the pressure she feels to improve the scores her ESL students receive on the English Regents exam – a test that was developed to measure the English achievement of native English speakers. Many ESL teachers and administrators in this study say that ESL classes have grown increasingly similar to English language arts classes because of the testing movement. Furthermore, the New York State mandate in the Commissioner's Part 154 that one advanced level ESL course be taught by a certified English language arts teacher rather than by an ESL teacher has added to the push for ESL to become more like English language arts courses for native English speakers.

The focus on developing 'communicative competency' in English (Hymes, 1972) has been a popular approach of ESL classes for the past 25 years, whereby authentic communication by students or 'communicative language teaching' replaced previous rote memorization and repetition approaches (Richards & Rodgers, 2001). However, as the example above shows, ESL pedagogy in the high-stakes testing era has now moved away from a focus on communicative competence to a focus on essays and literary elements, as well as memorization, signifying a major change in both the content and approach of ESL classes. The problem with this change is that topics such as persuasive writing and literary elements are not explored in addition to developing core academic literacy skills and communicative competency in English, but rather have largely replaced those skills. In addition, infusing an English language arts focus into ESL instruction limits the possibility for content-based language instruction such as teaching language through math activities or art, which is an effective approach for second language learning (Richard-Amato & Snow, 1992; Richards & Rodgers, 2001).

Educators are often frustrated by the ways that their own teaching practice must conform to the demands of high-stakes testing. In New York City there has been an increase in state mandated, prescriptive curricula since the passage of *No Child Left Behind*, and teachers note how testing rewards teacher-centered styles of teaching which emphasize rote memorization and skills. A common complaint is that ESL teachers who wish to focus on the cultural diversity of their students must turn their backs on these external pressures to do so. As Kleyn argues, based on her research in New York City,

> Currently, there is no reward system or even acknowledgement associated with teaching from a multicultural framework, perhaps because there is no standardized test to measure it. If teachers take on this challenge, they must 'teach against the grain'. (Kleyn, 2007: 274)

In essence, the Regents exams in New York City are redefining ESL, making ESL classes in every way more like the English language arts classes taken by native speakers of English. This reflects a change in language acquisition policy, whereby literature and literary analysis are now the central aspects of the English language an ELL must acquire. Regents exams do not fully address the needs of English learners to acquire both written and oral English, in an academic register and also spoken for daily use, because this exam was not intended to do so.

Narrowing of curriculum content to exam material: 'No time for the atom bomb'

As schools work to align their practices to the tests, a topic that frequently arose in interviews with teachers is how the exams have narrowed the curriculum and, correspondingly, teaching. The example below illustrates 'teaching to the test' in a classroom with ELLs. Figure 6.1 is an excerpt from

████████████ HIGH SCHOOL   MS. G. ███████ PRINCIPAL
SOCIAL STUDIES DEPARTMENT   MR. L. ███████, A.P.
AMERICAN HISTORY   MR. B. ███████

FINAL EXAM *(3 Pts. w)*

DESARROLLO DE DESTREZAS: INTERPRETACION DE UNA CARICATURA

Basa tus respuestas a las preguntas 1 y 2 en la caricatura dada y en tu conocimiento de estudios sociales.

1   La base para el uso de la señal de alto por el Tío Sam se encuentra en
   1 el Acuerdo de Mayflower   3 las Resoluciones de Virginia y de Kentucky
   2 la Doctrina Monroe   4 el Compromiso de 1820

2   La idea principal de la caricatura es que
   1 los Estados Unidos deben evitar alianzas embrolladoras
   2 el Hemisferio Occidental está cerrado a nueva colonización europea
   3 los estados tienen el derecho a desafiar las decisiones del gobierno nacional
   4 la esclavitud queda prohibida en los estados del Oeste

Figure 6.1 Final exam question, Bilingual US History Course, School #1

a final exam I collected at the focal school, written by a Spanish bilingual teacher of US History. Figure 6.2 is an actual test item from the Spanish translation of the US History and Government Regents Exam.

Even a reader who does not speak Spanish can look at these and see how similar they are. Both are test items containing political cartoons which pertain to some aspect of US history, followed by a set of multiple-choice questions which require students to interpret the cartoon. As can be seen, the

Base su respuesta a la pregunta 10 en esta ilustración y en sus conocimientos de estudios sociales.

Fuente: Justus, *Minneapolis Star* (adaptado)

10 ¿Cuál es la idea principal de esta ilustración?
    (1) Los estadounidenses no pudieron sustentar adecuadamente los gastos de los candidatos políticos.
    (2) La publicidad de campaña no influye en la cantidad de votantes que asisten a las urnas.
    (3) Los costos de campaña son una de las principales causas de la deuda interna.
    (4) Los altos costos de campaña afectan adversamente al proceso político.

Figure 6.2 Question 10, June 2003 US History and Government Regents Exam, New York State Deparment of Education

final exam given to bilingual students in this example mirrors the high-stakes test they need to take to graduate from high school. The separation between classroom-based assessments and external standardized tests has become blurred; this is a clear instance of how testing and curriculum become synonymous when tests are high stakes.

However, preparing students for the tests comes at a cost, as teachers are simply unable to prepare students for the exams without cutting out aspects of broader learning. This point is exemplified in the following quotation:

> I came here a little angry and flustered today. I was teaching my Regents Four class and we were talking about the atomic bomb, and the students were really interested. But at some point I felt we have to wrap this up and move on. This isn't on the curriculum ... It's not even an 'aim'. They give out the aims, you get a list of aims you need to cover, so you know it's part of the Regents. The tests have taken more importance in the sense that if I don't cover Regents material, have I shortchanged these points? If I'm just doing breadth and no depth, have I shortchanged the kids? It's a no win situation ... And I've had to make choices, and eliminate things. (Ms M, Bilingual Social Studies Teacher, School #9, interview notes)

School #9 infuses into their Social Studies curriculum a prescribed set of aims to ensure teachers remain focused on Regents preparation. In order to prepare for the Global History and Geography Regents exam, 'Ms M' explains how certain topics must be reduced or cut completely; as such, the curriculum is narrowed to those topics on the test. This quotation provides a clear instance of 'teaching to the test' where the test limits the number of concepts studied in class and/or the depth of study, and topics that are not part of the exam are seen as 'off task' and only covered in a cursory way, if not dropped completely.

This issue is critiqued as much by educators as by students interviewed for this research. The following passage was taken from a focus group interview with nine ELLs at School #3, where Regents preparation is concentrated into later grades, in what is called the 'Senior Institute':

> *['Ms J' is the Social Studies teacher, 'S1' is from Sierra Leone and 'S2' is from the Dominican Republic]*
> **Ms J:** Moving from Junior to Senior Institute is a big change. Tell Kate what classes were like before, in Junior Institute. What was it like before, what is it like now, and what do you think of it?
> **S1:** ... But now it's a big change, because now all the classes we are taking now they are all prep classes. We not really learning anything, we're only learning the content of the tests and not what we're supposed to

know and go to college. So now this Regents things is making our classes be prep classes. Not like real classes I'm supposed to be taking, so I feel very bad staying in class.

... **S2:** In the ninth grade we used to, like, work on projects that we enjoyed and really feel like you're learning. But now you just get into something, but by the time you start enjoying it, it's over. You just understand it and the teachers they say, 'We don't have time, we need to move on'.

(11th Grade ELLs and their teacher, School #3, interview transcript)

In this passage, students share how the need to prepare for Regents exams has changed their educational experiences in school. The students discuss how quickly they must learn each topic that is presented, in order to cover everything they need for the exams, and how the topics that are studied are limited only to those that will be on the exams. The students and teacher quoted above express their frustration at the limitations of narrowing the curriculum in this way.

Discussion

This chapter has detailed how standardized tests become *de facto* language policy when attached to high-stakes consequences, shaping what content schools teach, how it is taught, by whom it is taught, and in what language(s) it is taught. Schools and individual educators in the sample changed their language policies because of the Regents exams, increasing how much English or native language is taught. In the case of bilingual educators, 'teaching to the test' has meant creating and adopting language policies in their classrooms where language is purposefully used as a test preparation strategy. While most schools and educators have created language policies promoting English to meet testing demands, others have found ways to preserve native language instruction. Some bilingual teachers do not alternate languages at all, finding monolingual instruction in the students' native language to be the best strategy for ELLs who will take a version of the exam that is translated into their native language. Curriculum and teaching for ELLs are now aligned to Regents exams, which has resulted in a narrowing of the curriculum to the material on the tests and a new definition of English as a Second Language that is more similar to English language arts classes taken by native English speakers. These changes are troubling because they are being driven by the tests, which were not developed to meet the specific educational needs of ELLs; as a result, many of these changes reduce the quality of education that ELLs receive.

For example, while it sets high expectations for ELLs to strive to pass the English Regents, it is pedagogically unsound to place beginning level ESL students in daily English Regents preparation courses like those native English speakers take; instead, teachers of English language learners must have the space for pedagogy that goes beyond testing 'drill and kill', allowing for individualized instruction. Similarly, school language policies should be carefully planned and decided upon by educators, administrators, and community members to meet the individual needs of the students (Corson, 1999), instead of being determined in an ad hoc way by high-stakes testing. Moreover, tests now are a great influence on choices about how and what ELLs are taught, which undermines years of research and educational practices which have proven effective. While the recent passage of anti-bilingual education legislation in the states of California, Arizona and Massachusetts offer explicit examples of language policymaking, testing is also shaping language policy, albeit in an implicit way. The results are equally powerful.

Chapter Summary

- High-stakes tests have become *de facto* language education policy, shaping what content is taught in school, how it is taught, by whom it is taught, and in what language(s) it is taught. 'Teaching to the test' is commonplace in classrooms serving ELLs, resulting in changes to language education policy. Most ELLs now experience a test-focused education.
- While most schools studied increased how much English instruction ELL students receive, one school instead increased native language instruction as a test preparation strategy, with very promising results.
- Many bilingual teachers use the tests to determine language of instruction, highlighting the mismatch between testing that is monolingual and instruction that is bilingual. Some bilingual teachers have chosen to teach monolingually in either English or the students' home language to ensure the language of teaching and testing are the same.
- English Regents preparation starts at the beginning levels of ESL class and the ESL curriculum looks similar to that of English language arts for native English speakers, where genres of literature rather than communicative competence are now studied. Curricula and testing across subjects have become synonymous, and teachers employ numerous test preparation strategies; many of these changes are inappropriate for ELLs.

Part 3

Expansion and Recommendations

Chapter 7

Higher Expectations vs. Language as Liability: Why the Drawbacks of Accountability Outweigh the Benefits for English Language Learners

As different school districts and state departments of education implement the accountability systems required by *No Child Left Behind*, standardized test scores are turned to as an easy yardstick for measuring the educational achievements of a student, teacher, administrator, school, city or state. The previous chapters of this book have detailed the linguistic demands of tests such as New York's Regents for English language learners, and the many ways that the exams shape both the educational experiences and instruction of these students. This chapter builds on the findings reported thus far, and considers the benefits and drawbacks of the changes that have occurred in schools since the passage of NCLB, within the framework of statewide accountability.

This chapter details some of the intended and unintended consequences of this accountability system, taking the case of high school ELL students in New York City as the starting point. As described previously, the scores that New York City high school students receive on their Regents exams is a primary measure used for citywide accountability to the state. Likewise, statewide scores on the Regents are reported to the US Department of Education, so that the state can continue to receive federal funding without sanctions. Schools receive a schoolwide accountability score determined by the state to show they have made adequate yearly progress (AYP) under *No Child Left Behind*, and if schools do not meet their progress goals, they risk being placed on a list of 'schools under registration review'. While Chapter 5 focuses mainly on students, and Chapter 6 focuses mainly on teachers and administrators, this chapter moves outward to examine this system of accountability more widely.

Specifically, the chapter is divided into the following four sections: (1) Raising Standards and Expectations for ELLs, (2) Language as Liability, (3) How Schoolwide Accountability Leads to Negative Consequences for ELLs, and (4) Where are Opportunities to Learn? The first section of this chapter explores the vision and ideal behind the inclusion of ELLs into statewide assessments for accountability purposes, and describes the benefits of doing so for these students. A positive finding commonly reported by educators and students in New York City is that standards and expectations for ELLs have become higher since it was required that they also pass the Regents to graduate, resulting in a curriculum for these students that is more academic and challenging. Supporters of NCLB argue that highlighting the achievement gap between minority and majority students will result in closing that gap. Findings from research I conducted, however, are unable to substantiate this argument, as this research indicates instead that the inclusion of ELLs in statewide accountability has been primarily punitive. While it is undeniable that *No Child Left Behind* has increased the attention now being paid to ELLs in school, the problem is that most of this attention is negative, and thus more harmful than helpful.

As discussed in the second section of this chapter, a major problem with the current national accountability model is caused by the constant change among ELLs as a group who must make annual improvement under NCLB. In compliance with the law, rapid acquisition of English is a goal for ELL students, and English proficiency is an indicator of their performance. Within this framework, ELLs exit the 'ELL subgroup' once they have acquired English, which means they are then no longer classified as ELLs in performance data. In this way, the gains made by ELLs who acquire English do not actually get counted in ELL data. Together with the addition of newly arriving ELLs into the subgroup, this causes a downward pressure on test scores by ELLs (Abedi, 2004; Abedi & Dietal, 2004). Thus, ELLs as a group are always, by definition, 'low performing'. Research by Escamilla *et al.* (2003) found that school report cards, part of statewide accountability under *No Child Left Behind*, showed lower scores in schools with large numbers of ELLs. Schools with large numbers of ELLs may also be required to make greater gains in 'adequate yearly progress' reporting, increasing pressure caused by NCLB mandates on these schools (Abedi, 2004). In this way, the law's accountability provisions can punish, rather than support, schools and districts with large numbers of ELLs.

The later sections of this chapter highlight the most commonly cited negative effects of including ELLs in Regents testing, as study participants in New York more often felt that effects were negative. A negative finding is that language has become a liability for ELLs within the accountability system, and they are frequently penalized for their English 'deficiency', limiting their opportunities in school and life, and leading to test-driven teaching that is often inappropriate. A further negative finding is that the accountability system is prejudicial against ELLs and the schools that serve them, because the exams measure whether a student receives a passing score, rather than annual growth, and because ELLs as a group will by definition consistently receive low test scores. The accountability system punishes schools serving large numbers of ELLs, and offers schools an incentive not to serve ELLs or allocate resources towards their education. This chapter concludes that the drawbacks of including ELLs within the accountability system outweigh the benefits. Each year, test scores show a wide achievement gap, and this is unlikely to change until sufficient attention is paid to providing ELL students with opportunities to learn what the exams assess.

Raising Standards and Expectations for ELLs: From 'Mickey Mouse' Instruction to Requiring that Everyone Joins the 'Olympic Team'

The National Academy of Education Panel on Standards-Based Education Reform articulates the vision driving current reforms in the following passage:

> Internationally competitive standards for what American students should know and be able to do are expected to improve the substance of school curricula and to increase the motivation and effort of students, teachers, and school systems. (McLaughlin & Shepard, 1995: 7)

The belief behind standards-based reform is that expectations for student performance must be articulated and made explicit, thereby providing a set target that makes it easier to measure growth. Standards offer a means to hold students, teachers, schools, districts, and states accountable for that growth (Menken, 2000).

For students with special needs such as ELLs, the rationale for their inclusion in assessment and accountability systems is to improve the quality of educational opportunities available to them.

> Inclusion in the testing program helps to remind districts and schools that students will need to receive at least the same quality and the same amount of content instruction as is given to other students. (Rivera & Stansfield, 1998: 67)

As Goertz and Duffy (2001: 9) summarize, 'Holding educators accountable for test scores, the theory goes, will increase these students' access to a high-quality, standards-based general education curriculum'.

The data from this research indicate that standards and expectations for what ELLs should know and be able to do have indeed risen since it was mandated that all students must take five Regents exams to graduate from high school. When asked, teachers and administrators in the New York City high schools studied point to higher standards as the key benefit of the emphasis on standardized testing for ELLs.

Do you think the English Regents [exam] is a challenge for ELLs?
Ms V: Oh, yeah. In general, it's a challenging test for a few things. It's all higher order thinking for the student who is well-prepared and above. But never before has everyone been required to be at this high level. When I was in school, it was a certain portion of students taking the Regents. It's so important now. Everyone has to be on the Olympic team! … Now if you look in [Beginning ESL] Level One, you can have a kid here only a few months who can read and say who is the character. We've gone from 'Kate and Lucille are sitting' to the ability to analyze whatever they are reading. Of course there's also the ability of the teacher, but it proves that if you expect more you can get more. That is something good my whole life I've fought for.
(Ms V, ESL/Bilingual Coordinator, School #9, interview notes)

Throughout the interview from which this quotation was taken, 'Ms V' repeatedly comments on how low expectations for ELLs used to be, and the ways that they have risen since ELLs were required to also take the English Regents exam. Specifically, she refers to how ESL instruction at her school used to be grammar-based and simplistic, whereas now she believes it to be more challenging.

Below is another example of how testing has served to raise expectations for ELLs at the school level:

Do standardized tests such as the Regents affect the education of ELLs? If so, how?
Mr B: It's had a good effect. It forces the standards for ELLs because too many people have come with the notion that people who don't speak English aren't bright, and we know this is garbage. This forces a higher level of instruction. Kids are kids are kids is our attitude here, and ESL students are expected to perform to the same level as all students. There was this perception, when I first became principal, there was a very negative attitude about ELLs. We've moved far off that.
(Mr B, Principal, School #4, interview transcript)

'Mr B' is the principal of a large and diverse New York City high school, where he has seen standards and expectations for ELLs become higher since it was required that they be included in Regents exams. While later in the interview he is also critical of the rigidity of the accountability system, he praises the positive effect this policy has had in 'raising the bar' for ELLs.

The increasing rigor of ESL classes is a common topic in interviews with teachers in this area, particularly among those who have been teaching since 1999 and before. Many teachers see the new emphasis on literature in place of grammar (described in Chapter 6) as a positive change, in the belief that making ESL more like English language arts classes is emblematic of higher standards for ELLs. In the following excerpt, an experienced ESL teacher describes the level of books she is currently using in her ESL Level Four class at Focal School #1, as compared to before it was required that ELLs be included in the English Regents exam:

> **Ms R:** On this level [Level Four], we used to use grammar books. This book we're using in Level Four [she shows me the book], it was used in Level Seven for the RCT [Regents Competency Test].[15] So we brought everything down, every book I taught in Level Six, to lower levels now.
> *Why is that?*
> **Ms R:** I think we want kids to read more, and make the classes just generally harder. And there's just a sense that we have to prepare them for this stuff.
> (Ms R, ESL Teacher, Focal School #1, interview transcript)

'Ms R' describes here how books that previously were used in teaching more advanced levels of ESL at her school are introduced at lower levels now. This shows how ESL classes have become more difficult in order to prepare ELLs for the English Regents exam.

This trend in rising expectations also carries through to other subjects, such as Math.

> Math has always been the gatekeeper. It has never been democratic, no matter how far you go back. But we can't have dropout rates, everyone has to do it. You know, we used to do Mickey Mouse math. Many of them come in at too low a level, they shouldn't come into high school at [Math] Level One and Two, but they arrive with a history of failure. And now everyone has to pass the same exam. So do you dumb it down or bring up the student? We'd like to bring the student up.
> (Ms S, Math Assistant Principal, Focal School #1, interview notes)

Many Math teachers and administrators such as 'Ms S' note how the inclusion of ELLs into high-stakes exams has galvanized changes at the school level by moving from a 'dumbed-down' curriculum to higher expectations for these students. As she explains, the law now pressures schools to perform.

As shown here, standards and expectations for ELLs have risen and instruction has become more demanding. I would argue that this is a positive finding, and that expectations for ELLs should be high. This change is one way that NCLB and test-based accountability has benefited ELLs. As will be discussed below, however, often the benefits of elevated standards come at a very high price for ELL students, who are held accountable for their lack of English proficiency. The instruction of ELLs has also radically changed because of the Regents exams in ways that are not always suitable for their educational needs, in large part because the tests being used were developed to assess monolingual students and not ELLs.

Language as Liability: The Downside of Accountability for ELLs

After remarking that people on both sides of the high-stakes testing debate are in favor of high standards and accountability, Sobol (2004a) noted that this is not the central issue. As he writes, 'The question for me is not whether we should have standards, assessment, and accountability. The question is what kinds of standards, testing, and accountability shall we have?' (Sobol, 2004a). *No Child Left Behind* is increasingly receiving criticism for its top-down approach to accountability and corresponding lack of attention to providing the necessary resources, structures, and opportunities to ensure that all students can attain the rigorous standards that have been set (Sobol, 2004a, 2004b). Additionally, test-based accountability offers schools incentives to reduce the numbers of low-performing students, such as ELLs, from taking the test or, worse, to avoid serving these students at all (Rotberg, 2000).

While teachers and administrators see raised standards and expectations as a major benefit of high-stakes testing for ELLs, they are also very critical of numerous drawbacks created by this recent educational reform. Educators in New York City repeatedly discuss ways that current testing policies are discriminatory against ELLs and the schools that serve them, such that language has become a liability in our quest for accountability. In addition, many argue that current testing policies are driven more by politics than by what is educationally sound, resulting in educational decisions that are not best-suited to meeting the needs of ELLs. A serious problem is that accountability, as states have interpreted it, is based on standardized test scores. As previous chapters in this book have noted, the tests being implemented are typically those intended for native English speakers, which threatens the validity and reliability of an English learner's test score. This places ELLs at an unfair disadvantage, and greatly limits their future opportunities when test scores are attached to high-stakes decisions like graduation, as is the case in New York. In interviews for this research, educators in New York repeatedly draw into serious question the validity of including ELLs in the English Regents at all. This is supported by research which states that testing ELLs in English mainly measures English proficiency, not content knowledge, and therefore threatens test validity (Abedi & Dietal, 2004; Abedi *et al.*, 2004; Council of Great City Schools/National Clearinghouse for English Language Acquisition, 2002; Escamilla *et al.*, 2003; García & Menken, 2006; Menken, 2000; Solano-Flores & Trumball, 2003; Valenzuela, 2005).

The following is a quotation from an interview with an ESL coordinator, who is also an experienced teacher, about the validity of including ELLs in the English Regents exam:

> **Ms K:** When we go to graduate school, we learn that the test has to be valid and reliable! In order to be valid and reliable we have to test what was taught, so a test designed for eleven years of English language arts [ELA] is used with kids who haven't had eleven years of ELA. So, it's not valid! ... [The Regents have] changed the curriculum a lot. In some ways, that's good. But they ask ESL students to accomplish too much in too short a time. This is backed by studies saying it takes seven to ten years to acquire English ... They can't learn a second language that fast.
> (Ms K, ESL Coordinator/Teacher, Focal School #1, interview notes)

In this quotation, 'Ms K' shows how the mandate that ELLs pass the English Regents does not take into consideration research showing the length of time it typically takes students to acquire a second language (e.g. Cummins, 2000; Thomas & Collier, 1997). As she points out, requiring ELLs to pass the English Regents holds them accountable for learning English, a language that they simply have not had the opportunity to acquire yet.

The following quotation offers further support for the preceding critique:

> *You said you resent this [that ELLs are required to pass the English Regents]/*
> **Ms O:** I think it's ridiculous that we're told to give a [Regents] task for our final exams for an L3 [Level Three] class! These kids have been in the US for a year and a half and you want them to do a task on the final exam about the Regents that's taken other kids eleven years in school to do? ... For ESL students, it's English as a *foreign language* and it's not fair they should be held to the same requirements as everybody that was born here ... I'm not saying their exam shouldn't be equal to the English ELA exam, but it should be different. They should have the option of taking an English foreign language exam or an English Regents exam ...
> (Ms O, ESL Teacher, School #2, interview transcript)

As 'Ms O' argues, the English Regents exams were developed to assess knowledge of English language arts (ELA) by native English speakers on such topics as literary elements and different writing genres, and were not designed to measure the English proficiency or growth of ELLs. Echoing Ms K's argument above, Ms O draws parallels between ESL and foreign language study, and both educators note that ELLs have not had the 11 years of preparation to learn the material on the English Regents exam that native English speakers have had. The teachers cited here challenge the validity of including ELLs in the English Regents, even with the accommodations ELLs are permitted such as extended time and the use of bilingual dictionaries.

The findings from this research show that the decision to include ELLs in Regents exams has galvanized many changes in the instruction and curriculum that these students receive, and has resulted in 'teaching to the test'. Chapter 6 details the many ways that educators and school administrators align teaching and learning to the Regents exams across subject areas, as a result of the pressure to perform well on measures of accountability. The trouble with teaching to the test where ELLs are concerned is that the exams currently driving these educational decisions result in educational practices that are not deliberate to meet the specific educational needs of these students. Regents exams are geared towards the assessment of monolingual, native English speaking students and not necessarily suitable for guiding the instruction of ELLs or as the sole means of evaluating them within an accountability system.

The quotation below summarizes this aspect of the tension between the benefits and the drawbacks of including ELLs into a system of accountability which relies on test scores as the primary indicator of performance.

Do standardized tests such as the Regents affect the education of ELLs? If so, how?

Ms K: The Regents has been a blessing and a bane. It has certainly raised standards for ESL students when that needed to be the case. When I came to teaching ESL over a decade ago before all this, I was an English major before TESOL, so I saw the value of literacy. So I did that as a teacher, I found books that could be done at a low level. Then five years down the road it's literally being shoved down our throats ... For me, seeing Regents exams, that was a good thing in that respect. But what's bad is kids are being coached to pass the test rather than focus on language acquisition. (Ms K, ESL Assistant Principal, School #8, interview notes)

Based on this passage, 'Ms K' believes that the new emphasis on literature in ESL classes is positive and indicative of higher standards for these students. On the down side, however, she acknowledges how 'teaching to the test' has overshadowed a focus on helping ELLs actually acquire the English language.

While many educators question the validity of including ELLs in Regents exams from a psychometric perspective, others ague further that their inclusion is a social justice concern, that it is discriminatory in its results and driven by political incentives. Chapter 5 details how the Regents exams limit the life choices of ELLs when they are unable to pass and graduate from high school, and how the exams are related to high dropout rates and increased GED enrollments. Within the current accountability system, ELLs and the schools that serve them are punished because the students have not had sufficient time to acquire English. This is a point made in the first interview I had with the principal and assistant principal at Focal School #1, when they discussed the school's low 'adequate yearly progress' scores for the ELL subgroup.

> (*'Ms A' is the principal and 'Ms N' is the ESL/foreign language assistant principal*)
> **Ms N:** The test of math is strongly linguistically based, it's all about language. ELLs will make mistakes with more frequency. Krashen, Cummins, they show the amount of time it takes; we know that research shows it takes five to seven years for a student to learn English and when a student comes within high school or junior high school years, it's not setting high standards
> **Ms A:** It's discriminatory!
> **Ms N:** It is discriminatory. No one's measuring these students after eleven years in their native language. You have to succeed at English Regents. It statistically can drag down a school and puts a warp on what's going on, and no one at the state level has addressed this. They don't want ELL Regents.
> **Ms A:** ... It's the subgroups that are killing the school.
> (Principal and ESL/Foreign Language Assistant Principal, Focal School #1, interview notes)

Using research on second language acquisition in support of this point, the principal and assistant principal argue that including ELLs in exams before they are proficient in English is discriminatory against students and also the schools that educate them. Students in the ELL subgroup and their schools struggle to make annual progress requirements because the students have not had enough time to acquire the language needed to perform well on the exams.

Furthermore, the accountability system in New York is prejudicial against schools with large numbers of ELLs because it cannot measure the full progress of this 'subgroup'. In New York as elsewhere across the United States, once students pass an English proficiency assessment they exit the ELL subgroup. Plus, the Regents exams solely measure outcomes, and do not measure progress. This is explained below by a school administrator in a school with a large ELL population:

> If there's a kid in the class comes in and averages 28, and later averages 41, what am I giving the kid? No, nothing, failure! Still 55 in bold, nothing shows me – It's just about value added, but there's no progress. With the Board of Ed, we have no way to show progress.
>
> (Mr C, Assistant Principal of Organization, School #2, interview transcript)

As 'Mr C' explains, there is a set passing score for the Regents examinations, which is 55. There is no way to show the city or state Department of Education if an ELL has improved their performance on a Regents exam from, for example, a score of 28 to a score of 41, because both of these are still failing scores. In this regard, progress on the Regents is not counted in the current accountability system. This is unfortunate at Mr C's school, where many ELL students are making substantial annual gains. The gains they make are simply not enough to pass the test, and therefore only reflect negatively on the school.

In interviews, educators of ELLs in New York City quickly link testing policy to political incentives. The quotation below exemplifies this, and shows how many educators locate current testing practices within the history of marginalization and discrimination against immigrant students in US public schools (for more description of this, see Crawford, 1999; Ricento, 1995). In the passage that follows, teachers in a focus group at School #3 discuss the Regents exams, and link testing to the political incentives of New York City Mayor Bloomberg and Schools Chancellor Klein. It is important to clarify that these officials are evaluated by the performance of city schools.

> (*'Ms N' teaches Science, 'Ms M' teaches Global Studies, 'Ms J' teaches US History and 'Mr R' teaches Math*)
> **Ms M:** It's all political.
> **Mr R:** They want their numbers. The New York City Department of Education wants high numbers to show Klein and Bloomberg are doing such a good job. So they lowered down the passing grade and they can say, 'Whoa, look at the high pass rate we have!' It's all part of the deal to make it look good.
> **Ms M:** What's sad for me is students feel so disempowered.
> **Ms J:** As do I.
> ... **Ms J:** Some of the politics of it is the students who were affected, in this case for our school ELL students. But in general usually/

Mr R: Minority students
Ms J: Minority students, marginalized students, yeah.
(Teachers of ELL Science, Social Studies, and Math, School #3, focus group interview transcript)

Teachers serving ELLs in New York City are aware of the ways that politicians and school officials such as Mayor Bloomberg and Schools Chancellor Klein are involved in the accountability system, and judged on the basis of students' test scores. A point made by the teachers cited here is that Regents testing in New York is political rather than educational in the current high-stakes testing climate, and driven by political incentives rather than a desire to provide the best possible education.

This is explained further in the following quotation:

What do you perceive to be the benefits and drawbacks of standardized testing for you, ELL students, your school?
Ms Y: I think up there in Albany or wherever this is a minor problem to them. They don't know my school or about Chinese students. But even for Spanish students, they're still not up to the standard. They still don't consider us as important, so what can you do? New York State they look at the whole state, like Westchester they have 90% students who can do it, so they don't consider minorities.
(Ms Y, Chinese Bilingual Math Teacher, School #8, interview notes)

'Ms Y' feels that the needs of her students and other ELLs in New York City are just a small part of the statewide accountability system, which also includes affluent suburban districts like Westchester where students are overall doing well on the tests. The teachers cited in this section repeat the theme heard elsewhere that testing furthers the marginalization and disempowerment of immigrant and minority students in public schools, instead of redressing this problem.

How Schoolwide Accountability Leads to Negative Consequences for ELLs: 'Lame Horses' in the Race

While certain stakes are obvious when an ELL is included into an accountability system that is based on high-stakes testing – for instance, that they will not graduate from high school or will need to stay in school longer than the traditional four years – there are also a number of more covert negative side-effects that were uncovered in this research. Because of schoolwide accountability, schools experience pressure to either exclude those students who are hardest to teach or deny them resources.

For example, the year that I began collecting data for this research was the first year of a 'small schools initiative', which divided large New York City high schools into several smaller schools. Some of the high schools I was studying were large, and therefore not part of this initiative. In September of that year, the numbers of ELLs at the large schools where I was conducting research dramatically increased – by several hundred ELLs apiece – because ELLs were being denied admission to the new, smaller schools that had just opened. In the passages below, school administrators explain how this affected School #2:

> Our new number is more than 1,000 ELLs and last year it was around 700, because these students are coming. The other schools have become small schools but the way the grants are written they don't allow ELLs in the new small schools. That's not fair or where this country's policy is! For example, [school name] is now five schools. They fired all of their ESL teachers. So this year I have two new teachers from that school, but ELLs aren't going there.
> (Ms M, ESL Assistant Principal, School #2, interview transcript)

> *It seems that your number of ELLs has increased [this year].*
> **Mr C:** Absolutely. Last year it was 740 ELLs and now it's 1,000. This school will become all ELLs. Why do I have 1,000 ELLs if all these small schools are opening up? They should have the same percentage of ELLs as other schools. They're not dealing with them because, off the record, it was their philosophy that small schools can't handle it. I'm waiting for the lawsuit. Special ed, too. And our school will continue to go down. You've created a situation where all kids doing well go to these small schools. They select every single kid. Small schools have to succeed because there's money attached to it ... Schools look worse if you add ESL and special ed.
> (Mr C, Assistant Principal of Organization, School #2, interview notes)

These administrators disclose that new small high schools in New York are not admitting ELLs, off the record. As 'Mr C' explains, the small high schools are under public scrutiny and therefore need high test scores. ELLs, however, typically do not perform as well as native English speakers on Regents exams, and therefore pull a school's overall test scores down. The New York City Department of Education in fact adopted an official policy in 2006 that new small high schools are permitted not to accept ELLs during their first three years of operation. This example shows how including ELLs in the testing system can act to deny these students of certain educational opportunities such as being in a small school, because schools often take aggressive steps to be perceived as 'high-performing' and are under tremendous pressure to maintain high test scores.

High-stakes testing thereby creates a disincentive to serve certain students, which is particularly problematic for those who have had limited or interrupted formal schooling, as described below by a school counselor:

> **Ms F:** . . . Students with a strong background in Spanish, they pick English up so quick. But if they're deficient in their native language, then they can't. Some of these students, no other schools would accept them. One girl in my Spanish class wasn't accepted anywhere, that happens. I talk to my friends at another school and they say, 'You accept students with just two years of education?' It's very difficult to, they don't accept kids. *Why?*
> **Ms F:** Your school is accountable. These kids come in, and they look at how many kids each year graduate. And they rate you on this about how successful you are. If you're in a race and you start this race with a horse who is lame, then the chance to succeed is very slim. But we've been taking all these horses!
> (Ms F, Spanish Bilingual Counselor/Spanish Teacher, School #7, interview notes)

School #7 admits a significant number of students who have had limited schooling previously, when few other New York high schools would admit them. As Ms F explains in her racehorse analogy, the reality is that these students are unlikely to pass the Regents exams and graduate on time, which creates a pressure on schools not to admit or serve these students.

Similarly, including ELLs into the accountability system by requiring them to participate in Regents exams impacts the allocation of school funding, a further covert side-effect of this reform. The following quotation offers an example of how this occurs:

> If the goal is Regents there will always be limited services for [ELLs], because the kids will never pass. If you tell the school you have to pass all these kids and you know they're not going to pass and the kids are a negative on the cohort. So what will the school do, put in a lot of money to make smaller class sizes knowing after four years, no matter what, they'll show zero on the cohort?! Or put all their resources where the kids have a chance at passing the English and the Math Regents? These kids are a negative on the cohort. And that's why high-stakes assessments don't work. Same stupidity. You heard me, the same stupidity!
> (Mr C, Assistant Principal of Organization, School #2, interview transcript)

In this passage, a school administrator explains how using high-stakes tests as the basis for accountability can worsen rather than improve the situation for ELLs in schools. In specific, he shows that schools will choose to allocate the limited resources they have to serving mainstream students who, because they are not ELLs, are more likely to perform well on the tests – particularly if they benefit from programs devoted to improving their test scores. Again, the constant influx of new ELLs in combination with the fact that ELLs who acquire English exit the subgroup creates a downward pressure on ELL test scores overall (Abedi, 2004; Abedi & Dietal, 2004). Within the current accountability system, schools choose to allocate their funds to students who will be able to pass the tests with the appropriate preparation, rather than to fund students who will simply improve, but are unlikely to pass within the required time period.

A related side-effect of schoolwide accountability for ELLs is the limitation it creates on the types of courses these students can take. One of the findings from this study is that bilingual education content-area courses are typically only offered for low level Regents courses needed in order to meet the minimum requirements for graduation, such as the Math A course.

> **Ms A:** ... What happens is we offer bilingual classes up to Math A. After Math A, the advanced math classes are not offered in bilingual ...
> *Why are bilingual classes only at the lower level?*
> **Ms A:** I guess that is a matter of resources. They have them only at the lower levels.
> (Ms A, Math Assistant Principal, School #2, interview transcript)

Schools are under great pressure for all of their students to pass the Math A Regents so that they can graduate, but they are under far less pressure to prepare students for higher levels, such as the Math B Regents, because higher level math is not a graduation requirement. As a result, bilingual content-area courses are only available in the lower levels at School #2 and elsewhere. ELLs are unable to benefit from bilingual courses at the higher levels because the present accountability system focuses attention on the lower levels. As seen here, accountability in New York has created a number of unintended side-effects for ELLs that limit the educational opportunities available to them, and pull resources away from students who need them most.

Where are Opportunities to Learn?

As current education reforms in the United States focus on outcomes and accountability, far less attention has been paid to ensuring that ELL students are provided every opportunity to attain the standards that have been set, through the provision of resources and quality programs. Every state has academic standards in accordance with *No Child Left Behind* and the federal legislation which preceded it. Accordingly, the New York State Education Department established 28 learning standards in such areas as English Language Arts, Math, Science, Social Studies, Languages Other than English and the Arts. However, there is another type of standards particularly applicable to ELLs: *opportunity-to-learn standards*. The purpose of these standards is to guarantee 'the level and availability of programs, staff, and other resources sufficient to meet challenging content and performance standards' (McLaughlin & Shepard, 1995). No states have adopted these, as the requirement to do so was long ago removed from federal legislation after heated debate (Pitsch, 1996).

Without question, ensuring that ELLs meet the same challenging standards that have been set for native English speakers is fully reliant on the presence in our schools of high-quality programming, teachers, and all of the other resources necessary to meet their learning needs. Yet, in its focus on outcomes and testing for accountability purposes, the process for achieving these outcomes and the provision of real opportunities to learn has been overlooked in federal legislation (Rothstein, 2002). As Heubert (2002) notes, opportunity-to-learn is also at the core of 'disparate impact' claims which argue that policies and practices have the effect of discriminating even if they are not overtly discriminatory; this was the underlying argument in the *Lau v. Nichol* ruling in 1974, which proved that educational programming for ELLs had discriminatory effects.

In New York City and elsewhere, the argument can easily be made that ELLs are not provided adequate opportunities to learn with regard to teacher quality, resources, and programming as examples. Nationally, only 2.5% of teachers who instruct ELLs possess a degree in ESL or bilingual education, and just 30% of all teachers with ELLs in their classrooms have received any professional development in teaching these students because only a very small minority of teacher education programs require it (Antunez & Menken, 2000; National Center for Education Statistics, 1997). The shortage of qualified teachers for ELLs is most acute in urban areas, where the majority of ELLs reside (Urban Teacher Collaborative, 2000). ELLs also typically attend the most impoverished and under-resourced schools, which is directly related to poor academic performance on standardized tests (Orfield, 2001). Furthermore, these students often are not permitted to remain in language support programs for the amount of time sufficient to acquire enough English to succeed in school.

In New York City, learning opportunity issues in the education of ELLs is a topic that frequently arises in interviews with teachers and school administrators. The example below is one ESL teacher's response to a question I posed regarding the benefits and drawbacks of including ELLs in Regents testing:

> ... So do the benefits outweigh the drawbacks? ... In an ideal school, where perhaps it was smaller and there was more individual accountability and knowledge of each student, programming was done on a more individualized level, supports were more individualized instead of these mass Saturday meetings, things like that, I think it could work and benefits would outweigh. But in a school like this which I think is too large and impersonal, and where students even have trouble accessing their counselors and transcripts to discuss their progress, I don't think it works. I think it overall at this school would be better if testing didn't exist.
> (Ms K, ESL Teacher, School #4, interview transcript)

Many city high schools like the one where 'Ms K' works are large and overcrowded, and there simply are not enough resources to go around.

In fact, this lack of resources in New York City schools has recently been recognized in the courts. The Campaign for Fiscal Equity is an organization that seeks to reform the State of New York's school finance system to provide more resources to New York City. In the United States, per pupil expenditures are typically determined by local property taxes; as a result, per pupil expenditures in New York City are far less than in wealthier parts of the state (and this is similar for other urban areas in the United States). In the case of *CFE v. State of New York*, the New York State Court of Appeals sided with the Campaign for Fiscal Equity on 26 June 2003, ordering the state to reform its educational funding system to ensure that city schools have the resources they need to provide the opportunity for a sound basic education, which the court defined as a 'meaningful high school education'. It was also recognized in this ruling that ELLs, along with impoverished and disabled students, have the greatest needs, and that these have not been met due to a lack of sufficient funding (Campaign for Fiscal Equity, 2004).

There is also a shortage of teachers in New York City prepared to teach ELLs. García and Trubek (1999) explain that the shortage of urban minority educators for urban minority children has resulted from the fact that schools of education now implement entrance exams their candidates must pass to be admitted, as a way to ensure that these institutions have high pass rates on state certification exams and are thus evaluated favorably. However, like language minority students, language minority teacher candidates also do poorly on standardized tests (García & Trubek, 1999). As a result, few bilingual teacher candidates are able to graduate and become certified teachers.

While several of the schools studied for this research have bilingual programs on paper, they actually do not have the teachers to support their programming. This is the case at School #10, which can only offer bilingual content-area classes in Haitian Creole for certain subjects.

What do you perceive to be the benefits and drawbacks of standardized testing (for you, ELL students, your school)?
Ms C: What are the benefits? To have benefits, you have to address the issues. But it hasn't been done, basically because there's no money. That's what happened. The kids are not graduating, and parents are frustrated. Earth Science is now in Creole. There aren't enough qualified bilingual teachers, so there aren't bilingual classes for all subject areas, they don't have it. This year they offered Earth Science in bilingual, when it used to be always ESL. But in math now they still don't have a bilingual teacher, that's an issue.
(Ms C, Haitian Bilingual Counselor, School #10, interview notes)

Here a bilingual counselor shows how the lack of prepared bilingual teachers negatively affects the graduation rates at her school. Similarly, although there are enough students at School #4 to warrant a Bengali bilingual program, a program is not offered because Bengali bilingual teachers are not available.

In addition to a shortage of trained teachers, there is a lack of bilingual materials needed to support bilingual education programs in New York City high schools. The excerpt that follows illustrates this point:

We have no resources for bilingual students. I found students were not passing the [Living Environment] Regents exam ... [Y]ou need materials in both languages. And if we don't have books, you won't be able to excel as you would if you had those books. That's been my fight with all the assistant principals we've had. We've gotten some books, but it's not enough ... [She shows me a book that says 'edition in Spanish and English'] But see this book, we can't get it! This is what I need, for them to have it in English and Spanish.
(Ms A, Spanish Bilingual Science Teacher, Focal School #1, interview notes)

The lack of bilingual materials in content-area subjects is a topic which bilingual teachers frequently discuss, and this shortage will only grow worse as more states in the United States have prohibited bilingual education, discouraging publishers from producing bilingual materials. Teachers were often found having translated materials into a minority language themselves, in order to support their bilingual instruction and help their students. In New York City there is a lack of prepared teachers, appropriate materials, and high-quality programs needed to provide ELLs the opportunity they need to succeed within the current accountability system.

Discussion

There is no disagreement that *No Child Left Behind* has served to focus the attention of the education system on ELLs, yet we have to ask ourselves if that attention has been beneficial or harmful. Unfortunately, the findings from this research indicate that the impact of this law is in the latter category. Including ELLs in New York's Regents exams has served to raise standards for these students on one hand, yet sufficient opportunities-to-learn have not actually been provided to ensure that students can pass the exams. Instead, large numbers of ELLs are being penalized and barred from graduation because they have not yet had the opportunity to become fluent in English. Schools are discouraged from serving high needs students who pull their test scores down, so in New York ELLs are not admitted to small high schools and, within schools, schools feel pressured to spend less funding on these students.

Of great concern is that within this 'language as liability' framework, ELLs are seen through the lens of the deficit model. The following quotation supports this concern:

> Ironically, although the intention in testing is to 'level the playing field', it is common knowledge that tests have become the instruments to confirm unconscious assumptions about the unacceptability of some students and legitimate their exclusion. (Reid & Valle, 2004: 12)

Researchers point out how US schooling has traditionally approached multilingualism as a 'problem' that must be resolved through educational programs emphasizing English acquisition (Crawford, 1998; García, 1997; Ruiz, 1984). Within the climate of high-stakes testing fueled by *No Child Left Behind*, the accountability framework highlights the 'problems' and 'deficits' of ELLs. While states and school districts have focused attention on holding students accountable for their educational progress by denying high school graduation or grade promotion when they fail to achieve a certain test score, insufficient attention has been paid to ensuring that ELLs actually have the opportunity to attain the standards that have been set, for example through high-quality curricula, qualified teachers and schools with ample resources. The provision of opportunities to learn is simply not the current national focus.

Although the emphasis on testing for accountability holds the potential to not only raise expectations for ELLs but also greatly improve the opportunities offered to them in school, it has serious consequences when implementation is solely punitive in its results. We are at a key moment in the standards-based reform movement, as education policy can turn attention to ensuring opportunity to learn provisions for all students, and particularly those with the greatest needs, or too many ELLs will simply continue to fall through the cracks in the name of accountability, when they are systematically denied the opportunity to meet or exceed the standards.

Chapter Summary

- Two main benefits of test-based accountability for ELLs in the United States are that greater national attention is now being paid to these students, and expectations for their performance in school have increased. However, the drawbacks of accountability are found to outweigh the benefits, and the greater attention ELLs currently receive is primarily punitive.
- Because tests in English are required for accountability purposes, ELLs are by definition always labeled 'failing'. This is not because ELLs are failing to progress in the ways they should towards acquiring the English language, but rather because the tests solely measure outcomes rather than progress. This has negative consequences for ELLs and the schools that serve them.
- Schools serving large numbers of ELLs are at greater risk of failing to meet federal accountability requirements, and thus losing funding or being closed. This creates a disincentive for schools to admit ELLs and/or allocate resources towards their education.
- The focus on testing outcomes has overshadowed adequate attention being paid to the provision of opportunities for ELLs to learn, which includes the financial and human resources schools need (e.g. materials, facilities, high-quality books and qualified teachers).

Chapter 8

High-Stakes Testing and Language Un-Planning: Theoretical Implications of Testing as Language Policy

Earlier in this book, I explained how conducting research in language policy requires quite a bit of detective work on the part of the researcher, as this is the only way to expose and ultimately understand covert language policies. In the United States, where there is no official national language or national language policy, implicit policies are pervasive and extremely significant for understanding national priorities. In this chapter, the findings from this study are now located within language policy research and discussed.

Specifically, this chapter considers the different language policy implications of high-stakes testing in the US case, and what this means for the field. First and foremost, *No Child Left Behind* is a language policy, even though it is not presented as such and rarely seen in this light. At every level of the educational system, the law's top-down testing policies are interpreted and negotiated, such that all of the individuals involved become language policymakers, with teachers acting as the final arbiters of policy. Tests are *de facto* language policy in schools, and essentially become policy for language education when curriculum and teaching are aligned to the tests. Testing and accountability under the law ultimately reflect a 'language-as-problem' or 'deficit model' orientation in recent US language policy, where language has become a liability for ELLs.

The chapter is organized into the following sections: (1) New Orientations, (2) Testing and the Negotiation of Language Status in Schools, and (3) New Conceptions of Language Policy. The first section explores how tests have become *de facto* language policy, by showing how *No Child Left Behind* reflects a 'language-as-problem' orientation, and by beginning to examine different language policy byproducts of testing beyond the impact on curricula. Testing has narrowed which variety of the English language is valued and promoted as the standard; this creates a sorting mechanism that positions ELLs and speakers of non-standard varieties of English at the bottom. The second section goes on to describe how testing entails the negotiation of language status: On one hand, the existence of exam translations has created an official place for certain minority languages in school and supports bilingual education programs in these languages; on the other hand, translations participate in the creation of language hierarchies in schools with English at the top, and minority languages without translated exams at the bottom.

In light of these findings, this chapter concludes by offering a new perspective for the field of language policy in the third section, which challenges the notion of language 'planning' within the United States, making the argument that it is a misnomer to refer to these language changes as 'planned' in this context. In addition, this chapter proposes a new way of thinking about language education policy, whereby individuals at every level of the educational system are seen as potential language policymakers, as is appropriate for situations in which neither language policies nor language education policies are explicit or centrally planned. The language policies created as a result of testing are first elaborated in this chapter, before turning attention towards these new conceptions for the field.

New Orientations: Tests as *De Facto* Language Policy

As noted in Chapter 2 of this book, which provides a detailed history of federal education policy in the United States and how *No Child Left Behind* compares to previous legislation, NCLB reflects a shift in orientations towards language planning and policy in recent US history. As discussed by Hornberger (2006a), the Civil Rights Act of 1964, the passage of the Bilingual Education Act of 1968, and the *Lau v. Nichols* ruling of 1974 reflected a *language-as-resource* orientation (using the terminology of Ruiz, 1984). By contrast, NCLB symbolizes a return to the *language-as-problem* orientation towards US language policy that drove decisions to restrict language usage during the Americanization campaign of the early twentieth century, in the period after the United States entered World War I.

The history of education in the United States is characterized by a tension between equality and excellence, and shifts in our federal educational policy are described as a cyclical swing with these values at opposing ends (Fowler, 2000; Kaestle, 2001). Federal educational policy both reflects and affects the social context from which it emerges. For example, the *Civil Rights Act* and *Bilingual Education Act* clearly promoted equity within the context of a society deeply concerned by social inequity at that time. We have now swung into a time in which educational policies promote excellence through an emphasis on standards, standardized assessments and accountability, as more immigrants arrive in the United States than ever before.

It is highly symbolic that NCLB mandated several significant name changes; these changes marked the official end of the Bilingual Education Act, when the term 'bilingual' was removed from all federal legislation. For example, what was called the *Bilingual Education Act* was renamed *Language Instruction for Limited English Proficient and Immigrant Students* (Title III) in NCLB. Similarly, as described previously, what was then called the National Clearinghouse for Bilingual Education was required to change its name to the 'National Clearinghouse for English Language Acquisition'. Amidst this emphasis on educational excellence in federal education legislation, 'bilingual education' has been erased.

While Title III of NCLB did not outlaw bilingual education outright, it does seem to encourage English-only policies because of the accountability provisions, as supported in recent research (Crawford, 2002b; Evans & Hornberger, 2005; Wiley & Wright, 2004). Although the legislation mandates that states identify the languages needed for assessment purposes, states are not required to use native language assessments. In addition, states must prove progress in English but not in students' native languages. In an informal interview, US government officials described English to me as 'the gateway to content-area knowledge', as opposed to students' native languages serving that purpose (Office of English Language Acquisition administrators, US Department of Education, interview notes). Implicit within current legislation is the promotion of English, leaving it to states to decide whether other languages 'count'. Because many local districts like New York City implement bilingual education programs, the promotion of English-only in statewide assessments is often at odds with school-level bilingual policies.

In the case of New York, the Regents exams are the state's interpretation of NCLB, and Regents scores are reported for federal 'adequate yearly progress' and accountability requirements. Because the exams are based heavily on language, they by definition frame ELLs as 'deficient', or 'below standard'. This *language-as-problem* orientation negatively impacts and penalizes students who are ELLs, as described in the previous chapters of this book, because most of these students do not possess the language proficiency needed to pass the tests and graduate from high school. This book has also described the myriad ways that educators and school administrators have changed the curricula and instruction in English as a Second Language and bilingual classes. The research findings detail how standardized tests have become *de facto* language policy in the US because they are attached to high-stakes consequences, and thus shape what content schools teach, how it is taught, by whom it is taught, and in what language(s) it is taught.

The connection between high-stakes testing and *de facto* language policy is supported by the Center on Education Policy (2005), in their discussion of high school exit exams. This study surveyed all 25 states with exit exam requirements, and asked the following question: 'Does the state have an official position (e.g. law or policy) stating that students must be competent in the English language in order to receive a high school diploma?' (Center on Education Policy, 2006: 102). Of the states that responded to the survey, 21 indicated that English proficiency is simply an implied requirement, in that all students must pass an exit exam to graduate and English is one of the main subjects in that exam. Only three states indicated that English competency is not a graduation requirement; New Mexico is one of these, which makes sense as the state has adopted an 'English Plus' policy and, accordingly, permits ELLs to take all parts of the high school exit exam in Spanish to receive a diploma. As the authors write:

> [M]ost states with exit exams do not exempt English language learners from testing, do not allow special alternate routes to a diploma, and do not provide translations of the tests (at least of English language arts tests). These policies are consistent with the implicit understanding among most exit exam states that English proficiency is a requirement for graduation. (Center on Education Policy, 2005: 102)

The states requiring ELLs to take an English language arts test in order to graduate from high school do not have explicit language policies and yet, through their testing requirements, competency in English is necessary to graduate.

The research presented in this book offers new support for prior research conducted by Shohamy (2001: xiii) in Israel, from which she concluded that 'language testing policy' is the *de facto* 'language policy'. Even though these two contexts differ greatly, this conclusion remains the same. In the US case, the changes to language policy being negotiated were not the result of language planning. Rather, teachers and administrators at all levels of the educational system were found in this research to be responding to testing mandates under *No Child Left Behind* and the inclusion of ELLs in Regents exams. They then created educational policies within which implicit language policies were embedded. This fits with the distinctive history of the United States, where an elaborate combination of court rulings, state mandates, educational policies and complex language practices have defined language policy – in the absence of an official national language or some government body responsible for language planning (Crawford, 2000; Spolsky, 2004).

The lack of unified planning defines the United States case where Israel, by contrast, is often characterized as a language planning 'miracle' (Cooper, 1989). In a language shift that took only 50 years, what was a pluralingual Jewish community shifted to one where the vast majority of the population spoke Hebrew by the time the State of Israel declared independence in 1948 (Spolsky & Shohamy, 1999). Furthermore, Hebrew had been revitalized in the latter half of the 19th century from a religious biblical language that people 'knew but did not speak' to one suitable for daily use (Ben Rafael, 1994; Glinert, 1995; Spolsky & Shohamy, 1999). In this case, the Zionist ideology actively and effectively promoted Hebrew monolingualism, upholding the symbolic, political connection between Hebrew and national identity in the creation of that country. More recently, the Ministry of Education's 1995–1996 Policy for Language Education acknowledged the loss of immigrant languages and encouraged multilingualism (Shohamy, 2001; Spolsky & Shohamy, 1999).

The type of planning on a national level in the Israeli case is entirely absent in the United States. Language 'planning' is not part of the equation, and instead the tests – not language – are the starting point. Although the cases of the United States and Israel differ in significant ways, what holds both together is the power of tests to become *de facto* language policy.

Standardizing the standard

Not only do tests shape many decisions regarding language policy in education, such as what language will be the medium of instruction, they also narrowly define the language aspects and varieties that are valued and that students need to know. Chapter 4 detailed the different tasks on the English Regents exam, and Chapter 6 described how ESL teachers prepare English learners for that test. The language of the English Regents exams is a highly prescribed version of Standard English, emphasizing literacy skills such as persuasive writing, literary analysis, and the comprehension of non-fiction passages as well as texts from different literary genres. These skills then become encoded in classroom instruction, as teachers and school administrators focus their energies on ensuring their ELL students can pass the tests that count for high school graduation. This decidedly formalized and rigid variety of Standard English is promulgated by the English Regents, which becomes a sorting mechanism positioning English language learners and students who speak a non-standard variety of English at the low end of a hierarchy that values the standard.

In the case of US Latinos, who are permitted to take content-area Regents exams that are translated into Standard Spanish, testing emphasizes ever narrowing definitions of literacy. García and Menken (2006) argue that in cities like New York where English and Spanish speakers are in close contact, speakers move along a 'bilingual and bidialectal continuum' in their interactions. Yet testing fabricates a dichotomy with Spanish on the one hand and English on the other – using traditional models with some in the group speaking one or the other standard and others speaking both – which is purely academic and conflicts with the far more dynamic and complex sociolinguistic situation of US Latinos today (García & Menken, 2006). Schools have responded to an increasingly fluid sociolinguistic situation by adopting restricted definitions of academic language, assessed in Standard English or Standard Spanish by high-stakes tests that focus on literacy, and widening the gap between the language use of Latino students and the language of the tests.

Testing and the Negotiation of Language Status in Schools

Language status and acquisition planning are cited in research as primary goals of language planning and policy (Cooper, 1989; Haugen, 1972). This section of the chapter explores how testing also involves changes in language status in New York City. Specifically, this section clarifies how certain languages enjoy privileges in schools that others do not, as a byproduct of testing policies. These changes to language status evolved from efforts to meet the demands of high-stakes tests, but were not the result of careful language planning.

Official support for 'the top five' minority languages by exam translations

When the New York State Department of Education decided to translate the Regents exams in subjects other than English into Spanish, Chinese, Haitian Creole, Korean and Russian, they gave these languages an official status in schools that was not offered to other minority languages, thereby creating a language hierarchy. This side-effect of translations offers an interesting example of the types of incidental language policies that result from testing policies. While test translations offer assistance to ELLs on Regents exams, they are very important in supporting and preserving bilingual education programs in these languages. The following interview excerpts show the importance of Regents exams to ensure that schools offer bilingual education programs (first quote), and to ensure that instruction within those programs actually uses the minority language (second quote):

> The language policy now depends on each individual school. If Regents didn't exist I'd get rid of bilingual education and just keep a native language literacy piece, and do content-area instruction in English. (Mr C, Assistant Principal of Organization, School #2, interview notes)

> So I teach more Spanish now because English is no longer an issue on the Regents. When the state said you can take this exam in the student's language, I saw it as a green light to go ahead and teach in that language. (Ms M, Bilingual Social Studies Teacher, School #9, interview notes)

As these quotations show, the translations go beyond just making the exams more accessible to ELLs, to actually offering support for minority language instruction. Chapter 4 explored the use of Regents exam translations and concluded that although the translations do help ELLs improve their test scores, the help they offer is limited because they cannot truly 'level the playing field'. It seems instead that a major significance of exam translations is actually sociopolitical, and relevant to language policy: they serve to sustain bilingual education programming. Chapter 6 showed the great extent to which educators align curriculum and teaching to the test and, where language is concerned, this affects language policy decisions – as exemplified in the second quotation above. Because the exams are available in certain minority languages, the state has offered a 'green light' to teach in those languages, even if that was not necessarily the state's intention.

On the other hand, if Regents exams were only available in English, the tests would undermine existing bilingual programs and teachers would be forced to use more English or only English in their instruction. This is what occurs in states that do not permit translations. For example, Gutiérrez *et al.* (2002) note how difficult it is for schools in California to retain native language instruction when tests are only offered in English, and Alamillo and Viramontes (2000) describe the pressure on teachers to teach more English in states with English-only state assessments. Crawford (2004) offers the example of a dual language bilingual education program in Montgomery County, Maryland, where instruction was equally balanced between English and Spanish prior to mandatory testing. After the introduction of high-stakes tests in English, the school became worried about poor performance, and decided to increase the amount of English instruction offered by adding two and a half hours of English phonics each day. These examples show how English-only testing can easily evolve into English-only language policy in schools.

In contrast to these examples, New York is one of a very small minority of states permitting and implementing test translations (Rivera & Collum, 2006; Stansfield & Rivera, 2002). Therefore, one implication of high-stakes testing for language policy in New York is systemic support for bilingual education programs in Spanish, Chinese, Korean, Russian and Haitian Creole, even within this period of English-only policies and language restriction in US history.

Speakers of minority languages other than 'the top five' in New York: The marginalized of the marginalized

A further language policy byproduct of testing is a language hierarchy in schools which locates the speakers of minority languages that are not recognized by Regents exam translations at the bottom. Interestingly, the five languages into which Regents exams are translated do not actually represent the most commonly spoken minority languages in New York City schools. As reported in Chapter 3, the top five languages spoken by ELLs in New York City are (in order of largest to smallest): Spanish, Chinese, Russian, Urdu and Bengali. Test translations are not offered in Urdu or Bengali even though these languages are more widely spoken than either Haitian Creole or Korean. The reason for this is that the five languages of the translations are the most commonly spoken minority languages in New York State as a whole, as reported by the National Clearinghouse for English Language Acquisition (1999). As such, while translation policy matches state demographics, it does not match the demographics of New York City.

This leaves large numbers of ELLs – approximately 20% of the total ELL population in New York City – at a great disadvantage, because no extra help on assessments is offered to speakers of languages other than the five for which there are Regents translations. The many speakers of minority languages such as Vietnamese, Bengali, Twi, Mandingo and Urdu in city high schools must take Regents exams in English. Furthermore, unlike ELLs who speak a language like Spanish that is acknowledged by the system, they must also fulfill high school foreign language requirements because their mother tongue is not recognized. As a result, these students must take foreign language courses at the schools they attend, usually Spanish, while simultaneously learning English. Students who speak these languages are very aware of their disadvantage in comparison with their ELL peers who can use translated exams, as indicated in the following interview quotation:

[S1 is from the Dominican Republic, S2 is from Bangladesh, S3 is from Guinea, and S4 is from Bulgaria]
S2: It's good though, it's easy for them [Spanish speakers].
… How do you feel you can't take it in your language?

S3: You feel left out, like when the Math Regents comes ... See, they're giving them a better opportunity to pass that [we] don't have.
... Do you have any recommendations about the Regents for policymakers?
S2: They should make, like, like all the languages, the majority of people living in New York, all those languages.
S4: They should make it equal for everybody!
(11th and 12th grade ELLs, Focal School #1, interview notes)

A teacher at a school with a significant West African population explains this further:

Another interesting political dynamic in terms of how the state is trying to help ELLs is they provide Regents in five different languages, but what that's turned into here is a sense of unfairness. Most of our students speak Spanish and then French, and the languages [of the Regents] are Spanish and Haitian Creole but not French. It turns out the state is only helping some of our students – the majority of our minority groups. Not that it's divisive, but it's unfair.
(Ms J, Regents Social Studies Teacher, School #3, interview transcript)

As these quotations show, speakers of languages not offered as Regents translations are at the lower end of a language hierarchy in New York City public schools. The decision by the New York State Department of Education to offer translations in five minority languages was not the result of language planning, but was driven by the need to resolve the problems associated with including ELLs in tests that were not intended for this student population. The end result, however, is language policy, in the complex articulation of the status of different minority languages.

Even with translations, English is what counts (and minority languages do not)

Even though New York deviates from the national norm and Regents for subjects other than English are translated, the message that the exams seem to convey to educators and students is still that English is what counts. This is shown in the following interview excerpt, which arose when I asked the same group of students quoted on the preceding page about this topic:

What is the message the Regents send you about language, which languages are important and why?
S2: English, because you talk that language you could go to any country and just speak English.

S1: English.
S3: The message is you got to know English. If your English is not good you won't be able to do these tests right here. Where you got to try hard even though you're not from this country because you came here to stay. (11th and 12th grade ELLs, Focal School #1, interview notes)

In the preceding passage, the importance of English is a belief shared by all the students interviewed, including 'S1' who can take the exams in Spanish.

This point is further supported by educators with regard to the message of the Regents exams:

... [W]hat do you think are the language policy implications of the tests? What is the message the tests send you about what language is important and should be emphasized in the classroom?
Mr C: English only. With the math, what do they end up teaching? English. What language do they all end up teaching? English. Mr B [who teaches mainly in Spanish] is the rare exception.
(Mr C, Assistant Principal of Organization, School #2, interview transcript)

I also have, it's sort of a language policy question. Do the Regents exams send students a message about language?
Ms K: I think it very clearly sends the message that English is the language of instruction here. And English is the language of transforming and processing knowledge. In particular, this English Regents.
(Ms K, ESL Teacher, School #4, interview transcript)

The responses to questions about the intersection between language policy and the Regents exams were consistent that English is the most important language because, even though some students can take translations, all students must pass the English Regents exam.

The dominance of English within the United States and as an international language of wider communication is widely documented (Crawford, 1998, 2000; Cummins, 2000; Fishman, 1991; Fishman *et al.*, 1996; García, 1997; Phillipson, 1992; Phillipson & Skutnabb-Kangas, 1996; Ricento, 1995; Skutnabb-Kangas, 2000; Wiley & Lukes, 1996; Wiley & Wright, 2004), and strongly felt by ELL students and those who educate them in New York City schools. The fact is that English is currently being spoken in over 113 territories where it holds official, co-official, *de facto* official, lingua franca, additional language, in-government, official second language, or official third language status (Fishman *et al.*, 1996). This power of English threatens the use of minority languages as a medium of instruction in the United States, where educational policies favor English and immigrants typically lose their mother tongue by the third generation (García, 1997; McCarty,

2004; Rumbaut *et al.*, 2006). An added pressure in favor of English in New York City schools is the frequent reports by bilingual teachers during interviews that most of the classroom materials and texts available to them were provided in English only, making native language instruction difficult or impossible. The power of English within the United States and elsewhere, in combination with English language arts testing requirements, as well as other factors such as limited minority language resources, sends students and teachers alike the message that English is what counts.

At the same time that testing mandates are clarifying the high status of English in US public schools, knowledge of a minority language does not help ELLs meet the requirements of either *No Child Left Behind* or New York's graduation requirements. It is a great irony in the United States that native English speakers spend years in school studying foreign languages such as Spanish, and yet so little is done to help immigrant students maintain their native languages. As stated above, NCLB evaluates English proficiency but does not require native language proficiency. Similarly, while high school students must study a foreign language in high school, passing a foreign language Regents exam is not actually a high school exit exam requirement. Time and again, I was told by teachers and administrators at the different high schools in this study that most Spanish-speaking students do very well on the Spanish Regents exam, yet this does not carry nearly the weight that their scores on the English Regents do, because the Spanish Regents exam is not tied to high school graduation. Similarly, a schoolwide score on the Spanish Regents is not a measure of adequate yearly progress within the city or statewide accountability systems. Knowledge of a minority language simply does not count within the current high-stakes testing and accountability context. Instead, for ELLs it is mainly a liability.

The hierarchy of languages in New York City high schools

These findings show how a linguistic hierarchy has been created in schools where English is at the top, the five languages of the exam translations are in the middle, and the remaining minority languages are at the bottom. This is depicted in Figure 8.1.

Figure 8.1 is a reflection of the power dynamics, politics, and numerical population of minority language speakers, and displays the current status of different minority languages in relation to English in New York City schools. As shown in the figure, English is at the top of the hierarchy. The five languages in the middle are those which are offered as Regents translations, and therefore hold some official status in school. Though these five minority languages are the most widely spoken after English in the state of New York, as explained above, they are not the most widely spoken in

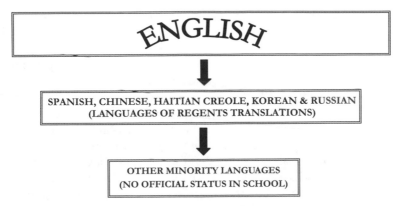

Figure 8.1 The Regents language hierarchy in New York City high schools

New York City (where, for instance, Urdu is in the top five numerically). This is indicative of how the state currently has more power over determining testing policy than the city, and how much influence the state therefore has in affecting language policies in schools. The remaining minority languages – spoken by about 20% of ELLs in New York City – are at the bottom of the hierarchy and hold lower status, because they have not been officially recognized in any way. As such, sustaining bilingual education programs in these languages is more difficult, and ELLs who speak these languages receive fewer supports on tests than other students.

New Conceptions of Language Policy: Language Un-Planning and Language Education Policy

This chapter concludes by offering a new perspective for the field of language planning and policy. Specifically, I argue here that language 'planning' is a misnomer in the US context, where language policies are created at every level of the educational system in *ad hoc*, uncoordinated and often competing ways. Although there are many differing definitions of the term 'language planning' offered in the literature, the findings from this research indicate that these definitions fail to portray the US context accurately. In the United States, standardized testing affects classroom practice every day, and it is misleading to state that language is truly 'planned'. I argue instead that individuals at every level of the educational system are involved in unplanned language policymaking as they negotiate recent mandates to include English language learners in high-stakes exams, and the tests become *de facto* language policies in reality. If anything, the negotiation of testing has required schools to undo the language programs they had in place previously; as described in this book, ESL classes have become like English language arts classes, in many ways removing the language learning supports that had been in place since the *Lau vs. Nichols* ruling. Language learning is often relegated to a secondary concern, when the curriculum and instruction by necessity involve test preparation. In sum, this research exemplifies the sorts of *ad hoc* language policymaking that occurs in the United States, in the absence of any concerted efforts at language planning.

Accordingly, the perspective on language education policy that is proposed here accounts for the reality that there are language policymakers at every level of the education system. *No Child Left Behind* is a top-down policy, and it is characterized by increased federal involvement in public education, making it the most invasive federal education policy ever in US history (Hill, 2000). While the United States has a decentralized education system, NCLB demands greater centralization by attaching strings to federal Department of Education funding, to be sure the mandates are followed. However, even educational policies which attempt to control implementation are negotiated at the classroom level, and rarely applied exactly as policymakers intended (Canagarajah, 2005; Cuban, 1998; Steiner-Kahmsi, 2004). In his discussion of 'how schools reform education reform', Cuban (1998) identifies a key division between policymakers and practitioners. While policymakers evaluate an educational policy's effectiveness by the extent to which it achieves the desired goals, practitioners evaluate a policy's effectiveness by its adaptability in implementation. Cuban (1998) argues that the practitioner's perspective is neglected, and in fact that effective education reforms are those which can be modified to best fit each context and sustained over time.

Current federal education policy is interpreted and negotiated at every level of the educational system and, where the education of English learners is involved, has resulted in the creation of incidental language policies. Below is a summary of the key language policymakers at the different levels of the educational system in this research, and their language policymaking activities in New York are briefly reiterated. To use the metaphor offered by Ricento and Hornberger (1996), these are the different layers of New York's language policy 'onion'. This description moves from the national to the local level, as *No Child Left Behind* is funneled down through the system to classroom teachers:

US Department of Education – The US Department of Education has no official language education policy statement, but rather has implicit language policy through the adoption of *No Child Left Behind*. NCLB removed 'bilingual education' from federal legislation and promotes English through its accountability mandates. The US Department of Education requires all ELLs in New York to participate in English language arts exams annually.

New York State Department of Education – The state has interpreted NCLB by including ELLs in Regents examinations and increasing the amount of English instruction ELLs receive in high school. The requirement that ELLs must pass the English Regents exam is tantamount to making English proficiency a requirement for high school graduation. The state has aligned ESL standards and instruction to English language arts. ELLs are permitted test translations as an accommodation, and translations support bilingual education, yet also contribute to a language hierarchy.

New York City Department of Education – The *ASPIRA Consent Decree* of 1974 and the *Lau Plan of 1977* require services be provided to ELLs and favor transitional bilingual education. The city mandated that elementary test scores be used as a criterion for grade promotion.

Parents/Community – In New York City, bilingual education programs have historically been started or ended as the result of parental pressure, so parents and community play an essential role in the creation of school-based language policies. However, parents and community members were not involved in the state or city's interpretations of NCLB; instead, schools were required to balance state mandates with parental concerns.

Administrators of New York City Public High Schools – High schools determine programming and policies for the education of ELLs. Few high schools have schoolwide language education policies, though small schools serving entirely ELL populations are more likely to have them (e.g. School #5 is a dual language school). Schoolwide language policies often conflict with state and national policies, and many schools with bilingual programs are feeling pressured to increase English and reduce native language instruction to improve their test scores.

Assistant Principals – Large high schools have assistant principals for each subject area, who play a key role in determining language education policy; they interpret state policies and must prepare ELLs for the Regents exams, so they design educational programming accordingly. Within a school, these policies are often not schoolwide and can be contradictory; for example, at School #1 there is strong support for bilingual instruction by the ESL/Foreign Language Assistant Principal, while the Math Assistant

Principal systematically requires bilingual teachers to use mostly English in instruction.

Teachers – Teachers are the final arbiters of policy implementation. The language policies they adopt are often driven by their own language ideology as well as by school policies. Even in schools with clear schoolwide language education policies, teachers have their own interpretations of the demands of testing, and their own beliefs about language, so determine language education policies for their individual classrooms. Teachers instruct in English and/or the students' native languages, and usually decide the quantity of instruction in each. There is often tension between teachers' policies and those of the school, city, state, or country.

All of this variation details the complexities of language policy within the US context, and shows why notions of language planning are insufficient to capture these variances. The figure that follows pays homage to Ricento and Hornberger's (1996) onion metaphor, connoting the layers of language policy, and visually depicts the language policymakers at the different levels of the public education system in the wake of recent testing mandates. The two-way arrows in the figure below show how top-down policies are not simply implemented as the policymakers intended, but rather are interpreted and negotiated every step of the way. It is worth noting that students are not considered language policymakers here, indicated by the one-way arrow in Figure 8.2, showing how they are mainly the recipients of the complex array of policies that come down to them from above.

Redefining language policy

To clarify the new perspective proposed here, it is important to first identify recent definitions of language planning and policy offered in the literature, in order to clarify why they are not entirely suitable for the US testing case. It was explained in Chapter 1 that within the field of language policy, which is still quite new, there is a lack of unity with regard to how 'language planning' and 'language policy' are defined. Based on their review of the many definitions, Kaplan and Baldauf (1997: xi) define language planning as an activity 'intended to promote systematic linguistic change in some community of speakers', that is usually 'top-down' and leads to, or is directed by, the dissemination of language policy by government or some other power. Cooper (1989) provides a broader definition, which also includes 'bottom-up' language planning. The problem with these definitions is that in the case of testing in New York City schools, the many language changes adopted to prepare students for the Regents exams are rarely systematic or organized.

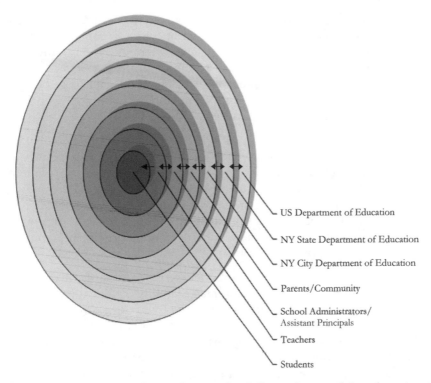

Figure 8.2 Language policymakers at the different layers of the educational system

For Ager (2001: 5), language planning is defined as the ways communities 'consciously attempt to influence the language(s) their members use, the languages used in education, or the ways in which Academies, publishers or journalists make the language change'. And, he defines language policy as 'official planning, carried out by those in political authority' (Ager, 2001: 5). From his perspective, language planning involves unofficial influence on language, while language policy is official. This definition is insufficient to describe educators' responses to the inclusion of ELLs into high-stakes tests, where teachers or assistant principals adopt language policies that are completely unofficial, and *ad hoc* to such an extent that they often vary from classroom to classroom within the same school.

Representing a different viewpoint, McCarty (2004) offers a broader definition of language policy whereby unofficial activities are just as important as official ones. Referring to the US context, she defines language policy as a 'sociocultural process' that 'includes public and official acts and documents, but, equally important, it constitutes and is constituted by the practices each of us engages in every day' (McCarty, 2004: 72). Fettes also pays attention to the reality that policies are frequently adopted without any planning whatsoever. The passage below is his response to the definition of language planning as involving 'systematic' language policy development:

> The principal difficulty with this interpretation is that a great deal of language policy-making goes on in a haphazard or uncoordinated way, far removed from the language planning ideal. Therefore language planning in this wider sense must be linked to the critical evaluation of language policy: the former providing standards of rationality and effectiveness, the latter testing these ideas against actual practice in order to promote the development of better (more sophisticated, more useful) language planning models. (Fettes, 1997: 14)

Recognizing that most schools adopt policies that are not planned, Corson (1999: 17) suggests a process for language planning that includes language policymaking, and thereby offers a 'planned way for schools to extend high-quality education to all their students without discrimination'.

Many authors simply use the terms language planning and policy interchangeably in the literature, and there has been recent movement in the field to refer only to language policy. Spolsky (1998: 66) explains that while the term 'planning' was preferred earlier on, the many failures of national language planning efforts caused people to favor the term 'language policy' in the late 1980s. In fact, Spolsky and Shohamy (1999: 32) do not distinguish between the terms, and define language policy as 'an explicit statement, usually but not necessarily written in a formal document, about language use'. In more recent work, Spolsky (2004: 39) notes four main features in his theory of language policy: '[T]he tripartite division of language policy into language practices, language beliefs and ideology, and the explicit policies and plans resulting from language management or planning activities that attempt to modify the practices and ideologies of the community'. Spolsky (2004: 222) concludes that 'the real language policy of a community is more likely to be found in its practices than its management'. In applying these definitions to current language policies in the United States, the decisions made to declare English the official language in certain states and the passage of anti-bilingual education legislation in California, Arizona and Massachusetts are examples of explicit language policies. Testing policy, however, is implicit in that the tests were not developed with the goal of affecting language change or use; what Spolsky (2004) terms 'language management' is absent. In fact, ELLs are now being included into tests intended for native English speakers simply as an afterthought. In this regard, we have to look at the language practices in order to infer the underlying language policy.

The New York City case exemplifies the type of haphazard language policymaking that Fettes (1997) describes, and the language policies that are adopted are unsystematic and often contradictory. They are also implicit in New York, embedded within educational policies that are explicit. And, they are frequently not 'conscious' or 'official' decisions to affect or manage language change. The Regents exams were not developed to evaluate ELLs, but ELLs were included so that there would be accountability for their performance in accordance with federal mandates. As a result, this testing policy became the *de facto* language education policy, when schools began to realize the changes that needed to occur to prepare students for the tests. In this way, school language policies are often unplanned, and it is a misnomer to discuss 'language planning' in cases such as that of high-stakes testing in the United States where the policy comes first, leaving the possibility for planning only as an afterthought.

Redefining language education policy

In her research, which exposes all of the different ways that language practices are overtly and covertly regulated, Shohamy (2003, 2006) offers the following distinction between language policy and language education policy:

> [Language policy (LP)] is concerned with the decisions that people make about languages and their use in society, whereas [language education policy (LEP)] refers to carrying out such decisions in the specific contexts of schools and universities in relation to home languages and to foreign and second languages ... In general, LPs and LEPs are stated explicitly through official documents such as national laws, declarations of certain languages as 'official' or 'national', language standards, curricula, tests, or other types of documents. At times, LPs and LEPs are not stated explicitly but must be derived implicitly by examining a variety of *de facto* practices. In these situations, the LP and the LEP are more difficult to detect because they are 'hidden' from public eyes. (Shohamy, 2003: 279)

Shohamy's (2003) definition of language education policy is very helpful in describing the situation in New York, which is unique because there is neither an explicit language policy nor a language education policy, making examination of *de facto* practices a central concern.

The definition of language education policy I propose offers several main distinctions from those presented above. First, like Shohamy (2003, 2006), McCarty (2004) and Spolsky (2004) I also favor the use of the term 'language policy' without a clear link to 'language planning' because so much of the decisionmaking that occurs is unplanned, as described in the preceding section of this chapter. Second, language policymaking can occur at every level of the educational system, as shown in Figure 8.2. In describing the role of teachers, Shohamy (2006) describes how educators carry out language education policies 'with no questions asked' and thus 'serve as 'soldiers' of the system who carry out orders by internalizing the policy ideology and its agendas' and 'as bureaucrats that follow orders unquestioningly' (Shohamy, 2006: 79). This characterization of teachers in not supported in my research. Instead, as described previously, teachers are in fact the final policymakers. For example, there were several teachers and administrators who resisted the pressures created by testing to increase English in instruction, and increased native language instruction instead. In this way, my view of language education policy recognizes both 'top-down' and 'bottom-up' policies.

Third, I argue here that the distinction between language policy and language education policy is actually quite often blurred. Shohamy (2006) draws a clear separation between language policy and language education policy, based primarily on contexts with official language policies and/or language education policies. In discussing the areas of intersection and disconnection between 'language education policy' and 'language policy', one of the editors of this book, Nancy Hornberger, offered an alternative explanation of this relationship, as best depicted by a Venn diagram; my interpretation of her image can be seen in Figure 8.3.

As shown in Figure 8.3, some aspects of language education policy are self-contained, such as language curriculum and medium of instruction. Yet, as in the case of testing, language education policy can also involve areas such as language standardization and the creation of linguistic hierarchies, which extend beyond education into the broader rubric of language policy. This seems particularly to be the case in places where language policies and language education policies are mainly *ad hoc*. The ways that language education has been reshaped as a result of recent education reform efforts provides an example of how language educational policy can simply be a byproduct of educational policy, in the absence of an overt language policy or language planning. As I have discussed throughout this book, high-stakes testing in the United States is an educational policy which has resulted in *de facto* language policy.

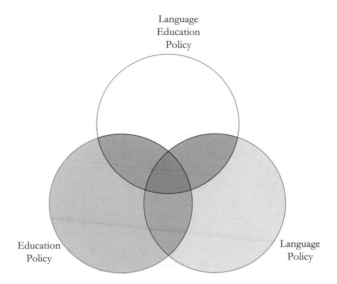

Figure 8.3 The relationship between language policy, education policy, and language education policy

Discussion

This chapter has outlined several of the language policy implications of standardized testing in the United States. Testing has become *de facto* language policy, greatly impacting language education, and resulting in the standardization of test languages and the creation of linguistic hierarchies when some minority languages are officially recognized through test translations and others are not, and the dominance of English is reinforced. This chapter shows how there are language policymakers at every layer of the educational system, as *No Child Left Behind* is interpreted, negotiated, and implemented, with teachers characterized as the final arbiters of policy.

In light of these findings, it is imperative that language policies in education are considered in definitions of language policy within this field, as time and again the research notes the absolutely central role that schools play in language policy (Cooper, 1989; Corson, 1999; Cummins, 2000; Fishman, 1991, 2001; Hornberger, 1996; Kaplan & Baldauf, 1997; Phillipson, 1992; Phillipson *et al.*, 1995; Spolsky, 2004; Tollefson, 1991). Because so many of the recent changes to language policy in schools are simply incidental results of education policy without careful planning for language, I have used the term 'language policy' instead of 'language planning and policy' in this book. In addition, I argue for fluidity between definitions of the terms 'language policy' and 'language education policy', as there are areas of intersection as well as distinction.

With this perspective in mind, I would align myself with Corson (1999) and advocate for carefully planned, considered and developed language policies in schools that are closely matched to local needs and preferences. However, like Fettes (1997), it does need to be acknowledged that planning in the creation of language policy reflects an ideal, and simply is not our current reality. It is an ideal worth pursuing, however, as careful planning could prevent the adoption of educational policies that have an enormous impact on language simply because it was never considered at the outset, and which can carry negative consequences for language minority students in school. The next chapter offers a set of recommendations with regard to high-stakes testing and language policy in the education of ELLs, drawing upon the theoretical implications outlined in this chapter.

Chapter Summary

- There are numerous language policy byproducts of *No Child Left Behind*, supporting the argument in this book that testing results in *de facto* language policy. Testing lends itself to language standardization in increasingly restrictive ways.
- Testing, and particularly the support for test translations in state policy, have contributed to the creation of a language hierarchy in New York City schools with English at the top, the five minority languages into which tests are translated in the middle, and the languages without the benefit of translations at the bottom.
- Individuals at every layer of the educational system are involved in language policymaking, from the federal government to the state commissioner and into classrooms, as federal policies are interpreted, negotiated, and localized. Teachers are the final arbiters of language education policy implementation.
- The term 'language planning' is a misnomer within this context, and the research presented in this book offers grounding for a new conception of language policy that accounts for *ad hoc* and often contradictory policymaking in schools, and encompasses all forms of negotiation and policymaking – both from the top-down to the bottom-up. Careful language planning is an ideal worth pursuing, though it does not reflect the current reality.

Chapter 9

Moving Forward: Embracing Multilingual Language Policies from the Top-Down to the Bottom-Up

The impact of high-stakes testing on the instructional practices and learning experiences of English language learners has been dramatic, affecting language policies in schools and future opportunities for English language learners. Without question, tests have become a strong presence in the everyday lives of ELLs and educators. And, while their implementation has generated multiple interpretations and variations in classroom practices, they have been a central mechanism for the spread of English-only policies in US schools. This chapter offers a brief overview of topics discussed in this book, and then provides a set of recommendations.

The first part of this book clarified the significance of the assessment mandates within *No Child Left Behind* for English language learners, locating this law within the history of language policy in the United States. Immigrants have historically entered the United States during periods of alternating restriction or tolerance in the treatment of their languages. More immigrants arrived in the United States during the past decade than ever before, and it has become apparent that the current period is one of language restrictionism.

No Child Left Behind requires that ELLs participate in assessments and demonstrate growth in their English proficiency and content knowledge. While not a language policy at face value, because English is the language that 'counts' on tests, these assessments in schools have resulted in English-only approaches and the reduction of bilingual education programs. In New York, the state now requires ELLs to pass five Regents exams to graduate from high school. Although New York City has historically been supportive of bilingual education, the number of bilingual programs has decreased since the passage of *No Child Left Behind* in 2001, while English-only ESL programming has increased. Without supports in schools for minority languages, schools perpetuate the current cycle in which the languages of immigrants to the United States are typically lost by the third generation (Fishman, 2001; Rumbaut *et al.*, 2006).

A detailed analysis of high school exit exams from New York, Texas and California reveals how all of the exams are linguistically complex for ELLs, regardless of the subject being tested. ELLs in New York and elsewhere perform far below native English speakers on the standardized tests being used. New York's English Regents exam demands that students write four essays; yet, research shows that ELLs develop receptive skills more rapidly than the productive skills needed to write essays in academic English (Cummins, 1992; García & Menken, 2006). The English Regents exam also involves listening comprehension of lengthy non-fiction passages, knowledge of literary elements and genres, and synthesizing different texts around a common theme. The Math exams in New York and elsewhere are also highly dependent on language and literacy skills, and involve many word problems and text-based questions, where students must decipher the language to determine the math calculations that correct answers require. The tests are very difficult for ELLs, who are not yet fully proficient in the English language. Test translations are a popular test accommodation, yet provide only limited help when students do not possess a high level of content-specific vocabulary in their first language, so language remains a threat to test validity even when the test is provided in a student's native language.

The second part of this book highlights findings from a year-long qualitative research study conducted in New York City high schools. In their own words, students explain the challenges that the Regents exams pose, particularly the English Regents, and the pressures they feel to pass. Retaking all of the exams is commonplace, and high rates of exam failure among ELLs have created an incentive for them to leave school to pursue a Graduate Equivalency Degree or simply drop out; their stories confirm quantitative studies which show ELLs currently have the highest dropout rates of all students in New York City. Those who remain in school often experience a test-focused curriculum; some have passed all of the necessary course requirements and even been admitted to college, but attend Regents preparation courses each day in order to pass and graduate.

The findings from this research show how high-stakes tests have become *de facto* language policy in schools, shaping what content schools teach, how it is taught, by whom it is taught, and in what language(s) it is taught. This research found that school administrators and educators changed their language policies to respond to the demands of the exams, most often by increasing the amount of English instruction students receive. However, one school instead increased native language instruction as a test preparation strategy; finding that the skills the Advanced Placement Spanish exam demands are similar to those on the English Regents, the school began requiring Latino ELLs to enroll in Advanced Placement Spanish courses as a strategy to improve their pass rates on the English Regents, which they succeeded in increasing by 50 points. Such practices are supported by research which states that literacy skills developed in a student's native language transfer to their second language (Cummins, 1992, 2000). Bilingual teachers are in a complicated position, trying to balance bilingual instruction with monolingual testing, and some choose to teach monolingually so the language of instruction matches that of the exam.

Because of their high-stakes consequences, tests have become *de facto* language policy in schools, and shape the following:

- what content schools teach,
- how it is taught,
- by whom it is taught, and
- in what language(s) it is taught.

Educators thus become language policymakers, deciding how native language is used in the classroom, if at all, and using an array of strategies to prepare their students for the exams. 'Teaching to the test' is common, and the curriculum in all subject areas has often been narrowed to focus on the material required by the tests. Teachers report how English as a second language classes in New York have become much like English language arts classes taken by native English speakers. Overall, this is problematic when it is the exams that drive these choices rather than best practices for the education of ELLs doing so, particularly because the exams were not developed for these students.

The third part of this book expands these findings to the wider policy context. While *No Child Left Behind* has benefited ELLs by increasing their national exposure and expectations for their performance, the findings from this research highlight several main failings of the law for ELLs. Tests scores are the gauge of a school's success or failure within this accountability system, yet once ELLs pass an English language proficiency exam, they exit the ELL subgroup. This, combined with the arrival of new ELLs who do not yet speak English, causes overall group test scores to always remain low (Abedi, 2004; Abedi & Dietal, 2004). In addition, the exam policies establish a cutoff passing score that serves as the minimum required for a student to graduate from high school. Even when students' performance increases each time they are tested, if their scores remain below the cutoff score there is no measurement of growth or progress. As such, ELLs by definition are considered low performing, and schools serving large numbers of these students are at greater risk of failing to meet federal accountability requirements. This creates a disincentive for schools to serve ELLs, and fosters a deficit perspective.

There have been numerous language policy byproducts of testing. In addition to tests driving instruction and thus determining language education policy, they have contributed to the creation of language hierarchies in schools whereby English and certain minority languages are afforded higher status than other minority languages. Individuals at every layer of the educational system, including teachers, are involved in language policymaking as educational policies are interpreted, negotiated and implemented. Due to the complexity of these intersecting and often conflicting language policies, the findings from this research highlight how language policymaking often occurs in the absence of language planning; thus, this research promotes a new perspective for the field to capture such complexities in language education policy.

Recommendations

The power play between educational policy and language policy is thus complex, as top-down education policies often assume the place of language policies in schools. When this happens, top-down policies overpower local practices and it can become difficult for schools to provide quality educational programming for their language learners; all too often, such policies directly disadvantage these students. Specifically, the assessment and accountability mandates of *No Child Left Behind* are 'leaving behind' alarming numbers of English language learners. This is enabled by high-stakes testing, as ELLs are required to receive the same passing scores as other students on linguistically challenging exams which evaluate language proficiency as much as content knowledge. Not surprisingly, ELLs perform far below other students on standardized exams across subject areas in New York and elsewhere. When test scores are attached to high-stakes decisions like high school graduation, they can limit the future opportunities of ELLs.

Yet top-down educational policies need not undermine the quality of programming a school provides to its ELLs. The schools which are most vulnerable to the influence of testing as *de facto* language policy are those which do not have strong language policies and programs in place to counterbalance recent federal mandates. Therefore, the following are two main protections to the services a school offers language learners:

- Strong, coherent, clearly articulated and implemented schoolwide language policy.
- Top-down educational policies that support local language policies and practices.

A clear and cohesive school-based language policy which is consistently implemented on a schoolwide basis with a collective vision for the education of ELLs, is the greatest way to protect programming and negotiate top-down reforms and policies in ways that make sense for ELL students. Freeman (2004) and Corson (1999) offer clear guidance on the creation and implementation of school language policies. In the ideal world, all new educational policies would consider ELLs, support the language programming a school provides and improve local practices. While this latter recommendation is perhaps idealistic, and may be more difficult to attain than establishing strong school-based language policies, it is nonetheless essential to pursue.

With these fundamental points in mind, the following are recommendations based on the research shared in this book. These recommendations are relevant to *No Child Left Behind*, yet are also related to any context where high-stakes testing, language policy, and language learning intersect. Some recommendations mainly pertain to New York, as noted, though these also have implications elsewhere. The following recommendations are divided into those for educational policymakers, and those for schools and teachers:

Recommendations for educational policymakers

- Support schools in their development of clear and cohesive schoolwide language policies and in their decisions to teach language minority students in their native languages. Adopt only those testing and other educational policies which support a school's language policy, particularly if that policy involves native language instruction.
- Shift the paradigm to focus on the provision of opportunities to learn for ELLs. Ensure schools have all of the resources needed, through the provision of superior programming that is long enough in duration to offer sufficient support for English acquisition and native language development, superb instruction, high-quality materials in the language(s) of instruction, ample funding, and other necessary features.
- Move away from an over-reliance on standardized tests to allowing for the use of multiple measures of student achievement in addition to the tests (e.g. an array of samples of student work, grades, classroom performance, teacher recommendations) when assessing a student. Redesign the accountability system to also include district, school,

and classroom-based measures of student performance. Permit portfolios or other performance assessments which yield more accurate results with regard to ELLs than traditional assessments.

- Include ELLs into accountability systems in ways that are valid, appropriate, and fair for this student population. Develop assessments with ELL students in mind from the outset, rather than trying to include them as an afterthought into assessments developed for native English speakers. These assessments should be in English and students' native languages, and designed to determine content knowledge and language development separately. Assessments should offer information that is helpful to teachers, for example in identifying areas for future instruction.
- Allow for the measurement of *progress* rather than simply of *outcomes* on high-stakes exams, by showing annual growth in exam scores as well as performance in relation to a set bar for achievement, particularly on English exams.

[The recommendations below focus mainly on New York, though they have implications elsewhere]:

- While it is acceptable for ELLs to take the English Regents or other exams in English as an academic exercise, their scores should not be used to determine high school graduation nor as the basis for any other high-stakes decisions.
- Exam translations should be provided in all languages spoken by ELLs in high school. Provide clear guidance to schools on how and when translations should be used. In specific, students should receive English and native language versions so that they can use *both* during the exam session. And, permit students to respond in both languages. Ensure that exam translations are accurate.
- Minority languages should count. Performance by ELLs on language arts exams that are in their native language, such as the Chinese Regents or Spanish Regents should count within the accountability system. Much like English Regents exams for native English speakers, these exams display important literacy skills in a student's native language.

Recommendations for schools and teachers

- Develop schoolwide language policies that are consistent and cohesive, which support the desires of the community the school serves. A school's language policy should be used to establish coherent K-12 language programming for ELLs in which language learning is consistent and diversity is regarded as a resource.

- Even though *No Child Left Behind* accountability requirements implicitly promote English, schools should be able to support native language instruction. As shown at Focal School #1 in this research, doing so will aid rather than hinder students' development of English literacy.
- Although it is clear that educators need to address exam skills in their instruction, given the realities of high-stakes testing, tests should not drive instruction for ELLs. Rather, research on the effective education of ELLs should. For example, while it sets high expectations for ELLs to strive to pass the English Regents, it is pedagogically unsound to place beginning level ESL students in daily English Regents preparation courses or to center the English instruction they receive on these tests. Furthermore, teachers must have the space for instruction that goes beyond test preparation.
- Bilingual teachers should match their language(s) of instruction to the language(s) in which students will be tested, to yield valid scores on the tests that count. That said, and recognizing how current policies catch bilingual teachers in a difficult bind with regard to language alternation, the demands of the tests should also be balanced with other demands such as the knowledge required of students' futures in the United States.

Assessment and the evaluation of students, educators, and schools can be extremely valuable in improving our educational system in positive ways. However, this cannot be achieved by relying solely on standardized tests; this research documents how the drawbacks of accountability under *No Child Left Behind* outweigh the benefits for ELLs at present. It is of concern that test scores are closely aligned to race, class, and English proficiency level, yet serve as the indicator for accountability measures. As the system is now, we are simply perpetuating the inequities of students when they enter school, through the inequities of their test scores when they leave. Moreover, implicit language policies which emerge as byproducts of testing policies cannot rival the results of careful planning in providing the best possible education to ELLs.

Within the trajectory of education policy in the United States, we have arrived at a critical crossroads with regard to testing and accountability for students who are English language learners. On one hand, we have raised our expectations for these students. Yet on the other hand, we have created test-based systems that build barriers which are equally likely to impede upon the success of these students. In light of these realities, we must ensure that this becomes a time of possibility rather than liability for students who are English language learners in public schools, by creating systems that not only include but, further, promote the ideal education for these students. Doing so, as indicated in the recommendations above, is entirely feasible.

Notes

1. Language minority students in the United States are typically students living in households in which a language other than Standard English is spoken. Language minority students in need of language support services to succeed in English-medium classrooms are referred to as English language learners (ELLs) in this book. While I think the term is problematic because it makes English the sole focus (rather than home language) and because even native speakers of English are in a sense English language learners, this term is adopted here because it is an improvement over the prior term, 'limited English proficient', and because it is currently favored in the New York City school system and elsewhere in the United States.
2. Many languages have been displaced and subsequently died out as a result of linguistic contact, when languages compete to serve the same functions within the same community. Often, entire communities move from speaking one language to another through a process of 'language shift', resulting in communal loss of the first language over time. 'Reversing language shift' is a process promoted by Joshua Fishman (1991, 2001) 'to understand, limit, and rectify the societal loss of functionality in the weaker language' (Fishman, 2001: 2).
3. Ruiz (1984) argues that US language policy has typically regarded multilingualism as a 'problem' in education that must be solved by promoting English. He counters this *language-as-problem* orientation by advocating a *language-as-resource* orientation which would view each language as a resource to be managed, developed, and conserved. Likewise, research by García (1992) posits the need for careful language planning and offers a language garden analogy, with the view that language is something to be tended and cultivated.
4. To learn more about *No Child Left Behind* and ELLs in states other than New York, see the following websites:
   Center for Equity and Excellence in Education http://ceee.gwu.edu/
   Institute for Language Education Policy http://users.rcn.com/crawj/Announcing.pdf
   Jim Crawford's Language Policy Website http://ourworld.compuserve.com/homepages/JWCRAWFORD/
   Language Policy Research Unit, Arizona State University http://www.language-policy.org/blog/
   National Clearinghouse for English Language Acquisition http://www.ncela.gwu.edu/resabout/nclb/
   Teachers of English to Speakers of Other Languages (professional association) http://www.tesol.org

U.S. Department of Education http://www.ed.gov/nclb/landing.jhtml
University of California Linguistic Minority Research Institute (UC LMRI)
http://lmrinet.gse.ucsb.edu

5. Staten Island is not listed as a borough where ELLs attend school in New York City, because few ELLs live there (though this appears to be beginning to change).

6. Most English language learners take the Math A Regents exam, which is the first in the series of Math Regents exams and fulfills the minimum graduation requirement for mathematics.

7. Social promotion refers to the practice of advancing students in grade each year according to their age, rather than their academic achievement, such that students who fail might be able to move onto the next grade regardless.

8. ESL and foreign language coordinators in most cases are also teachers, whereby they teach students several periods of the day and devote the remainder of the day to administrative work.

9. All schools included in this study are located in Manhattan, the Bronx, Brooklyn, or Queens; Staten Island was not included because so few ELLs live there (New York City Department of Education, 2002).

10. This chart uses the terminology of the New York City Department of Education (2004a). Certain data were not available, because at the time this study was conducted these schools had not been in existence long enough to provide four-year pass rates or free lunch eligibility. This is indicated in the table by 'N/A' for 'not available'.

11. In the United States, free lunches are provided by the school to students from low-income families, so this category is a proxy for poverty because eligibility is based on family income.

12. Hymes (1972) defines 'communicative competence' as a speaker's ability to use language in ways that are not only grammatically correct but also contextually appropriate.

13. More advanced students can later also take the Mathematics B Regents which would make them eligible for an Advanced Regents diploma instead of a general Regents diploma.

14. It is worth noting that in spite of this principal's efforts at the time of this study to curtail the impact of the Regents exams on the school's programming by limiting preparation to the later years of high school, I have learned that the school administration has now begun preparation for the Science Regents exam in the ninth grade, driven by a need for high passing rates.

15. As detailed in Chapter 3, the RCT refers to the Regents Competency Test and is a test of basic skills that was the minimum exam requirement for a high school diploma in New York prior to 1999 and the passage of *No Child Left Behind*.

References

Abedi, J. (2001) Assessment and accommodations for English language learners: Issues and recommendations. *CRESST Policy Brief 4*. Los Angeles: National Center for Research on Evaluation, Standards, and Student Testing.

Abedi, J. (2004) The no child left behind act and English language learners: Assessment and accountability issues. *Educational Researcher* 33 (1), 4–14.

Abedi, J. and Dietal, R. (2004) Challenges in the no child left behind act for English language learners. *CRESST Policy Brief 7*. Los Angeles: National Center for Research on Evaluation, Standards, and Student Testing.

Abedi, J., Hofstetter, C. and Lord, C. (2004) Assessment accommodations for English language learners: Implications for policy-based empirical research. *Review of Educational Research* 74 (1), 1–28.

Abedi, J. and Lord, C. (2001) The language factor in mathematics tests. *Applied Measurement in Education* 14 (3), 219–234.

Advocates for Children. (2004) *An Overview of Research on the Effectiveness of Retention on Student Achievement for New York City Schoolchildren*. New York: Advocates for Children.

Ager, D. (2001) *Motivation in Language Planning and Language Policy*. Clevedon: Multilingual Matters.

Alamillo, L. and Viramontes, C. (2000) Reflections from the classroom: Teacher perspectives on the implementation of proposition 227. *Bilingual Research Journal* 24 (1 & 2), 1–13.

Alexander, N. (1999) English unassailable but unattainable: The dilemma of language policy in South African education. Paper presented at the Biennial Conference of the International Federation for the Teaching of English. On WWW at http://www.nyu.edy/education/teachlearn/ifte/war99.htm. Accessed 6.4.02.

Amrein, A. and Berliner, D. (2002) *An Analysis of Some Unintended and Negative Consequences of High-Stakes Testing*. Tempe: Education Policy Research Unit, Arizona State University. On WWW at http://www.asu.edu/educ/epsl/EPRU/epru_2002_Research_Writing.htm. Accessed 15.3.03.

Anstrom, K. (1995) New directions for Chapter 1/Title I. *Directions in Language and Education* 1 (7), 1–11. Washington, DC: National Clearinghouse for Bilingual Education.

Antunez, B. and Menken, K. (2000) *An Overview of the Preparation and Certification of Teachers Working with LEP Students*. Washington, DC: NCELA. On WWW at http://www.ncela.gwu.edu/pubs/reports/teacherprep/teacherprep.pdf. Accessed 8.4.03.

Arenson, K.W. (2003a) Education dept. test chief has resigned, regents say. *New York Times.*

Arenson, K. (2003b) Math failures are raising concerns about curriculum. *New York Times.*

Arenson, K. (2004) More youths opt for G.E.D., skirting high-school hurdle. *New York Times.*

Artiles, A. and Trent, S. (1994) Overrepresentation of minority students in special education: A continuing debate. *Journal of Special Education* 27 (4), 410–437.

August, D. and Hakuta, K. (eds). (1997) *Improving Schooling for Language-Minority Children: A Research Agenda.* Committee on Developing a Research Agenda on the Education of Limited-English-Proficient and Bilingual Students, Board on Children, Youth, and Families, National Research Council. Washington, DC: National Academy Press.

Baker, C. (1995) Bilingual education and assessment. In B.M. Jones and P. Ghuman (eds) *Bilingualism, Education and Identity* (pp. 130–158). Cardiff: University of Wales Press.

Baker, C. (2001) *Foundations of Bilingual Education and Bilingualism* (3rd edn). Clevedon: Multilingual Matters.

Ben-Rafael, E. (1994) *Language, Identity, and Social Division: The Case of Israel.* Oxford: Oxford University Press.

Blank, R., Manise, J. and Brathwaite, B. (1999) *State Education Indicators with a Focus on Title I.* Washington, DC: Council of Chief State Schools Officers, Planning Evaluation Service of the U.S. Department of Education.

Brisk, M. (2005) *Bilingual Education: From Compensatory to Quality Schooling.* Mahwah, NJ: Lawrence Erlbaum Associates.

California Department of Education (2004) Questions and answers about the California high school exit examination (CAHSEE) test variations. Sacramento, CA: California. Department of Education. On WWW at http://www.cde.ca.gov/ta/tg/hs/documents/qandatestvar.pdf. Accessed 20.3.06.

California Department of Education (2005a) California high school exit examination (*CAHSEE*) October 2005 English language arts released test questions. Sacramento, CA: California Department of Education. On WWW at http://www.cde.ca.gov/ta/tg/hs/elartq.asp. Accessed 20.3.06.

California Department of Education (2005b) California high school exit examination (*CAHSEE*) questions and answers for parents/guardians. Sacramento, CA: California Department of Education. On WWW at http://www.cde.ca.gov/ta/tg/hs/documents/infoparents05.pdf. Accessed 20.3.06.

Cameron, S. and Heckman, J. (1993) The nonequivalence of high school equivalents. *Journal of Labor Economics* 11 (1), 1–47.

Campaign for Fiscal Equity. (2004) *The CFE Decision: What Did the Court Decide and What Does it Mean for You and Your Community?* New York. On WWW at http://www.cfequity.org/. Accessed 21.11.04.

Campanile, C. (2004) Higher 'degree' of HS kids seek GED. *New York Post.*

Canagarajah, S. (ed.). (2005) *Reclaiming the Local in Language Policy and Practice.* Mahwah, NJ: Lawrence Erlbaum Associates.

Capps, R., Fix, M., Murray, J., Ost, J., Passel, J. and Herwantoro, S. (2005) *The New Demography of America's Schools: Immigration and the No Child Left Behind Act.* Washington, DC: Urban Institute.

Center for Applied Linguistics (2002) *Directory of Two-Way Bilingual Immersion Programs in the U.S.* Washington, DC.

Center on Education Policy (2005) States try harder, but gaps persist: High school exit exams. Written by P. Sullivan, M. Yeager, N. Chudowsky, N. Kober, E. O'Brien and K. Gayler. Washington, DC.

Cheng, L. and Watanabe, Y. (eds), with Curtis, A. (ed.) (2004) *Washback in Language Testing: Research Contexts and Methods.* Mahwah, NJ: Lawrence Earlbaum Associates.

Cooper, R.L. (1989) *Language Planning and Social Change.* Cambridge: Cambridge University Press.

Corson, D. (1999) *Language Policy in Schools: A Resource for Teachers and Administrators.* New Jersey: Lawrence Erlbaum Associates.

Council of the Great City Schools and National Clearinghouse for English Language Acquisition and Language Instruction Educational Programs. (2002) *Assessment Standards for English Language Learners: Executive Summary.* Published draft. On WWW at http://www.ncela.gwu.edu/ncbepubs/assessmentstandards/execsum/executivesummary3.htm. Accessed 10.10.02.

Crabtree, B. and Miller, W. (eds). (1992) *Doing Qualitative Research: Multiple Strategies.* Newbury Park: SAGE Publications.

Crawford, J. (1992a) *Language Loyalties: A Sourcebook on the Official English Controversy.* Chicago: University of Chicago Press.

Crawford, J. (1992b) *Hold Your Tongue: Bilingualism and the Politics of English-Only.* Reading, MA: Addison-Wesley.

Crawford, J. (1998) Language politics in the United States. In C. Ovando and P. McLaren (eds) *The Politics of Multiculturalism and Bilingual Education: Students and Teachers Caught in the Cross Fire* (pp. 107–147). New York: McGraw Hill.

Crawford, J. (1999) *Bilingual Education: History, Politics, Theory and Practice.* Los Angeles: Bilingual Education Services Inc.

Crawford, J. (2000) *At War with Diversity: US Language Policy in an Age of Anxiety.* Clevedon: Multilingual Matters.

Crawford, J. (2001) *Proposition 203: Anti-bilingual Initiative in Arizona.* On WWW at http://ourworld.compuserve.com/homepages/JWCRAWFORD/az-unz.htm. Accessed 11.11.04.

Crawford, J. (2002a) Making sense of Census 2000. Tempe, AZ: Language Policy Research Unit, Education Policy Studies Laboratory, Arizona State University. On WWW at http://www.asu.edu/educ/epsl/LPRU/features/article5.htm. Accessed 19.7.06.

Crawford, J. (2002b) OBITUARY: The bilingual ed act, 1968–2002. *Rethinking Schools Online,* 16 (4), 1–4. On WWW at http://www.rethinkingschools.org/archive/16_04/Bil164.shtml. Accessed 25.7.06.

Crawford, J. (2004) No child left behind: Misguided approach to school accountability for English language learners. Paper for the Forum on ideas to improve the NCLB accountability provisions for students with disabilities and English language learners. Washington, DC: Center on Education Policy & National Association for Bilingual Education.

Cuban, L. (1998) How schools change reforms. *Teachers College Record* 99 (3), 453–477.

Cummins, J. (1992) Language proficiency, bilingualism, and academic achievement. In P. Richard-Amato and M. Snow (eds) *The Multicultural Classroom: Readings for Content-Area Teachers* (pp. 16–26). White Plains, NY: Longman.

Cummins, J. (2000) *Language, Power, and Pedagogy: Bilingual Children in the Crossfire.* Clevedon: Multilingual Matters.

Dale, T. and Cuevas, G. (1992) Integrating mathematics and language learning. In P. Richard-Amato and M. Snow (eds) *The Multicultural Classroom: Readings for Content-Area Teachers* (pp. 330–348). White Plains, NY: Longman.

Davila, J. (2004) *Ready or Not: On Eve of English Regents Exam, Immigrant Groups Protest Unfair Test, Poor Preparation of Students, and Dropout Crisis*. Press Release. New York: New York Immigration Coalition.

Dee, T. and Jacob, B. (2006) Do high school exit exams influence educational attainment or labor market performance? *NBER Working Paper*, No. W12199 (April 2006). On WWW at http://ssrn.com/abstract = 900985. Accessed 11.7.06.

Del Valle, S. (2002) *A Briefing Paper of the Puerto Rican Legal Defense Fund on the New English Regents Exam and Its Impact on English Language Learners*. New York: Puerto Rican Legal Defense and Education Fund.

Education Trust. (2003) *"Don't Turn Back the Clock!" Over 100 African American and Latino Superintendents Voice Their Support for the Accountability Provisions in Title I (NCLB)* (press release). Washington, DC: Education Trust.

Elmore, R. and Rothman, R. (eds) (1999) *Testing, Teaching, and Learning: A Guide for States and School Districts*. Committee on Title I Testing and Assessment, the National Research Council. Washington, DC: National Academy Press.

Escamilla, K., Mahon, E., Riley-Bernal, H. and Rutledge, D. (2003) High-stakes testing, Latinos, and English language learners: Lessons from Colorado. *Bilingual Research Journal* 27 (1), 25–49.

Evans, B. and Hornberger, N. (2005) No child left behind: Repealing and unpeeling federal language education policy in the United States. *Language Policy* 4, 87–106.

Fettes, M. (1997) Language planning and education. In R. Wodak and D. Corson (eds) *Encyclopedia of Language and Education, Volume 1: Language Policy and Political Issues in Education*. Boston: Kluwer Academic.

Fishman, J. (1979) Bilingual education, language planning and English. *English World-Wide* 1 (1), 11–24.

Fishman, J. (1991) *Reversing Language Shift*. Clevedon: Multilingual Matters.

Fishman, J. (ed.) (2001) *Can Threatened Languages be Saved? "Reversing Language Shift" Revisited*. Clevedon: Multilingual Matters.

Fishman, J., Conrad, A. and Rubal-Lopez, A. (eds). (1996) *Post-Imperial English. Status Change in Former British and American Colonies, 1940–1990*. Berlin and New York: Mouton de Gruyter.

Fowler, F. (2000) *Policy Studies for Educational Leaders: An Introduction*. Upper Saddle River, NJ: Merrill.

Freeman, R. (2004) *Building on Community Bilingualism: Promoting Multiculturalism Through Schooling*. Philadelphia: Caslon Publishing.

Gàndara, P. (2000) In the aftermath of the storm: English learners in the post-227 era. *Bilingual Research Journal* 24 (1 & 2), 1–13.

García, O. (1992) Societal bilingualism and multilingualism (mimeo). Cited in C. Baker, *Foundations of Bilingual Education and Bilingualism, 1996*. Clevedon: Multilingual Matters.

García, O. (1997) Bilingual education. In F. Coulmas (ed.) *The Handbook of Sociolinguistics* (pp. 405–420). Oxford: Blackwell.

García, O. (2002) New York's multilingualism: World languages and their role in a U.S. city. In O. García and J.A. Fishman (eds) *The Multilingual Apple: Languages in New York City* (2nd edn) (pp. 3–50). Berlin and New York: Mouton de Gruyter.

García, O. and Fishman, J. (eds) (2002) *The Multilingual Apple: Languages in New York City* (2nd edn). Berlin and New York: Mouton de Gruyter.

García, O. and Menken, K. (2006) The English of Latinos from a plurilingual trans-cultural angle: Implications for assessment and schools. In S. Nero (ed.) *Dialects, Englishes, Creoles, and Education.* Clevedon: Multilingual Matters.

García, O., Morín, J. and Rivera, K. (2001) How threatened is the Spanish of New York Puerto Ricans? In J. Fishman (ed.) *Can Threatened Languages be Saved?* (pp. 44–73). Clevedon: Multilingual Matters.

García, O. and Trubek, J. (1999) Where have all the minority educators gone and when will they ever learn? *Educators for Urban Minorities,* 1, 1–8.

García, P. (2003) The use of high school exit examinations in four southwestern states. *Bilingual Research Journal* 27 (3), 431–450.

Garcia, P. and Gopal, M. (2003) The relationship to achievement on the California high school exit exam for language minority students. *NABE Jounral of Research and Practice* 1 (1), 123–137.

Gardner, N. (2000) *Basque in Education in the Basque Autonomous Community.* Vitoria-Gasteiz: Euskal Autonomi Erkidegoko Administrazioa.

Glinert, L. (1995) Inside the language planner's head: Tactical responses to a mass immigration. *Journal of Multilingual and Multicultural Development* 16 (5), 351–371.

Glod, M. (2007) Fairfax resists 'no child' provision: Immigrants' tests in English at issue. *Washington Post.*

Goertz, M. and Duffy, M. (2001) *Assessment and Accountability Systems in the 50 States.* Philadelphia: Consortium for Policy Research in Education, University of Pennsylvania. On WWW at http://www.cpre.org/Publications/rr46.pdf. Accessed 15.1.03.

Gormley, M. (2004) Bill exempts English learners from exam. *New York Newsday.* On WWW at http://www.nynewsday.com/news/education/ny-bc-ny-english learners0612jun12,0,4219897.story?coll=nyc-manheadlines-education. Accessed 12.6.04.

Government Accountability Office. (2006) *No Child Left Behind Act: Assistance from Education Could Help States Better Measure Progress of Students with Limited English Proficiency.* Washington, DC.

Gutiérrez, K., Asato, J., Pacheco, M., Moll, L., Olson, K., Horng, E., Ruiz, R., García, E. and McCarty, T. (2002) 'Sounding American': The consequences of new reforms for English language learners. *Reading Research Quarterly* 37 (3), 328–343.

Hakuta, K. (1986) *The Mirror of Language: The Debate on Bilingualism.* New York: Basic Books.

Halliday, M. (1975) Some aspects of sociolinguistics. In E. Jacobsen (ed.) *Interactions Between Linguistics and Mathematical Education: Final Report of the Symposium Sponsored by UNESCO, CEDO and ICMI,* Nairobi, Kenya. UNESCO report No. ED-74/Conf. 808 (pp. 25–52). Paris: UNESCO.

Harris, J. and Ford, D. (1991) Identifying and nurturing the promise of gifted black American children. *Journal of Negro Education* 60 (1), 3–18.

Haugen, E. (1983) The implementation of corpus planning: Theory and practice. In J. Cobarrubias and J. Fishman (eds) *Progress in Language Planning* (pp. 269–290). Berlin and New York: Mouton/Walter de Gruyter.

Hayes, B. and Read, J. (2004) IELTS test preparation in New Zealand: Preparing students for the IELTS academic module. In L. Cheng and Y. Watanabe (eds) with

A. Curtis (ed.) *Washback in Language Testing: Research Contexts and Methods* (pp. 97–112). Mahwah, NJ: Lawrence Earlbaum Associates.

Heath, S. (1983) *Ways with Words*. New York: Cambridge University Press.

Herszenhorn, D. (2006a) U.S. says language exam does not comply with law. *New York Times*.

Herszenhorn, D. (2006b) More students in New York will take regular English test. *New York Times*.

Heubert, J. (2002) First, do no harm. *Educational Leadership* 60 (4), 26–30.

Heubert, J. and Hauser, R. (eds) (1999) *High Stakes Testing for Tracking, Promotion, and Graduation*. Washington, DC: National Academy Press.

Heugh, K. (1999) Languages, development and reconstructing education in South Africa. *International Journal of Educational Development* 19, 301–313.

Hill, P. (2000) The federal role in education. In D. Ravitch (ed.) *Brookings Papers on Education Policy 2000* (pp. 11–40). Washington, DC: Brookings Institution Press.

Holmes, D., Hedlund, P. and Nickerson, B. (2000) *Accommodating English Language Learners in State and Local Assessments*. Washington, DC: National Clearinghouse for Bilingual Education.

Hornberger, N. (ed.) (1996) *Indigenous Literacies in the Americas: Language Planning from the Bottom Up*. Berlin and New York: Mouton de Gruyter.

Hornberger, N. (2006a) Nichols to NCLB: Local and global perspectives on U.S. language education policy. In O. García, T. Skutnabb-Kangas and M. Torres-Guzmán (eds) *Imagining Multilingual Schools: Languages in Education and Glocalization* (pp. 223–237). Clevedon: Multilingual Matters.

Hornberger, N. (2006b) Frameworks and models in language policy and planning. In T. Ricento (ed.) *An Introduction to Language Policy: Theory and Method* (pp. 24–41). Malden, MA: Blackwell Publishing.

Hull, D. (2006). Appeals court upholds exit exam: State schools superintendent hails ruling. *The Mercury News*. On WWW at http://www.mercurynews.com/mld/mercurynews/news/15259081.htm. Accessed 20.8.06.

Hymes, D. (1972) On communicative competence. In J. Pride and J. Holmes (eds) *Sociolinguistics: Selected Readings* (pp. 269–293). Harmondsworth: Penguin Education.

Judd, C., Kidder, L. and Smith, E. (1991) *Research Methods in Social Relations*. Fort Worth: Holt, Rinehart, and Winston.

Kabbany, J. (2006) Southwest County has at least 1,200 seniors yet to pass exit exam. *The Californian*.

Kaestle, C.F. (2001) Federal aid to education since World War II: Purposes and politics. In *The Future of the Federal Role in Elementary and Secondary Education* (pp. 13–35). Washington, DC: Center on Education Policy. On WWW at http://www.ctredpol.org/pubs/futurefederal_esa/future_fed_role_kaestle.htm. Accessed 7.1.03.

Kaplan, R. and Baldauf, R. (1997) *Language Planning: From Practice to Theory*. Philadelphia: Multilingual Matters.

Kindler, A. (2002) Survey of the states' limited English proficient students and available educational programs and services, 2000–2001 summary report. Washington, DC: National Clearinghouse for English Language Acquisition. On WWW at http://www.ncela.gwu.edu/states/reports/seareports/0001/sea0001.pdf. Accessed 2.4.03.

Kleyn, T. (2007) Multicultural education and bilingual teachers: An examination of convergence and divergence across ethnolinguistic groups. Unpublished doctoral dissertation, Teachers College, Columbia University.

Kloss, H. (1977) *The American Bilingual Tradition*. Rowley, MA: Newbury House.

Kuzel, A. (1992) Sampling in qualitative inquiry. In B. Crabtree and W. Miller (eds) *Doing Qualitative Research: Multiple Strategies* (pp. 31–44). Newbury Park: SAGE Publications.

Lakshmi, R. (2006) House committee reviews the case of making English the official language of the US. *Washington Post*.

LeCompte, M. and Preissle, J. (1993) *Ethnography and Qualitative Design in Educational Research* (2nd edn). San Diego: Academic Press.

Lewin, T. (2004) City resolves legal battle over forcing students out. *New York Times*. On WWW at http://www.nytimes.com/2004/06/19/education/19pushout.html. Accessed 19.6.04.

Liebowitz, A. (1969) English literacy: Legal sanction for discrimination. *Notre Dame Lawyer* 45 (1), 7–67.

Linn, R. (2000) Assessments and accountability. *Educational Researcher* 29 (2), 4–16.

Marketwire. (2007) Kansas house approves making English the official language: State could become 29th with official English policy. Washington, DC. On WWW at http://www.sys-con.com/read/340274.htm. Accessed 26.2.07.

McCarty, T. (2003) Revitalising indigenous languages in homogenising times. *Comparative Education* 39 (2), 147–163.

McCarty, T. (2004) Dangerous difference: A critical-historical analysis of language education policies in the United States. In J. Tollefson and A. Tsui (eds) *Medium of Instruction Policies: Which Agenda? Whose Agenda?* (pp. 71–96). Mahwah, NJ: Lawrence Erlbaum Associates.

McKay, S. and Weinstein-Shr, G. (1993) English literacy in the U.S.: National policies, personal consequences. *TESOL Quarterly* 27 (3), 1–14.

McLaughlin, M. and Shepard, L. (1995) *Improving Education Through Standards-Based Reform: A Report by the National Academy of Education Panel on Standards-Based Education Reform*. Stanford: National Academy of Education.

McNeil, L. and Valenzuela, A. (2000) The harmful impact of the TAAS system of testing in Texas: Beneath the accountability rhetoric. *Occasional Paper Series*, 1 (1). Houston, TX: Rice University Center for Education. In G. Orfield and M. Kornhaber (eds) *Raising Standards or Raising Barriers? Inequality and High Stakes Testing in Public Education* (pp. 127–150) Boston, MA: Harvard Civil Rights Project.

Menken, K. (2000) What are the critical issues in wide-scale assessment of English language learners? *NCBE Issue Brief No. 6*. Washington, DC: National Clearinghouse for Bilingual Education. On WWW at http://www.ncbe.gwu.edu/ncbepubs/issuebriefs/ib6.pdf. Accessed 2.5.02.

Menken, K. (2001) When all means all: Standards-based reform and English language learners. *NABE News* 24 (5), 4–7.

Menken, K. (2005) When the test is what counts: How high-stakes testing affects language policy and the education of english language learners in high school. Unpublished doctoral dissertation, Teachers College, Columbia University.

Menken, K. (2006a) Historical overview of policies for English language learners. In R. Freeman and E. Hamayan, (eds) *Educating English Language Learners: A Guide for Administrators* (pp. 1–5). Philadelphia, PA: Caslon Publishing.

Menken, K. (2006b) Teaching to the test: How standardized testing promoted by the No Child Left Behind Act impacts language policy, curriculum, and instruction for English language learners. *Bilingual Research Journal* 30 (2), 521–546.

Menken, K. (in press) High-stakes testing as de facto language policy in education. In E. Shohamy and N. Hornberger (eds) *Encyclopedia of Language and Education* (Vol. 7): *Language Testing and Assessment*. Netherlands: Kluwer.

Mensh, E. and Mensh, H. (1991) *The IQ Mythology: Class, Race, Gender, and Inequality*. Carbondale, IL: Southern Illinois University Press.

Miles, M. and Huberman, A. (1994) *Qualitative Data Analysis: An Expanded Sourcebook* (2nd edn). Thousand Oaks: SAGE Publications.

Mishler, E. (1986) *Research Interviewing: Context and Narrative*. Cambridge: Harvard University Press.

National Center for Education Statistics. (1997). *1993–94 Schools and Staffing Survey: A Profile of Policies and Practices for Limited English Proficient Students: Screening Methods, Program Support, and Teacher Training*. Washington, DC: U.S. Department of Education, Office of Educational Research and Improvement.

National Clearinghouse for English Language Acquisition. (1999) *State K-12 LEP Enrollment and Top Languages*. Washington, DC. On WWW at http://www. ncela.gwu.edu/pubs/reports/state-data/1998/index.htm. Accessed 20.12.99.

National Clearinghouse for English Language Acquisition. (2002) How has federal policy for language minority students evolved in the US? *AskNCELA No. 3*. Washington, DC. On WWW at http://www.ncela.gwu.edu/askncela/ 03history.htm. Accessed 10.1.03.

National Clearinghouse for English Language Acquisition. (2004) How many school-aged English language learners (ELLS) are there in the U.S.? *AskNCELA No. 1*. Updated October 2004 by Daniel Padolsky. Washington, DC. On WWW at http://www.ncela.gwu.edu/askncela/01leps.htm. Accessed 10.11.04.

National Clearinghouse for English Language Acquisition. (2006a) The growing number of limited English proficient students 1994/95–2004/05. Poster. Washington, DC. On WWW at http://www.ncela.gwu.edu/policy/states/ reports/statedata/2004LEP/GrowingLEP_0405_Nov06.pdf. Accessed 10.2.07.

National Clearinghouse for English Language Acquisition. (2006b) History. Washington, DC. On WWW at http://www.ncela.gwu.edu/policy/1_history.htm. Accessed 19.7.06.

New York City Department of Education, Division of Assessment and Accountability. (2003a) *2002–2003 Citywide and Statewide Assessment Calendar*. New York. On WWW at http://www.nycenet.edu/daa/schedule/index.html. Accessed 3.4.03.

New York City Department of Education, Division of Assessment and Accountability. (2003b) *2001–2002 Annual School Reports*. New York. On WWW at http://www.nycenet.edu/daa/SchoolReports/. Accessed 12.3.03.

New York City Department of Education, Division of Assessment and Accountability. (2004a) *2002–2003 Annual School Reports*. New York. On WWW at http://www.nycenet.edu/daa/SchoolReports/. Accessed 1.6.04.

New York City Department of Education, Division of Assessment and Accountability. (2004b) *The Class of 2003 Four-Year Longitudinal Report and 2002–2003 Event Dropout Rates.* New York. On WWW at http://www.nycenet.edu/daa/reports. Accessed 1.6.04.

New York City Department of Education, Division of Assessment and Accountability. (2005) *2004–2005 Annual School Reports.* New York. On WWW at http://www.nycenet.edu/daa/reports/Class%20of%202005_Four-Year_ Longitudinal_ Report.pdf. Accessed 26.6.06.

New York City Department of Education, Division of English Language Learners and Parent Outreach. (2002) *Facts and Figures 2001–2002.* New York. On WWW at http://www.nycenet.edu/offices/oell/Facts%20%20Figures%202001% 20%202002.pdf. Accessed 1.4.03.

New York City Department of Education, Directory of Offices and Divisions (2006a) *Statistical Summaries.* On WWW at http://www.nycenet.edu/offices/stats/ default.htm. Accessed 15.6.06.

New York City Department of Education, Office of English Language Learners. (2006b) *ELLs in New York City: Student Demographic Data Report.* New York: New York City Department of Education.

New York City Independent Budget Office. (2004) Can schools' ESL and bilingual programs make the grade? Written by N. Rivas Salas and M. Madrick. *Inside the Budget,* 128.

New York State Assembly Standing Committee on Education. (2003) *Regents Learning Standards and High School Graduation Requirements.* Notice of Public Hearing, New York City. New York: New York State.

New York State Department of Education. (2003) *English Language Arts Regents Examinations.* New York. On WWW at http://www.nysedregents.org/testing/ engre/arceng.html. Accessed 10.5.06.

New York State Department of Education. (2004a) *English Language Arts Regents Examinations.* New York. On WWW at http://www.nysedregents.org/ testing/engre/arceng.html. Accessed 10.5.06.

New York State Department of Education. (2004b) *Living Environment Regents Examination.* New York. On WWW at http://www.nysedregents.org/ testing/scire/regentlive.html. Accessed 10.5.06.

New York State Department of Education. (2004c) *Math A Regents Examinations.* New York. On WWW at http://www.nysedregents.org/testing/mathre/ regentmatha.html. Accessed 10.5.06.

New York State Department of Education, Bilingual/ESL Network. (2003) *Announcements.* New York. On WWW at http://www.emsc.nysed.gov/ciai/ biling/announce.html. Accessed 3.4.03.

New York State Department of Education, Commissioner of Education (1999a) Part 154. *Apportionment and Services for Pupils with Limited English Proficiency.* New York.

New York State Department of Education, Office of Bilingual Education. (1999b) *Testing Procedures for Limited English Proficient (LEP) Students.* Memorandum from Carmen Perez Hogan, Coordinator, Office of Bilingual Education to District Superintendents, Principals, and C.R. Part 154 contacts. On WWW at http:// www.emsc.nysed.gov/ciai/biling/pub/memo010499.html. Accessed 3.4.03.

New York State Department of Education, Office of Bilingual Education. (2002) *Application for Part 154 of the Regulations of the Commissioner (CR Part 154) and Title III, Part A of the No Child Left Behind Act of 2001 for the Education of Limited English*

Proficient (LEP) Students for the 2002–03 School Year. Memorandum from Carmen Perez Hogan, Coordinator, Office of Bilingual Education to District and School Superintendents. On WWW at http://www.emsc.nysed.gov/ciai/biling/CRPT154-TIII-RFP.doc. Accessed 3.4.03.

New York State Department of Education, Office of Curriculum, Instruction, and Assessment. (2003a) Regents and high school diploma/graduation requirements. *Section 100.5 of the Regulations of the Commissioner of Education Relating to General Education and Diploma Requirements*. On WWW at http://www. emsc. nysed.gov/part100/pages/1005a.html. Accessed 28.4.03.

New York State Department of Education, Office of Curriculum, Instruction, and Assessment. (2003b) *Component Retesting in Comprehensive English and Mathematics A in May 2003*. Memorandum to district superintendents and secondary school principals. Dated February 2003. On WWW at http://www.emsc.nysed.gov/ciai/testing/retest/memoretest03.htm. Accessed 28.4.03.

New York State Department of Education, Office of Elementary, Middle, Secondary and Continuing Education. (2000) *General Education and Diploma Requirements*. Albany, NY: New York State Department of Education.

Northeast Islands Regional Educational Laboratory at Brown University. (1999) Creating large-scale portfolio assessments that include English language learners. *Perspectives on Policy and Practice*. Providence. On WWW at http://www.lab. brown.edu/public/pubs/PolPerELL.pdf. Accessed 12.9.02.

Orfield, G. (2001) *Schools More Separate: Consequences of a Decade of Resegregation*. Cambridge, MA: The Civil Rights Project of Harvard University.

Padolsky, D. (2005) How many school-aged English language learners (ELLs) are there in the U.S.? *NCELA Frequently Asked Question #1*. Washington, DC: National Clearinghouse for English Language Acquisition. On WWW at http://www. ncela.gwu.edu/pubs/reports/state-data/1998/index.htm. Accessed 3.4.06.

Pennock-Roman, M. and Rivera, C. (2006) *A Review of Test Accommodations for ELLs: Effect Sizes in Reducing the Mean Achievement Gap*. Paper presented at the Annual Meeting of the American Educational Research Association, San Francisco, CA.

Phillipson, R. (1992) *Linguistic Imperialism*. Oxford: Oxford University Press.

Phillipson, R. and Skutnabb-Kangas, T. (1996) English only worldwide or language ecology? *TESOL Quarterly* 30 (3), 429–452.

Phillipson, R., Skutnabb-Kangas, T. and Rannut, M. (eds) (1995) *Linguistic Human Rights*. Berlin and New York: Mouton de Gruyter.

Pitsch, M. (1996) To placate conservatives, measure alters Goals 2000. *Education Week*.

Qi, L. (2005) Stakeholders' conflicting aims undermine the washback function of a high-stakes test. *Language Testing* 22 (2), 142–173.

Rappaport, S. (2002) *Beyond Bilingual Education: Meeting the Needs of English Language Learners in the New York City Public Schools*. New York: Puerto Rican Legal Defense and Education Fund.

Reid, K. and Valle, J. (2004) The discursive practice of learning disability: Implications for instruction and parent-school relations. *Journal of Learning Disabilities* 37 (6), 466–481.

Reyes, L. (2006) The Aspira consent decree: A thirtieth-anniversary retrospective of bilingual education in New York City. *Harvard Educational Review* 76 (3), 369–400.

Ricento, T. (1995) A brief history of language restrictionism in the United States. In S. Dicker, R. Jackson, T. Ricento and K. Romstedt (eds) *Official English?*

No!: TESOL's Recommendations for Countering the Official English Movement in the U.S. Washington, DC: TESOL.

Ricento, T. and Hornberger, N. (1996) Unpeeling the onion: Language planning and policy and the ELT professional. *TESOL Quarterly* 30 (3), 401–427.

Richard-Amato, P. and Snow, M. (eds). (1992) *The Multicultural Classroom: Readings for Content-Area Teachers.* White Plains, NY: Longman.

Richards, J. and Rodgers, T. (2001) *Approaches and Methods in Language Teaching.* Cambridge: Cambridge University Press.

Riddle, W. (1999) Education for the disadvantaged: ESEA Title I reauthorization issues. *Congressional Research Service Issue Brief.* Washington, DC: The Library of Congress.

Rivera, C. and Collum, E. (eds) (2006) *State Assessment Policy and Practice for English Language Learners: A National Perspective.* Mahwah, N: Lawrence Erlbaum Associates.

Rivera, C. and Stansfield, C. (1998) Leveling the playing field for English language learners: Increasing participation in state and local assessments through accommodations. In R. Brandt (ed.) *Assessing Student Learning: New Rules, New Realities* (pp. 65–92). Arlington, VA: Educational Research Service.

Rivera, C. and Stansfield, C. (2000) *An Analysis of State Policies for the Inclusion and Accommodation of English Language Learners in State Assessment Programs During 1998–1999. (Executive Summary).* Washington, DC: Center for Equity and Excellence in Education, The George Washington University.

Rotberg, I. (2000) Campaign 2000: Notes to the next president on education policy. *Education Week* 19 (28), 29 March 2000.

Rothstein, R. (2002) Lessons: States teeter when balancing standards with tests. *The New York Times.*

Ruiz, R. (1984) Orientations in language planning. *NABE Journal* 8 (2), 15–34.

Ruiz de Velasco, J. (2005) Performance-based school reforms and the federal role in helping schools that serve language-minority students. In A. Valenzuela (ed.) *Leaving Children Behind: How "Texas-Style" Accountability Fails Latino Youth* (pp. 33–56). Albany, NY: State University of New York Press.

Rumbaut, R., Massey, D. and Bean, F. (2006) Linguistic life expectancies: Immigrant language retention in southern California. *Population and Development Review* 32 (3), 447–460.

Rumberger, R. (2006) California's exit exam fails employers. *Los Angeles Times.*

Shohamy, E. (1998) Critical language testing and beyond. *Studies in Educational Evaluation* 24 (4), 331–345.

Shohamy, E. (2001) *The Power of Tests: A Critical Perspective on the Uses of Language Tests.* London: Longman/Pearson Education.

Shohamy, E. (2003) Implications of language education policies for language study in schools and universities. *Modern Language Journal* 87 (ii), 278–296.

Shohamy, E. (2006) *Language Policy: Hidden Agendas and New Approaches.* London: Routledge.

Skutnabb-Kangas, T. (2000) *Linguistic Genocide in Education – Or Worldwide Diversity and Human Rights?* Mahwah: Lawrence Earlbaum Associates.

Sobol, T. (2004a) No child left behind. Unpublished manuscript.

Sobol, T. (2004b) A president that "gets it." In C. Glickman (ed.) *Letters to the Next President: What We Can Do About the Real Crisis in Public Education.* New York: Teachers College Press.

Solano-Flores, G. and Trumball, E. (2003) Examining language in context: The need for new research paradigms in the testing of English-language learners. *Educational Researcher* 32 (2), 3–13.

Spolsky, B. (1995) *Measured Words: The Development of Objective Language Testing.* Oxford: Oxford University Press.

Spolsky, B. (1998) *Sociolinguistics.* Oxford: Oxford University Press.

Spolsky, B. (2004) *Language Policy.* Cambridge: Cambridge University Press.

Spolsky, B. and Shohamy, E. (1999) *The Languages of Israel: Policy, Ideology, and Practice.* Philadelphia: Mutilingual Matters.

Stansfield, C. and Rivera, C. (2002) How will English language learners be accommodated in state assessments? In R. Lissitz and W. Scafer (eds) *Assessment in Educational Reform: Both Means and Ends* (pp. 125–144). Boston, MA: Allyn and Bacon.

Steiner-Khamsi, G. (ed.) (2004) *The Global Politics of Educational Borrowing and Lending.* New York, NY: Teachers College Press.

Sullivan, P., Yeager, M., Chudowsky, N., Kober, N., O'Brien, E. and Gayler, K. (2005) *State High School Exit Exams: States Try Harder, But Gaps Persist.* Washington, DC: Center on Education Policy.

Texas Education Agency. (2004) *Texas Assessment of Knowledge and Skills (TAKS) Exit Level English Language Arts, Mathematics, Social Studies, Science.* Administered July 2004. On WWW at http://www.tea.state.tx.us/student.assessment/resources/release/taks/2004/gr11taksjulyb.pdf. Accessed 3.4.06.

Texas Education Agency, Student Assessment Division. (2004) *Texas Assessment of Knowledge and Skills (TAKS) Information Booklet.* Austin, TX. On WWW at http://www.tea.state.tx.us/student.assessment/taks/booklets/math/g11.pdf. Accessed 3.4.06.

Thomas, W. and Collier, V. (1997) *School Effectiveness for Language Minority Students.* Washington, DC: National Clearinghouse for Bilingual Education.

Tollefson, J. (1991) *Planning Language, Planning Inequality: Language Policy in the Community.* London and New York: Longman.

Uebelacker, K. (2005) *Fair Testing.* Teacher Action Research Paper. San Francisco: San Francisco Education Fund Leadership Institute. On WWW at http://www.teachersnetwork.org/tnli/research/prep/uebelacker.htm. Accessed 27.3.06.

Urban Teacher Collaborative. (2000) *The Urban Teacher Challenge: Teacher Demand and Supply in the Great City Schools.* On WWW at http://cgcs.org/reports/2000/RNT-0101.pdf. Accessed 20.7.00.

US Census Bureau. (2000) QT-P16 Language spoken at home: 2000. *Census 2000 Summary File 3.* Washington, DC. US Census Bureau.

US Citizenship and Immigration Services (2004) A guide to naturalization. Form M-476. On WWW at http://www.uscis.gov/graphics/services/natz/guide.htm. Accessed 14.8.06.

US Department of Education. (1994) *The Improving America's Schools Act of 1994: Summary Sheets.* Washington, DC.

US Department of Education. (2001) *The No Child Left Behind Act of 2001.* P.L. 107–110. Washington, DC.

US Department of Education, Office of English Language Acquisition, Language Enhancement, and Academic Achievement for Limited English Proficient Students. (2003) *DRAFT Non-regulatory Guidance on the Title III State Formula Grant Program. Part II: Standards, Assessments, and Accountability.* Washington, DC.

US Department of Education, Office of the Education Secretary. (2006) Secretary Spellings announces partnership with states to improve accountability for limited English proficient students. Press Release, July 27, 2006. On WWW at http://www.ed.gov/news/pressreleases/2006/07/07272006.html. Accessed 1.8.06.

Valencia, R. and Villarreal, B. (2005) Texas' second wave of high-stakes testing: Anti-social promotion legislation, grade retention, and adverse impact on minorities. In A. Valenzuela (ed.) *Leaving Children Behind: How "Texas-Style" Accountability Fails Latino Youth* (pp. 113–152). Albany, NY: State University of New York Press.

Valenzuela, A. (1999) *Subtractive Schooling: U.S.-Mexican Youth and the Politics of Caring*. Albany, NY: State University of New York Press.

Valenzuela, A. (2002) High-stakes testing and U.S.-Mexican youth in Texas: The case for multiple compensatory criteria in assessment. *Harvard Journal of Hispanic Policy* 14, 97–116.

Valenzuela, A. (ed.) (2005) *Leaving Children Behind: How "Texas-Style" Accountability Fails Latino Youth*. New York: State University of New York Press.

Warren, J., Jenkins, K. and Kulick, R. (2005) High school exit examinations and state level completion and GED rates, 1975–2002. Paper prepared for presentation at the annual meeting of the Population Association of America, Boston, April 2004. On WWW at http://www.soc.umn.edu/ ~ warren/WJK.pdff. Accessed 11.7.06.

Wiley, T. (1996) Language planning and policy. In S. McKay and N. Hornberger (eds) *Sociolinguistics and Language Teaching* (pp. 103–147). New York: Cambridge University Press.

Wiley, T. and Lukes, M. (1996) English-only and standard English ideologies in the U.S. *TESOL Quarterly* 30 (3), 511–535.

Wiley, T. and Wright, W. (2004) Against the undertow: Language-minority education policy and politics in the 'age of accountability'. *Educational Policy* 18 (1), 142–168.

Wright, S. (ed.) (1996) *Language and the State: Revitalization and Revival*. Clevedon: Multilingual Matters.

Wright, W. (2002) The effects of high stakes testing in inner-city elementary school: The curriculum, the teachers, and the English language learners. *Current Issues in Education*, 5 (5). On WWW at http://cie.ed.asu.edu/volume5/number5/. Accessed 1.12.02.

Wright, W. (2004) Intersection of language and assessment policies for English language learners in Arizona. Doctoral dissertation, Arizona State University.

Wright, W. (2005) Evolution of federal policy and implications of *No Child Left Behind* for language minority students. Policy Brief. Tempe, AZ: Language Policy Research Unit (LPRU), Education Policy Studies Laboratory, Arizona State University. On WWW at http://www.asu.edu/educ/epsl/EPRU/documents/EPSL-0501–101-LPRU.pdf. Accessed 19.7.06.

Yin, R. (1984) *Case Study Research: Design and Methods*. Beverly Hills: Sage.

Zehr, M. (2006a) New era for testing English-learners begins. *Education Week*.

Zehr, M. (2006b) New York, Arizona at odds with Education Department over English testing. *Education Week*.

Zehr, M. (2007) States adopt new tests for English-learners. *Washington Post*. On WWW at http://www.elladvocates.org/media/NCLB/EdWeek24jan07.html. Accessed 10.2.07.

Zelasko, N. and Antunez, B. (2000) *If Your Child Learns in Two Languages*. Washington, DC: National Clearinghouse for Bilingual Education.

Index

Subjects

Authors